Documenting Performance

Documenting Performance

The Context and Processes of Digital Curation and Archiving

Edited by Toni Sant

Bloomsbury Methuen Drama
An imprint of Bloomsbury Publishing Plc

B L O O M S B U R Y
LONDON · OXFORD · NEW YORK · NEW DELHI · SYDNEY

Bloomsbury Academic
An imprint of Bloomsbury Publishing Plc

50 Bedford Square   1385 Broadway
London   New York
WC1B 3DP   NY 10018
UK   USA

www.bloomsbury.com

**Bloomsbury and the Diana logo are trademarks of Bloomsbury
Publishing Plc**

First published 2017

British Library Cataloguing-in-Publication Data
A catalogue record for this book is available from the British Library.

ISBN: HB: 978-1-472-58818-0
       PB: 978-1-472-58817-3
       ePub: 978-1-472-58819-7
       ePDF: 978-1-472-58820-3

Library of Congress Cataloging-in-Publication Data
A catalog record for this book is available from the Library of Congress.

Cover design by rawshock design
Cover image © shutterstock

Typeset by RefineCatch Limited, Bungay, Suffolk
Printed and bound in Great Britain

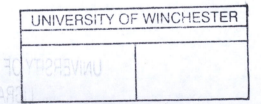

To Kekina

Contents

List of Illustrations

List of Tables

List of Contributors

Daisy Abbott is an interdisciplinary researcher and research developer based in the Digital Design Studio at Glasgow School of Art. Her current research focuses on interactive narratives, digital representations of ephemeral events, performing arts scholarship, digital heritage, digital and participatory culture, interaction design, 3D visualization methodologies and serious games.

Vanessa Bartlett is a researcher and curator based between Sydney and the UK. She is a PhD candidate at UNSW Art and Design where her research investigates connections between digital technologies and mental health through curatorial practice. Her most recent curatorial project *Group Therapy: Mental Distress in a Digital Age* was co-curated with Mike Stubbs for FACT (Foundation for Art and Creative Technology) Liverpool, UK, in 2015. Bartlett was formerly a Coordinator at Unfinished Histories, a project recording the history of Alternative Theatre in Britain 1968–88 through interviews and the collecting of archive material. In 2010–11, she served as Performance Programmer at Bluecoat, Liverpool's centre for the contemporary arts, where she curated live art, music, and dance.

Joanna Bucknall PhD is a senior lecturer in Drama and Performance at the University of Portsmouth. She is a practice-based scholar whose research interests include immersive performance practices, live art, practice-as-research, performance documentation and cognitive approaches to reception theory. She is the artistic director of Vertical Exchange Performance Collective, co-artistic director of KeepHouse Performance and an Associate Artist at the New Theatre Royal in Portsmouth. She has collaborated with venues such as The Barbican in Plymouth, Camden People's Theatre, The Basement in Brighton, Performing Arts Centre, Lincoln and more recently Battersea Arts Centre.

Gema Bueno de la Fuente holds a PhD in Library and Information Science (2010). She is currently serving as EU Projects Officer at LIBER. Since 2005, she has been assistant professor at the Library and Information Science Department, University Carlos III of Madrid in Spain, teaching on various undergraduate and postgraduate programmes. She has participated in several research projects, and published in national and international journals. She has also conducted research visits as a visiting scholar in the University of Minho (Portugal), the School of Information and Library Science of UNC-Chapel Hill (USA) and CAPLE/CETIS (UK). Her research interests are open access to science and education, digital libraries, digital preservation, vocabularies, semantic web standards, and linked data.

Alissa Clarke PhD is Senior Lecturer in Drama at De Montfort University, Leicester, UK. She has been practising Phillip Zarrilli's psychophysical performer training since 2002 and has been involved with Sandra Reeve's 'Move into Life' work since 2005. Alongside documentation of performance and psychophysical performance and performer training, her research interests include contemporary body-based performance practice, feminist and gender theory and performance practice (live and on film), and classical Hollywood cinema. She has published articles in these areas in journals including *Theatre, Dance and Performance Training, The Drama Review* and *The Journal of Writing in Creative Practice.*

Annet Dekker is a freelance researcher and curator. Currently she is Researcher Digital Preservation at Tate, London, Visiting Lecturer and research fellow at London South Bank University and The Photographers' Gallery, London, tutor at Piet Zwart Institute, Rotterdam, and fellow at Het Nieuwe Instituut, Rotterdam. She publishes widely on issues of digital art and preservation in international peer reviewed journals, books and magazines, and has edited several publications. Previously she worked as Web curator for SKOR, was programme manager at Virtueel Platform, and head of exhibitions, education and artists-in-residence at the Netherlands Media Art Institute. In 2014, she completed her doctoral research on conserving net art at Goldsmiths University of London.

Panayiota A. Demetriou holds a PhD awarded by the University of Bristol's Department of Theatre. Her thesis investigates performance approaches to exhibiting oral history archives through the use of sound art installations. Her research interests include HCI, archival and curatorial studies, audience participation and immersive practices, narratives/memories of war and practices of consumption, contested borders, gender and identity. Demetriou is also a freelance Live Art artist, performance photographer and the creator of the annual Cypriot non-profit festival Performance and Live Art Platform. She has also collaborated on international academic projects concerning the dissemination, accessibility and interaction with oral history collections of cultural heritage.

Miguel Escobar Varela is Assistant Professor of Theatre Studies at the National University of Singapore. He has worked as a theatre researcher, software programmer and translator in Mexico, The Netherlands, Singapore and Indonesia. His main research interests are Indonesian performance practices and the digital humanities. His articles have appeared in *Theatre Research International, Performance Research, TDR, Asian Theatre Journal, New Theatre Quarterly, Contemporary Theatre Review* and *Digital Scholarship in the Humanities.* He is the director and chief translator of the Contemporary Wayang Archive (http://www.cwa-web.org).

Gabriella Giannachi is Professor in Performance and New Media, and Director of the Centre for Intermedia at the University of Exeter. Her recent and forthcoming book publications include *The Politics of New Media Theatre* (Routledge 2007); *Performing Presence: Between the Live and the Simulated,* co-authored with Nick Kaye (MUP 2011); *Performing Mixed Reality,* co-authored with Steve Benford (MIT 2011); *Archaeologies of Presence,* co-edited with Nick Kaye/Michael Shanks (Routledge 2012); *Archive Everything* (MIT 2016) and *The History of Performance Documentation,* co-edited with Jonah Westerman (Routledge, forthcoming). She is an expert in performance documentation and is an investigator in the RCUK-funded Horizon Digital Economy Research Hub (2009–20). She collaborates with Tate and RAMM.

Lelia Green is a Professor of Communications at the School of Communications and Multimedia at Edith Cowan University, in Perth, Western Australia. She is the author of several publications including *Technoculture: From Alphabet to Cybersex* (2002) and *The*

Internet: An Introduction to New Media (2010), and also on the editorial board of the *Australian Journal of Communication* and *Media International Australia*. Her involvement in creative and performing arts research has seen her contribute to critiques of practice-led methods that lead to non-traditional research outputs.

Laura Griffiths is Senior Lecturer in Dance within the School of Film, Music and Performing Arts at Leeds Beckett University. In 2014, she completed an AHRC Collaborative Doctoral Award in partnership with the University of Leeds and Phoenix Dance Theatre, which focused upon notions of the body as archive and the intersection between dance practice and archival principles. Professional industry experience has encompassed project management within the arts, dance teaching in community settings, lecturing and research project assistance. Griffiths has project managed and undertaken Post-doctoral Research including for 'Respond' (www.respondto.org), a partnership with Yorkshire Dance, University of Leeds and Breakfast Creatives supported by the Digital R&D Fund for the Arts (Nesta, ACE, AHRC).

Cat Hope PhD is a musician and an Associate Dean at Edith Cowan University's Western Australian Academy of Performing Arts in Western Australia. Her compositions have been recorded for Australian, German and Austrian national radio, and her work has been awarded a range of prizes including the APRA|AMC Award for Excellence in Experimental Music in 2011, 2014 and the Peggy Glanville Hicks composer residency in 2014. Green has conducted extensive research into communication technologies, audio recording in forensic science, noise notation, low frequency sound, graphic scores and surveillance techniques for use in performance. She is also an active researcher in the area of music archiving, film music, digital art and electronic music performance.

Alvin Eng Hui Lim is Postdoctoral Fellow on the Theatre Studies Programme at NUS. He has recently completed his doctoral dissertation on popular religious practices and spirit mediums in Singapore. His key research interests are religious practices, spirit mediums and rituals, with emphasis on new media and digital technology. He is the Deputy Director and Online Editor (Mandarin) of the Asian Shakespeare

Intercultural Archive (A|S|I|A, http://a-s-i-a-web.org), and Editor of Theatre Makers Asia archive (http://tma-web.org). These are part of the Asian Intercultural Digital Archives (AIDA) project that aims to make some of the most notable contemporary theatre practices in Asia available online to a wide audience. He has also published on theatre, religious practices, and digital archiving.

Adam Nash PhD is an internationally recognized digital artist working in networked digital virtual environments. He is Lecturer and Program Manager of the Bachelor of Design (Digital Media) and Director of the Playable Media Lab in the Centre for Game Design Research, both at RMIT University, Melbourne, Australia.

Helen Newall PhD is a reader at Edge Hill University in northern England. Her writing includes new libretto, *Britten's Young Person's Guide to the Orchestra*, LPO, Carl Davis; *Frankenstein*, Chester Gateway; *Remote Control*, HTV Television Workshop; the award-winning *Dumisani's Drum*, Action Transport; *Anthem for Doomed Youth*, The Nuffield, Southampton; and for Theatre in the Quarter, Chester, *Silent Night: A Jacobean Christmas*, performed at Hampton Court; and the award winning *Over By Christmas*. Her photography *Dying Swans and Dragged Up Dames* has been exhibited in The Arts Centre, Ormskirk, and Bank Street Gallery, Sheffield. Her series, *Class; Rehearse; Perform*, featuring 12° North Dance Company, was exhibited at The Lowry, Salford and The Citadel, St Helens.

Alberto Pendón Martínez followed a philosophy degree with a Master's degree in Library and Digital Information Services. He is now the archivist in charge of the Pedro Aparicio documentation centre, which is a department of Teatro Municipal Miguel de Cervantes in Málaga, Spain. The centre is dedicated to investigate and spread the documentary heritage generated by the performance arts in town. It contains a graphic archive and a special library. His academic and professional activities spread across cultural heritage management within websites, the investigation of vocabularies and descriptive schemas applied to specific domains, and record management in e-government environments.

Claire Read researches the overlapping relationship between performance and documentation as a doctoral candidate at the

University of Roehampton in the UK. She argues that the use of technology in performance, specifically seen within the rise in live streaming, has altered the states of performance and documentation, and writes on the NT Live project as a key example. Her wider research involves media performances, archiving and performance writing. She is a member of the Theatre and Performance Research Association (TaPRA) and has spoken at the Documenting Performances working group's interim events. Claire is also a committee member for the New Researchers' Network, a sub-committee of the Society for Theatre Research (STR), and live streams the Society's annual lecture series for discrete online audiences.

Jeanine Rizzo LLD graduated as a lawyer from the University of Malta and furthered her studies in the fields of intellectual property law, and art and antiquity law at Masters level at University College London. While in London she was a research assistant to Norman Palmer, carrying out research on the law of bailment and on art law. She practices intellectual property law and art law at Fenech and Fenech Advocates in Valletta, specializing in copyright, trademarks, patents, design rights, entertainment law, music law and film law. Rizzo is also a lecturer and examiner at the University of Malta, and a member of the Chamber of Commerce RTDI Committee.

Daniela Salazar has an undergraduate degree in history and in 2013 she completed her MA in Museology at FCSH – New University of Lisbon in Portugal. During 2012 and 2013, she worked as a researcher in a project of the Association for the Study of Theatre and Performance in Portugal, funded by the Calouste Gulbenkian Foundation. Between 2010 and 2013, she conducted internships at the National Music Museum, and the National Theatre and Dance Museum in Portugal. The following year, Salazar was responsible for managing the collections, exhibition programme and educational service plan of the newly created Sumol Museum, managed by the company SUMOL + COMPAL. She is currently developing her PhD project as a FCT scholarship in Artistic Studies about exhibiting performativities: the place of performance in curatorial context.

Toni Sant is the artistic director of Spazju Kreattiv, Malta's national centre for creativity, which is based at St James Cavalier in Valletta.

His first book *Franklin Furnace and the Spirit of the Avant-Garde* (Intellect/University of Chicago Press, 2011) builds on his PhD from New York University. This was followed by *Remembering Rediffusion in Malta* (Midsea Books, 2016), which is the first book-length attempt to address issues around the management of Maltese audio-visual archives. He has lectured extensively on performance and technology in New York, Malta and the United Kingdom, most recently at the University of Hull's Scarborough Campus where he was Reader in Digital Curation and Executive Director of the Media and Memory Research Initiative. His writings on digital performance, live art and contemporary cultural heritage preservation have appeared in various journals and book chapters published internationally across the UK, USA, Norway, Switzerland and Malta.

Kirsty Sedgman PhD studies cultural value and theatre audiences. Her book *Locating the Audience* (Intellect 2016) is the first to explore in detail how people developed relationships with a new theatre company: National Theatre Wales. She now works with a range of cultural industry partners and government agencies, investigating how individuals and community groups find meaning in arts participation. Sedgman founded and chairs the Performing Audience Research Network, which brings together audience researchers from around the world, and she is the Membership Secretary and Treasurer of the Society for Theatre Research.

Amy Skinner PhD is a lecturer in Drama and Theatre Practice at the University of Hull. Her research interests include Russian and early Soviet theatre, theatre and fine art, and the interrogation of historiographic practices pertaining to theatre and performance. She has published on photography in Vsevolod Meyerhold's theatre from the perspective of the theatre historian, as well as on Meyerhold's directing and actor training practice. Her book *Meyerhold and the Cubists: Perspectives on Painting and Performance* was published by Intellect in 2015. Skinner is also a theatre director and scenographer specializing in the direction of multi-lingual theatre and theatre in translation, and as theatre maker and scholar, finds that performance photography is a vital concern in all of her working practice.

Ben Spatz is Senior Lecturer in Drama, Theatre and Performance at University of Huddersfield. He is the author of *What a Body Can Do:*

Technique As Knowledge, Practice As Research (Routledge 2015) as well as many shorter articles and essays published in both scholarly and artistic contexts. Spatz holds a PhD in Theatre from the City University of New York and was formerly a performer with the Gardzienice Theatre Association and a Fulbright Fellow at the Grotowski Institute in Wroclaw. He was a Movement Research Artist-in-Residence (2010–12) and has performed and presented work at numerous venues in New York City and beyond. Most recently he was selected as a UK Arts and Humanities Research Council Leadership Fellow (2016–18).

Allan Taylor is an academic and practitioner working across live art and photography. His research interests include photographing performance, the function of imagery in contemporary visual culture, photography as performance and the relationship between 'the performative' and photography. He is currently completing a PhD at Falmouth University in the UK and he lectures in media and cultural theory at University of East London.

Adam Trainer is a researcher, musician and broadcaster from Perth, Western Australia. He has taught film studies, cultural studies and popular music studies at Curtin University and Edith Cowan University. He has published on various aspects of digital media culture including the aesthetics of visual noise and post-ironic musical micro-genres. He has also published widely on the history of popular music in Western Australia. Trainer has worked as a researcher on several projects investigating specific Western Australian music communities. These include a critical social history of popular music in the state, and the Western Australian New Music Archive, which has seen the creation of an interactive web portal to house heritage materials that document the activities of the state's new music community.

Vivian van Saaze is Assistant Professor at the Faculty of Arts and Social Sciences at Maastricht University and co-founder and Managing Director of the Maastricht Centre for Arts and Culture, Conservation and Heritage (MACCH). Her research explores the challenges museums are facing in the wake of new artistic practices (such as new media, installation and performance-based art) and the implications of digitalization for museums. She is founder of the International Network for PhD and Postdoctoral Researchers in the Field of Contemporary Art Conservation, and was investigator in the Tate research network Collecting the Performative: a research network examining emerging practices for collecting and conserving performance-based art.

Laurene Vaughan PhD is Professor in Design at RMIT University. She is internationally recognized for her leadership in interdisciplinary design research. She is on the advisory board for the Centre for Design Research, Oslo School of Architecture and Design. Between 2005–10 she was Project Leader and Researcher within the Australasian Cooperative Research Centre for Interaction Design. She is currently co-leader of the Design Futures Lab at RMIT. She is also on the advisory board to the RMIT Design Archive. She was a Chief Investigator on The Circus Oz Living Archive Project. This research sought to develop a model for online digital engagement for the performing arts. This was funded through the Australian Research Council.

Professor **Sarah Whatley** is Director of the Centre for Dance Research (C-DaRE) at Coventry University, UK. Her research interests extend to dance and new technologies, intangible cultural heritage, somatic dance practice and pedagogy, dance documentation, and inclusive dance practice; she has published widely on these themes. Funded by the AHRC, European Commission and Leverhulme Trust, her current research projects focus on the creative reuse of digital cultural content, smart learning environments for dancers, reimagining dance archives, the generative potential of error in dance and HCI, and dancer imagery. She is also founding Editor of the *Journal of Dance and Somatic Practices* and sits on the Editorial Boards of several other Journals.

Acknowledgements

This book builds on work initiated by the Documenting Performance Working Group within the Theatre and Performance Research Association (TaPRA). This UK-based research association contained a similar working group, called Documentation of Performance, when it was first constituted in 2005. However, that group soon merged with the Theatre History and Historiography Working Group, partly because some members wanted to participate actively in both groups, while others felt that the documentation of performance was indeed just the sort of thing that the history and historiography working group would include as its broad area of focus. When Nicola Shaughnessy and I first convened the new TaPRA working group in 2010/11, we were driven by my distinct desire to focus not on documents as objects but on the processes of documenting as a practice. This is a subtle but essential shift that moves the centre of attention towards an activity that has hitherto been grossly underexplored in Performance Studies. In this context, documentation is not about the contents or objective qualities of a document but the making, preservation and potential reuse of that document. From a noun associated with documentary evidence to a verb describing the act of creating and collecting documents. The TaPRA working group on documenting performance has attracted interest and contributions from computer scientists, archaeologists, architects, visual artists, archivists and digital data preservation specialists. Not surprisingly, it has also drawn in participants from several other countries outside the UK, where the association holds all its events, some of whom have contributed directly to the contents of this book.

I must also extend my profound gratitude to Laura Molloy, who actively engaged with the TaPRA Documenting Performance

Working Group from its first public meeting at the University of Kent in 2011, sharing many valuable insights into documenting performance mainly from an information management perspective. She co-convened the working group with me from 2012 until 2015, when we passed the reins on to Georgina Guy and Johanna Linsley. Everyone who has ever presented their work through the working group meetings has helped shape my enthusiasm for the subject of this book, and also guided much of the field's current modes of thinking about the ways performance is documented. Special thanks to Sarah Whatley who has systematically changed the discourse on documenting performance remarkably through her extensive work on dance archives. I am genuinely thrilled that she is among the contributors for this collection of writings about documenting performance.

I am greatly indebted to Barry Smith who co-developed the Digital Performance Archive (now held by the University of Bristol) with Steve Dixon. Over a period of more than a decade, he inspired and encouraged me to think about performance archives beyond the theoretical engagement that was most prevalent in the 1990s. Before him, the late Brooks McNamara instilled in me the drive to look more closely at the ways performance documents are created and preserved. I will forever cherish my regular and frequent encounters with him as a graduate student at New York University's Tisch School of the Arts, particularly conversations on Broadway about the six million documents at the Shubert Archives, which he lovingly curated for many years. Martha Wilson and the staff at the Franklin Furnace Archive in New York City also deserve recognition for providing me unlimited access to one of the world's largest archives of ephemeral art. From their efforts I learned that performance archives are not merely what remains of live acts. I have already captured this experience in my book *Franklin Furnace and the Spirit of the Avant-Garde: A History of the Future*, but the Furnace has certainly continued to ignite much of the thinking that guided the way this book is edited and presented. Enriqué Tabone designed the first diagram in chapter 1 (with useful input from Andrew Pace) and all the graphs in chapter 11.

At the University of Hull, where I held the post of Reader in Digital Curation throughout most of the production of this book, my Media and Memory Research Initiative (MaMRI) colleagues enabled me to work in a professional environment where conversations about ways to document performance and how these relate to developments in data management and archival science are grounded in practical considerations. Special thanks to the University of Hull's Head of Information Services Chris Awre and Hull History Centre Senior Archivist Simon Wilson. Steve Borg, Rebecca O'Neill, and Darren Stephens are three of the doctoral researchers within MaMRI who have broadened my perspectives on documenting performance through their own work. They operate at the forefront of the emerging areas of inquiry around the context and processes of digital curation and archiving.

Documenting Performance: An Introduction

Toni Sant

This book addresses a significant need in both performance studies and performance practice to raise awareness on the impact that digital curation and archiving have on the past, present and future of field. The most significant point proposed in this book is a shift from using performance documentation as a generic (and frequently contentious) term to thinking about documenting performance as the simple process of creating and organizing documents towards providing documentation that is available for long-term access.

In this book, the use of the term documentation is avoided when it is a synonym for document/s or the basic processes of documenting. Throughout this book, documentation refers to the process of storing documents and preserving them in a systematic way for long-term access through an archive. To read this book in the spirit that it is presented, this distinction must be preserved. We avoid using the common term documentation when what is meant is simply document/s or the rudimentary process of creating documents.

The distinction is semantic but not trivial. It is how performance scholars and practitioners begin to understand how and why performance is documented: what happens and needs to happen when a document is created, how archives work, and what needs to happen to a document for it to become part of the documentation of a performance. The generic term documentation as widely embraced by performers, arts administrators and many performance scholars leads to relegating everything associated with documenting performance to a secondary concern in relation to the performance itself. We must focus less on documents that are commonly misconstrued as documentation and focus more on the processes of documenting where the ultimate aim is systematic documentation, ideally through standard methods of archiving proposed by library and information science.

The distinction between documents (in the sense of documentary residue) and documentation (the process of turning a collection into an archive that provides long-term access to documents) is possibly better described through a simple diagram that highlights the relationship between the different terms and their place in the overall practice of documenting performance.

An event or momentary experience is recorded through one or more means to create one or more documents. If a document is stored passively (i.e. without thought of the wider context for where and how it is stored) a collection is possibly created. If, however, the same document is stored actively (i.e. with the intent of doing more with it that merely keeping it) than it is archived. The interactive process of preparing the document to be accessed at a later date — ensuring that some of the context present in the original event but possibly

Table 1.1 Record – Store – Preserve: from document to documentation

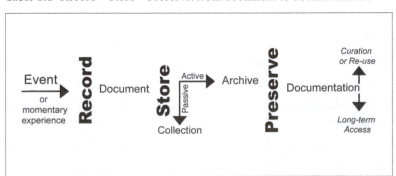

absent in the document itself is retained — constitutes the act of documentation or the creation of what may be called documentation. Through deliberate documentation, documents provide ways to access memories of performance events or momentary experiences of them. As with all documents, any performance document is subjective and open to interpretation, re-interpretation and other forms of re-use, either permitted by the originators or creatively derived by other users, regardless of the original context.

Common (back)ground

A wider concern with managing documents first became evident in the late nineteenth century. Paul Otlet (1868–1944) led the initial discussions on the relationship between documentation and documents. Otlet created the modern discipline we now call information science. He called it documentation. Suzanne Briet (1894–1989) elaborated on Otlet's initial position. In 1951, Briet published a manifesto on the nature of documentation — *Qu'est-ce que la documentation?* — claiming that a document is evidence in support of a fact because 'Latin culture and its heritage have given to the word *document* the meaning of instruction or proof' (2006: 9). For Briet, a document is 'concrete or symbolic indexical signs, preserved or recorded toward the ends of representing, of reconstituting, or of proving a physical or intellectual phenomenon' (10). She is the first to point out that this definition is 'most abstract, and thus, the least accessible'. In spite of this, it is clear that in her framework, documentation is a standardized approach to the management of documents. Following Briet, documentation should not be viewed as being concerned with texts but with access to evidence.

Many discussions on documenting performance (or, more vaguely, performance documentation) since the early 1990s cite a couple

of sentences written by Peggy Phelan in a critical assessment of
live art:

> Performance's life is only in the present. Performance cannot be
> saved, recorded, documented, or otherwise participate in the
> circulation of representations of representations: once it does so it
> becomes something other than performance.
>
> 1993: 146

Phelan's declaration that performance 'cannot be saved, recorded, [or]
documented" has led to more than two decades of benign resistance
from performance scholars and practitioners towards documentation
(in the Briet sense) of live performance. Much of this opposition is
clearly inflected by Walter Benjamin's widely embraced position on
the need to preserve the work of art's aura in the ever-expanding mass
media environment. However, the point that has very frequently been
overlooked is that although a recording or document is indeed
'something other than [the] performance' it has a value in its own
right. Performance scholars and practitioners often significantly
underplay the importance of performance documentation. This is
possibly because performance is rarely documented with the same
level of precision, commitment and discipline as the creation of the
other essential parts of the performance itself. It is as if documenting
performance is almost always an afterthought or, at best, a necessary
evil to ensure that there is some evidence that the performance
actually took place; but something far removed from the experience
of being in the same place and time as the original event. When
documentation is simply equated with the basic act of creating a
document, the precision, commitment and discipline of information
science rarely cross the minds of performance scholars or practitioners.

From around 1999, Philip Auslander's work on liveness became
cited frequently as an antidote to Phelan's earlier proclamation.
Auslander proposes that mediation of an event creates another

performance. Or, to paraphrase Rebecca Schneider (2011): the performance persists through its remains. However, for the most part, the argument remains on a theoretical level. What this book aims to provide is a practical recognition of the complexities of documenting performance as a significant practice that needs to do more than circulate what Phelan calls 'representations of representations'. More recently, Phelan appears to update her original position. Writing about performance photography in 2010, Phelan distinguishes between the making of a photograph and the viewing of the photograph at a later date, calling the relationship between them the 'photographic effect' (2010: 51). From her later writing, it has become fairly obvious that the recording of a momentary experience in the contemporary media-saturated performance ecosystem has intermingled with the experience of another present tense moment when the photo is viewed. For better or worse, performance arts now operate in a cultural economy that is hard to separate completely from media technology.

Going beyond the potentially simplistic dichotomy of the live event and what is recorded, this book brings together a number of new writings about the ways performance is documented and addresses some of the more significant issues arising out of the processes of documenting performance. While performance theorists have long argued that performance becomes something else whenever it is documented, the documents themselves cannot be regarded simply as incomplete remains from live events. The methods for preserving and managing them over time, ensuring easy access of such materials in systematic archives and collections, requires professional attention in its own right. Through the process of documenting performance, artists acquire a different perspective on their own work, audiences can recall specific images and sounds for works they have witnessed in person, and others who did not see the original work can trace memories of particular events, constructing their own viewpoint on them or using them to gain an understanding of something that would otherwise remain unknown to them and their peers.

How to document performance

Performance scholars are increasingly exploring the various ways performance documents are created and how documentation is reused by historians, artists and the general public to reframe the work preserved through writing, photos, video and other means. Such work also involves direct involvement in documenting different types of performances (theatre, dance, live art, stand-up comedy, live music, etc.) and analyzing the impact their presence may have on the work itself. Furthermore, people who did not attend the performance may experience it, or aspects of it, through the document/s produced.

A guidebook on documenting performance would be welcomed by professionals and amateurs alike. This book is not a guidebook but may be used as a core text on courses focusing on documenting performance or contemporary theatre and performance historiography. It offers insights into key considerations on the processes of documenting performance, and provides a number of useful case studies of good practice from around the world, even in cases where the most significant outcome is the lessons learned on what not to do or what works less effectively in the broader practices of performance documentation.

People involved in so-called 'Practice as Research' projects will find this book useful because it provides a professional framework for the type of documents they normally circulate as evidence of their outputs. To my mind, it is practice-based performance research where the acuteness of the problem of documentation can be perceived most clearly. The creation of documents is frequently deemed to be enough to document the practical work. Hundreds of hours of video footage from training or rehearsals sit unwatched after they have served their initial purpose, and this is usually because documents are mistaken for documentation. Think of it another way: how is anyone meant to find a specific sequence in the many hours of video recordings of physical movement, unless the document is processed in such a way as to provide a potential researcher with the information about what they can expect to see in the video recording other than, for example, contact improvisation between two performers on a given date. Context is an essential aspect for documents to be preserved for long-term keeping, along with other metadata, and for long-term accessibility plans.

Outside performance studies circles, this book should be of interest to archive professionals and arts administrators, seeking insights into the ways live performance is documented. Information managers particularly will find it useful to read how contemporary performance artists work in a range of forms including theatre, music, dance and live art, which frequently have different expectations from those for their primary documents. Here, for example, the subtle but significant ontological differences between a play script, a musical score, Labanotation or instructions for a live art installation immediately spring to mind.

One noteworthy way to think about documentation in a contemporary reality is through the evolving practice of digital curation, which the Digital Curation Centre (DCC) defines as an activity that 'involves maintaining, preserving and adding value' to digital data throughout its lifecycle.[1] The DCC's Curation Lifecycle Model is useful for understanding the actions and processes required to curate and preserve digital objects within this framework.[2]

The DCC's Curation Lifecycle Model has been used in digital curation skills development in the UK higher education sector across all disciplines, including in collaboration with other Jisc-funded digital

Table 1.2 The Digital Curation Centre's Curation Lifecycle Model

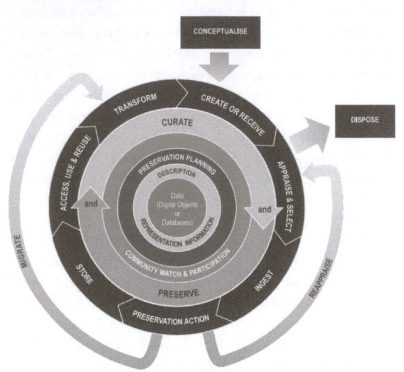

curation training resources such as those undertaken by the CAiRO (2011)[3] and KAPTUR (2013)[4] projects, which were specifically targeted at those engaging in creative arts research and Practice as Research. The relatively recent expansion in the availability of affordable digital technologies means that practitioners are now more likely to undertake the creation of digital objects in the production of creative work, including documenting work both in rehearsal and public presentation. As a result, new challenges are emerging for the sustainability of these burgeoning digital traces of performance.

In 2012, Laura Molloy examined digital curation awareness among a group of performance practitioners in the UK, who 'produce work outside institutional support structures such as those offered by academia or other large institution such as a national or regional theatre' (2014: 7). She found 'high confidence in [performance practitioners'] digital curation practices but– critically — [they] showed little awareness of the skills required for competent digital curation' (19). There is surprisingly little formal instruction on documentation in performance training and/or education. Frequently, both undergraduate and postgraduate courses in various forms of performance require documents to be submitted as part of the assessment of the live work. This is also common in Practice as Research projects, where the live work is habitually accompanied by documentary evidence of the performance.

Despite the prevalence of digital recording equipment, or perhaps even because of it, a renewed attention to training in documenting performance is also needed. Different institutions in Europe, Australia and North America, where similar approaches to the subject can be found, run classes on performance history (with different focal points on theatre, dance, music, live art — depending on the particular course) at different levels and in various formats. Some will have them as core study units for all students, others will have them as specialized/ optional courses at either undergraduate or postgraduate level. Increasingly, as anyone working in performance subject areas knows well, there has been a shift away from the traditional teaching of chronological histories and a move towards critical explorations of how histories are written and by whom. This approach requires a thorough discussion of the issue of performance documentation and the processes of documenting, which has previously taken place mostly at the postgraduate level.

The use of digital media has impacted both contemporary performance practices and strategies for documenting performance. We must now also consider a paradigm shift from documenting unique 'objects' to documenting multiple 'experiences' of 'objects'. In situations where participants are increasingly documenting their own presence, any ordinary person has the potential of entering the archive as documenter, bringing us closer to a democratic culture where documenting performance expands its hold from the controlled realm of performance production to include instant evidence gathered by people who were previously only expected to experience performance as passive beholders of the artists' intentions.

The main theoretical argument favoured by many academics revolves around physical 'presence' and relegates the cultural significance of documentation or the activity of documenting performance as secondary to the artists' works. It is no longer possible to regard live performance as something that is ontologically pristine and somehow believe that it can operate in a cultural economy separate from media technology. This book should help broaden the range of texts available for considering this shift. It provides a resource to potentially enable the required shift in perspective for the upcoming generation of performance practitioners and scholars. Theatre and performance studies are fast catching up with the emerging field of memory studies and the development of digital curation as a formal process of preservation and maintenance in archiving digital assets (texts, photos, videos, illustrations, sound recordings, etc.) for long-term access.

Structure

This book is divided into four parts for easy access to the main themes around which the contributors have been invited to write. Some of the contributing writers are key practitioners in documenting performance, involved in relatively high-profile projects. Others are early career researchers and practitioners involved in projects that indicate a long-term commitment to the evolving processes of documenting performance.

The first part presents the contexts for documenting performance in a contemporary reality. This is followed by a section that highlights how the methods of documenting performance have changed radically over the past hundred years or so. Part three provides a number of case studies illustrating the difference between documents, the process of documenting, and systematic examples of documentation offered through archives. The final part of the book features chapters that deal with different approaches to documenting the human body in motion. You will find an introduction to each of the four parts of this book, giving you some context for that cluster of chapters relating back to this general introduction.

Part One

Contexts for Documenting Performance

The contexts for documenting performance in a contemporary reality are very different than they were towards the end of the twentieth century. There are five key points that need to be taken into consideration now whenever any process for documenting performance is discussed. These are (1) the rise of memory studies, (2) the field of library and information science, (3) information management through popular web-based services, (4) alternative approaches to intellectual property management, and (5) the difficulties in preserving documents through digital media technology and other questions around preserving variable media art.

The study of memory as an interdisciplinary concern in its own right saw a rise in popularity around 2008 with the first issue of the peer-reviewed academic journal *Memory Studies*, from Sage Publications. Although primarily seen as a subset of sociology and psychology, it soon became evident from contributions to the journal that other areas as diverse as biological sciences and information management had interdisciplinary interests in the study of memory. The interdisciplinarity within this field of study was further emphasized with the release of the biannual *Journal of Educational Media, Memory, and Society* from Berghahn Books. This initial surge of interest was also reflected in the June 2009 issue of the *International Journal of Politics, Culture, and Society*, dedicated to the theme of Memory and Media Space. In their introduction to this issue, Brown et al. ask a fundamental question: 'is an interdisciplinary field of memory studies possible?' This turns out to be a quasi-rhetorical question, and their conclusion is that, 'on the arch that stretches between the interdisciplinary model that emphasizes commonalities and interactions to the proposal that focuses on differences, there are many opportunities for memory scholars, and especially for students entering the "field," to better comprehend, advance, and shape the study of memory' (Brown et al. 2009: 123). It is also useful to note that the authors of this journal contribution come from academic departments of psychiatry, sociology and psychology.

The rise of memory studies as a substantial area of research interest, is possibly best captured in the rather expansive list of books published in the Palgrave Macmillan Memory Studies series since 2010. The series editors are Andrew Hoskins and John Sutton, who are also editors of the *Memory Studies* journal. The list of topics covered in this book series goes well beyond the primary disciplinary areas mentioned earlier and include media studies, cultural history and theory, cultural and social anthropology, political science, and other arts and humanities subjects. The broad range of disciplinary aspects points to interdisciplinary possibilities, in the way that were captured in the special issue of the *International Journal of Performance Arts and Digital Media* on interdisciplinary approaches to documenting performance, which was published in 2014. What the various contributions in that issue made apparent is that the ubiquity of digital media technology must be taken into consideration more centrally in considering contemporary ways for documenting performance.

In this book, Daniela Salazar's 'Performance Arts and their Memories' (chapter 2) is a useful meditation on the relationship between memory and performance. The main chapter in this section that comes from the perspective of library and information science is called 'Description Models for Documenting Performance: Challenges and Current Trends' (chapter 3) and it is written by two library and information science professionals, Alberto Pendón Martínez and Gema Bueno de la Fuente.

It is rather obvious that library and information science as a discipline has much to offer the practice of documenting performance. Indeed, it is impossible to think of useful performance documentation outside its immediate circles of creation without some application of the processes and standards established through library and information science. It is easy to take this self-evident argument further and claim that it is through the discipline and standards arising out of library and information science that performance documents can be made readily available to future audiences. However, as Laura Molloy's research demonstrates, performance arts practitioners are not only untrained in library and information science, but for the most part they are also unaware that the standards and examples of good practice in other areas of activity driven by library and information science apply directly to performance arts.

The essential point to make here is that performance documentation arguably becomes most useful when handled in the context of library and information science (LIS). This does not mean that the creation of performance documents, whether by accident or by design, should be conducted by LIS professionals, but rather that they should at the very least be consulted in ensuring that documents are processed and preserved in ways that make them readily findable and available to future researchers.

Data management is directly related to all this. It is not irrelevant that the management of digital data has grown so rapidly over the past couple of decades. In some ways, library and information sciences are intrinsically related to data management, and perhaps the area where performance activities have had the least involvement in terms of the development of documentation arising from data generated either systemically or at random through performance work.

Information management through popular web-based services is something that probably makes many readers of this book think of Facebook, Twitter and other popular online social networking services. However, although such services are not to be overlooked, in the framework of this book and particularly in the context of documenting performance, it is rather more important to consider two ubiquitous popular online services that are directly involved in information management and sharing: Wikipedia and Google.

Wikipedia is the world's most popular non-commercial website, while Google is by far the most widely used online search service. This has now been the case for a number of years, and although it may stop being so for one reason or another, it is likely that the online data management models they provide will be around for many years to come. Wikipedia is built on free and open knowledge sharing and it is based on a number of guidelines that, over time, ensure more reliable data from verifiable sources on notable topics.[1] Google is foremost in exploiting the free and open knowledge provided by Wikipedia and other associated projects like Wikidata[2] and Wikimedia Commons[3] to provide useful basic information on the most searched for topics as effectively as for less well-known ones.

The most important feature of the interplay between Wikipedia and Google is that users are able to find basic information from an open database about rather specialized topics into which they may choose to delve deeper. Here an understanding of licences for the distribution of basic knowledge and intellectual property more broadly needs to be identified, especially as they relate to the possibilities for flexibility embedded in such licences to use, share and build work based on original work.[4] Jeanine Rizzo's 'Intellectual Property Matters for Documenting Performance' (chapter 4) serves as a primer on copyright and related issues as they pertain to various processes for documenting performance.

This section of the book closes with a chapter called 'Expanding Documentation, and Making the Most of the Cracks in the Wall' by Annet Dekker, Gabriella Giannachi and Vivian van Saaze. The authors provide an argument for new strategies for the creation and management of performance documents, questioning the very nature of documents, in a spirit not unlike Suzanne Briet's consideration of whether an antelope is a document.[5] Usefully, they do this through a careful discussion of three case studies of works that clearly problematize the boundaries of what constitutes a performance document. Richard Rinehart and Jon Ippolito have written a very eloquent discussion on the fundamental issues to consider in the preservation of art generated through, and with, digital media technology, which is not completely removed from the preservation of other forms of contemporary art involving variable media, including video art and art installations involving mutable elements. Simultaneously, however, their book, entitled *Re-Collection: Art, New Media and Social Memory*, sounds an alarm bell for the need to reconsider how media technology is used, especially by institutions, calling on legislative bodies to ensure that cultural preservation is handled more appropriately to safeguard long-term access to documents generated in the contemporary context.

Performance Arts and Their Memories

Daniela Salazar

This chapter aims to reflect on the role of museums and of their classification criteria not only in the light of their own collections but also through incorporating the participation of their visitors. The broader inquiry presented here addresses the lack of discussion about the role and function of existing museums of performance arts, which are dedicated to theatre, dance, music, or circus arts. How do performance arts museums explore and present memories of performance?

The conceptual relationship between memory, performance arts and exhibition

Through the construction of narratives and images about the past, the process of constructing memories only becomes meaningful in the present, and thus it plays with the temporal logic of events. Adding to this, and following Susan Crane, it is also 'an act of thinking of things in their absence',[1] which takes us to a phantasmagorical dimension of memory itself.

In this sense, this process has been the subject of various theoretical approaches, such as the personal, collective and/or cultural memory. However, and again according to Crane, one should notice that memory will always be individual because every person is mortal, i.e. memory '[is] linked to the brain and the body that bears it'.[2]

Still, even if memory is taken from the perspective of individual memory and of the Freudian unconscious; or from the perspective of the social production of memory – the concept of collective memory as introduced by Maurice Halbwachs; or from the approach of a personal or cultural memory produced through the historical construction discussed by Marita Sturken, it always strongly appears related with the distinction between the production of a written memory and of a performed memory. In this sense, it is relevant to underline Mary Carruthers' assertion that 'the metaphor of memory as a written surface is so ancient and so persistent in all Western culture that it must ... be seen as a governing model or "cognitive archetype".[3] This leads to essential questions like: which relationships can be found between the process of constructing memory and the artistic performance? And – which dimensions are shared between these two concepts and their practices? Which ones differentiate them?

Performance is an object of study and one that involves several forms of memory. These forms are, for instance, expressed through the gestural repetition and physical poses and movements enacted in social and/or anthropological contexts, and are linked to the emergence of processes of collective and/or cultural memory through the mediation of bodies. Still, as performance and construction of memory take place in different temporal settings, we also need to understand how a performance needs memory to produce its own meaning. Which memories are produced about an artistic performance and in which ways do they emerge or are preserved?

Richard Schechner underlines memory as one of the elements that constitute the performance ritual, whether social or artistic, emerging in the phase he designates as *aftermath*.[4] That is, Schechner argues how the memory of a performance is still part of that same performance, because it is from this process of constructing memory that one can appreciate what remains of who participated in it or has seen it.

The construction of memory in performance is one of the most unsettling questions discussed both by critics and practitioners: 'of painters the paintings remain, of sculptors the sculptures, of writers the books, of actors remains only the memory of the audience which time quickly takes charge of erasing'.[5] George Banu argues that memory will always be unfaithful to the live performance: 'Memory is unable to reconstructing the artistic event'.[6] However, if we compare artistic performance with everyday life, is the way in which the process of constructing memory occurs so different? Is the weight of the ephemeral nature of the performance not similar to historical experience? The main difference between the memories of performance arts and those of everyday life rests in the intentional, artistic and fictional dimension of performance and in the need to preserve a work of art that disappears as soon as the performance ends. In this sense, José Oliveira Barata classifies the memory of theatre, for instance, as an affective memory that should be preserved in the sense of acknowledging the stages, characters, actors and decors.[7] Additionally, for Osório Mateus, the memory of theatre '[is] a simultaneous memory that is not as the one in written chronicles, but as the ones of dreams.'[8]

In regard to performance arts, when the museum takes the role of collecting and preserving memories, the exhibition becomes a stage for those memories. In relation to this issue, Joan Gibbons invokes Pierre Nora's notion of 'lieux de mémoire', noting that 'artworks not only serve as location for the production and representation of memory but also that institutions such as the museum and gallery serve as locations in which already memory in the form of artworks are often housed'.[9] It thus becomes relevant to discuss the ways in which museums display memories produced about the creation of any artistic performance that does not subsist after its presentation except for material fragments and/or versions of their occurrence. When such memories are recognised, in which way might the performance itself be a means of preserving and displaying it?

In 1984, Stephan Bann proposed the concept of the 'ironic museum' based on the interaction between the metonym and the synecdoche. In his own words, this consists of 'the technique of dispersal and isolation as well as the technique of integration and combination of different things into a whole.'[10] Through this concept of the 'ironic museum', it becomes possible for one object on display to be the carrier of memories shared with the memories of other objects, and together they may shape a broader performance memory. For this encounter to take place, Diana Taylor suggests that we need to take advantage of objects included in archived memory – 'documents, maps, literary texts, videos, films, CDs,' as well as the repertoire – 'performances, gestures, orality, movement'.[11]

Thinking about exhibition displays of performance arts collections takes us to the articulation of its main features: the absence of a fixed temporality as well as its regular mutability. The curatorial approach for the display of the performance arts engages with events that take place in several temporal moments. It includes the moment of the artistic performance, of its reception when it is presented, of the subsequent production and preservation of its fragments, as well as of the documents that were created from that performance and, lastly, of the moment in which all these elements will construct the memory of the viewers. Furthermore, the nature of the exhibition, normally lasting several weeks or longer, and often consisting of a permanently static display, contrasts with the shorter duration of the original performance, its ephemeral nature, its circumscription and its openness to external factors, such as the presence of an audience.

Practices of documenting memories of performance arts at museums

The nature of live performance arts, namely their ephemerality, defines both the question about the preservation of memories of those manifestations and about other ways of 'memorializing' the moments that make up a live performance.

One of the clearest problems in this regard is the question of the recreation of the performance itself. How and through which means can one think about the reconstitution of an artistic performance? Thinking about this in relation to a particular example, such as a jamming session, an improvised and spontaneous musical moment, helps make the discussion clearer. A jamming session is clearly something that can be preserved (which is different from recorded, in this case) nor can it be repeated. What remains are only the memories of it, or, more precisely, moments from it.

When researchers use the recreation exercise, they have frequently not only taken advantage of the material devices used in the live performance such as setting, costumes, programmes, accessories, musical instruments, among others, but also documents that provide mediated access to the performance event such as photography, audio-visual recordings and personal and/or oral testimonies in several mediums. The mediated access of the latter kind has several advantages and disadvantages. For example, going back to the example of the jamming session, one could argue for the usefulness of the audio recording as a tool to document the artistic performance. Yet, although recording the location sound, the sound recording does not document the relationships established between the musicians, their interpretative expressions, or the reactions of whoever is in the live audience.[12]

In a similar way to audio recordings, photographic documents (which may include technical photography, and sometimes, artistic photographs too) are important resources for 'stored' memories of live performances, even though they only capture a partial document of that moment. Through photography, we are able to see the performer, the place of acting, the setting, the costumes and the audience, but we are not able to hear the voices of the performers, the applause, the emotional state of the audience or the background noise in the space where the original performance took place.

Performance arts practitioners, scholars and critics seem to favour video recordings as the best way to capture a sense of live performance, even if it cannot replace the original live performance. Taylor is quite explicit about this point: 'The live performance can never be captured or transmitted through the archive. A video of a performance is not a performance, though it often comes to replace the performance as a thing in itself (the video is part of the archive; what it represents is part of the repertoire)'.[13] One of the limitations of capturing live performances on video concerns the issue of the unique experience of being present for any performance arts event. This has implications particularly in relation to the live audience experience, which may differ from one live iteration to the next. To capture all the variations, one would need to record every occurrence of the same performance. Another issue that emerges relates to the role of whoever is operating the video camera or editing multiple camera captures together. Whoever is capturing a live performance through one or more video cameras is making an interpretation of what is happening, understanding the potential of the performance through their own perspective and personal sensibility. More than capturing it in an objective way, video documenters re-interpret it from their own language and through the technical means available.

Oral testimonies are another type of performance document that sometimes tends to be undervalued in the museum context. Some museums, such as the Museu Nacional do Teatro e Dança (National Museum of Theatre and Dance), in Lisbon, Portugal, have in their collections works linked to performing artists' own memories. The testimony in the first person, whether about the creative process of an artistic performance or about the reactions received through a member of the audience, enables further access that which cannot be recreated. It also makes the institutional approach to these memories more humane.

To adjust these methods of documenting performance to the display context, it is necessary to change the way in which the memories of the artists, of their audiences and of the museum objects interact with each other. A case study about the experiment of new means of conservation and display of this kind of memories and registers took place in May 2011, at the Museu da Música (Museum of Music; from here on referred to as MM) in Lisbon, Portugal, in the form of an exhibition called 'Cartão de Memória' (Memory Card).

In 2011, in the context of celebrating the International Day of Museums, the theme the International Council of Museums (ICOM) provided for museums all over the world to engaged with was 'Museum and Memory: objects tell our history'. The ICOM called on museums to pose the following question: 'How can we explore the concept of memory in a way that gives a new dimension to the museum itself?'[14]

With the aim of bringing to the MM a broader audience and their testimonies and of displaying a more experiential and sensorial dimension of music, the curators decided to develop an exhibition that explored musical memories told in the first person. The main feature of this exhibition was to ask visitors to share their memories with the MM, thus contributing to this initiative. This implied the need to involve the community directly in the MM exhibition. On location at the MM itself, visitors were invited to leave their musical memory at the end of their visit. There was also a link on the website of the MM for people to access and write their musical memory, mainly as a way of gathering the maximum number of testimonies and contributions possible for the project. Besides this online link and advertising on the MM website, the MM Facebook page also developed a strong communication campaign calling for contributions from the general public, including people who did not visit the exhibition at the museum. Beyond the memories on display, during the period in which the exhibition took place, the museum and website visitors could also download their own memory on a card, a memory that was, soon after, added to the ones already on display.

The particular way in which visitors were encouraged to relate on a personal level with this broad range of shared memories is worth underlining here. This had the positive consequence of solidifying the relation between the MM and its various visitors. If museums are in themselves a repository of memories and of objects that preserve and illustrate them, the exercise of looking for which memories were linked to the universe of the MM through its visitors augmented the information about both the museum and its visitors.

Memories of the body and embodied memories

The body is always present in the moment of artistic creation, being both one of its surfaces and tools, yet it often becomes absent from display in museum exhibitions. Even if we are able to display objects, testimonies or audio-visual records of live performances, the presence of the body is lost. Which memories get lost with this absence?

If we think about the role of the body in the practice of performing arts, it is only after the middle of the nineteenth century that a new space appears, a space, in the case of theatrical practices, to look at the actor not only as a voice and a vehicle of facial expression, but as a whole body. Emile Zola, for example, states that the theatre of his time 'uses the psychological man [yet] ignores the physiological men,'[15] and he was therefore one of the critics that open the space for this change of perceptions. Still, by the start of the twentieth century, Alfred Jarry noticed that 'the actor "puts in his head" the character yet he should do it with its whole body'.[16] Other contemporaries, like Adolphe Appia and Gordon Craig, defined the theoretical principles of the body of the actor as a plastic element and/or a machine-body that would later be put in use by the futurists, by the Bauhaus, or even by the live art happenings of the Fluxus movement.

In the latter half of the last century, performance arts used the body as a central tool in their practices, often putting the body in dangerous situations. Performers such as Joseph Beuys, Marina Abramovic, and the collective Fura dels Baus, for instance, put their bodies in the hands of their audiences or in quite adverse conditions as a way to test not only other possibilities of communication of sensorial processes but also to turn the creative process closer to the audience. More recently, we have seen practices that aim to show how the body is obsolete matter, linking a creative practice to the cybernetic and robotic experience – a noticeable case for such work comes from the contemporary artist Sterlac.

Maria Augusta Babo remarks on the feature that makes the body the central element of any performance practice: 'of the senses that open the body to the world, the optical and haptic reception are fundamental. [...] Touching is that precise gesture in which the body encounters the world.'[17] It is, then, in the haptic reception, in the desire to be connected and in the encounter of the subject with the world that this timeless attraction of the spectator with the body of the performer establishes itself. While being one of the main elements in the recording of the memories of artistic practices, it is, then, this tension between proximity and distance of the bodies that gets lost in the display context.

Echoing the deeply held belief of many physical performers and musicians, Marita Sturken argues that the body can be interpreted as a 'technology of memory' in a similar way to the processes of representation such as artefacts and images – i.e. elements through which memory can be produced. In Sturken's view 'the body has been perceived as receptacle of memory, from the memory of bodily movement such as walking, to the memory of past events in physical scars, to the memory of one's genetic history in every cell'.[18] The body is not only as a technology of memory but also as an agent of memories, both in its physical dimension of memories incorporated in gestures and in movements, and in its more subjective dimensions. The memories of the body and the embodied memories, be it in the performer, in the spectator or in the visitor, are transferred and shared in the body.

Description Models for Documenting Performance

Alberto Pendón Martínez and
Gema Bueno de la Fuente

Performing arts collections are composed of a wide variety of documentary resources that bear testimony to the performance activity. These collections are frequently distributed and held by institutions that do not necessarily belong to the classic triad of the LAM domain: libraries, archives, and museums. The organization and description of performing arts collections depend largely on the different cultural practices of their holding institutions and the work of exhibition institutions.

Some organizations encourage web dissemination of performing arts collections, developing and maintaining information products and services, such as the European Network of Information Centres for Performing Arts (ENICPA),[1] or the International Association of Libraries, Museums, Archives and Documentation Centres of the Performing Arts (SIBMAS),[2] and at a national level, institutions like the Spanish Theatre Documentation Centre.[3] There are also some initiatives in the area of performing arts information that are geared to the commercial sector, such as Digital Theatre;[4] but such projects are frequently not concerned with adopting documentation standards, as in the case of the Digital Dance Archives.[5]

The main weakness of all these initiatives and many others like them is the lack of shared conceptual models and descriptive vocabularies for the creation of structured information on their collections. The isolation of these institutions is a major threat that puts them at risk of being left out of the LAM environment, which is increasingly becoming hyper-connected by means of linked data technologies. However, there are also substantial strengths and opportunities. On the one hand, the ability of these resources to document and generate knowledge about the scenic event, a cultural object whose temporal nature makes it complex to record. On the other hand, the opportunity provided by a project like Europeana,[6] aggregators of content from various countries, aiming to improve and promote the visibility of specific collections. This happens through the standardization of descriptive data or metadata and the exchange of knowledge with other cultural heritage institutions through a semantic data model. In short, the wide typology of documents generated by performance arts, the heterogeneity of their holding institutions, the lack of common descriptive standards, and the temporary nature of the main object of interest set out the core challenges for performance arts to successfully enter an international network for the exchange and distribution of cultural heritage documents.

The performance event as a cultural object

Standardization of descriptive data for document retrieval is a common practice in the field of library information and archive science. Since the mid-twentieth century, libraries have adopted the International Standard Bibliographic Description (ISBD) mainly to establish library catalogues. In the archival sphere, the release of the General International Standard Archival Description (ISAD (G)) in 1994 marked a significant step forward in the standardization of administration and government records, allowing the exchange of information between archives and boosting public awareness of their collections. However, other memory institutions such as museums and information centres have adjusted less easily to the standardization of the description of their holdings, and therefore to exchange and disseminate information, thus frequently hampering the visibility of collections of potential interest.

In museums, three-dimensional artefacts constitute a particular type of cultural resource of unquestionable value. Through the significant efforts of the International Council of Museums (ICOM)[7] to develop conceptual models like CIDOC Conceptual Reference Model (CRM) and metadata schemas such as Lightweight Information Describing Objects (LIDO), this category of institutions has overcome its initial shortcomings. Their success can be useful for performing arts information collections, given the commonalities of their working subject, moving towards what we could call non-bibliographic cultural objects.

According to Saorín: 'Cultural objects are considered mainly those of historical and artistic value, although under the name of museum fall a number of scientific value pieces or even spaces for contemporary art, performing arts and music exhibitions'. (2010: 171)

A performance event could be defined as a specific type of cultural object, thus naming the features that qualify it as an information resource with its own structure:

- Uniqueness of the object: Its value derives from the singularity of its manifestation, created at a specific time and place. As such, the object is not reproducible in the same way as multiple copies of a bibliographic work.
- Cultural value: The staged event ceases to be the priority to satisfy the need for information, which is subject to proper organization and description of the associated documents that describe its history, participants and their relationship with other works.

- Complex entity: The logical unit is not always an individual object. It can also exist as part of a general work, forming collections and establishing relationships with associated images. Each of these components is subject to a separate description.
- Various uses: The information on these types of objects and their relevance is subject to their intended use: research, education, preservation, tourism, etc.
- Temporality: The duration of its manifestation means that the associated documents are usually limited to a time range that goes from conception to presentation, adding a residual character to this type of information resource.

Despite its residual and temporal nature, or precisely because of it, the associated information generated by the performance event becomes the only primary and recorded source available for the study and possible recreation of the performance or elements of it.

A collection of information resources associated with a performance event could comprise:

- Preproduction: notes, riders, costumes, plans and models.
- Production: scores, scripts, assembly drawings, wire drawings.
- Promotion: posters, press kits, promotional dossiers, press releases.
- Presentation: hand programmes, photographic and audio-visual records.

Performing arts digital information initiatives

The aforementioned qualities of performing arts events pose a challenge to the definition of optimum description models for information resources associated with this type of cultural object. In this sense, Doerr (2003) warns that the simplification to a common data format, as is usually the case with bibliographic and archival domains, may result in an inadequate approach. Performing arts information centres aim to include their collections in systems already in use by other cultural heritage institutions, while maintaining specific methods and procedures for their resources. In this context, the solutions proposed by two major international initiatives, namely GloPAC and ECLAP, are worthy of note.

The Global Performing Arts Consortium (GloPAC) is an international organization of institutions and individuals committed to using innovative digital technologies to create easily accessible, multimedia, and multilingual information resources for the study and preservation of the performing arts.[8] The project seemed to have stopped being active after the death of its director, Karen Brazell, in 2012, but it can be still considered a key model for the purpose of this chapter. Its main product is GloPAD, an online database of digital images, texts, video clips, sound recordings and complex media objects related to the performing arts, in English, Chinese, German, Japanese and Russian.

GloPAD's description model is based on a metadata application profile (GloPAC, 2006), which takes elements from various metadata namespaces such as Dublin Core,[9] Art Museum Image Consortium Data Specification (AMICO),[10] Categories for the Description of Works of Art (CDWA)[11] or VRA Core.[12] In the resulting schema, there are two main blocks of information: a group of elements that describes what is specifically represented in an item (audio, video, text or image), the Core Record; and another group that allows the description at the level of piece, person and production, setting the context and history of what is represented, but being not exclusive to that item, Background Record. The performance moment is the logical entity running through the centre of the whole database.

The Core Record could be a Performance Record describing the moment of performance represented in the digital object, or a Component Record, describing anything that is not a representation of a performance, but has been generated around it (rehearsals, press conferences, costumes, editing, etc.), or whose function is to promote or support it (posters, hand programmes and other promotional material). The resources included in the Background Record are contextual elements that must answer the standard questions: who, what, when, where and why.

The European Collected Library of Artistic Performance (ECLAP)[13] aims to foster access to European performing arts heritage by creating an online archive for all performing arts in Europe, and by providing solutions and tools to help them network and publish content collections on Europeana. By 2016, ECLAP was distributing more than a million items – images, video, documents, audio, e-book, ePub, animations, slides, playlists, collections, 3D, Braille music, annotations, etc. – coming from more than 32 established European institutions.

The ECLAP Metadata Schema is divided into four sections, which combine Dublin Core terms, technical metadata about the digital items and performing arts metadata. The latter records information about the first performance, 'place', 'city', 'country', 'date', and other properties such as Artsgroup, Plotsummary, Professionals, Cast, Crew, Object, Genre, PerformingArtType, HistoricalPeriod, PersonRecord, PieceRecord.

A new description paradigm: beyond resources types and domains

Traditionally in cultural heritage institutions, resource description standards have clearly distinguished between resources types (books, serials, printed music, sound recordings, etc.) and information domains (libraries, archives and museums). The current paradigm seeks to go beyond this through the reuse and sharing of descriptive schemes regardless of the resource's original context.

In libraries, over the past few decades, the MARC (Machine-Readable Cataloguing) and the ISBD formats have contributed to information exchange, data standardization and universal bibliographic control. As for archives, the ISAD family standards have allowed a wide harmonization in procedures and tools. Archival finding aids (guide, inventory and catalogue) have been renewed through the Encoded Archival Context (EAC) and Encoded Archival Description (EAD) standards, which have enabled their transition to digital environments.

Nevertheless, these models have encountered some limitations in the web era (Tillet 2010), both in satisfying the users' information needs, and in coping with the heterogeneous nature of web resources. This situation has provided the necessary impetus for the proliferation of new metadata models that are better adapted to this context.

In this sense, Functional Requirements for Bibliographic Records (FRBR) and CIDOC-CRM are two major initiatives coming from the library and museum domain respectively. Both are based on conceptual models that define the main concepts and relationships operating in a field of knowledge, acting as a structural framework for the development of metadata vocabularies for the description of cultural objects.

The FRBR entity-relationship model constitutes a new way to understand intellectual work, and therefore the bibliographic record. It proposes a structure consisting of entities, attributes and a set of relationships between them, organized into three groups:

- Group 1 are the products of intellectual and artistic endeavour named or described in bibliographic records: work, expression, manifestation and item;

Table 3.1 The FRBR entity-relationship model

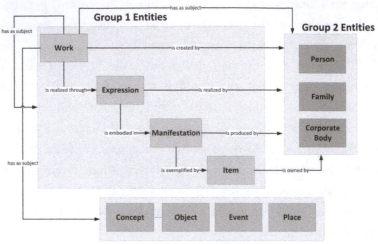

Group 3 Entities

- Group 2 are the entities responsible for the intellectual or artistic content, the physical production and dissemination or the custodianship of such products: person, family and corporate body;
- Group 3 are the entities that serve as the subjects of intellectual or artistic endeavour: concept, object, event, place, and any of the Group 1 or Group 2 entities.

Along with its extensions for Authority Data (FRAD) and Subject Authority Data (FRSAD), this model has served as a basis for new developments in cataloguing codes. As a result, the RDA (Resource Description Access) standard was published in 2010, though it has experienced uneven success in its adoption at libraries worldwide.

ICOM has adopted an object-oriented model for museums and published CIDOC-CRM in 1999, an ISO Standard since 2006: ISO 21117. According to ICOM, 'the primary role of the CRM is to serve as a basis for mediation of cultural heritage information and thereby provide the semantic "glue" needed to transform today's disparate, localized information sources into a coherent and valuable global resource' (Doerr and Crofts 1999).

Its structure consists of classes, subclasses and properties. It provides high flexibility allowing a subclass to belong to one or more classes and offering the possibility to refine it by adding additional classes for specific domains. Moreover, it is designed to represent the object/event context information, as well as its historical, geographical and theoretical background.

The versatility of the CIDOC-CRM model provides an excellent opportunity for those institutions and initiatives aiming to manage and disseminate performing arts collections without being isolated in the process of integration of European cultural heritage on the web. However, these are out of the scope of this model, as their definition of 'museum collections' does not explicitly mention them (Le Boeuf et al., 2015). This gap could be filled by the harmonization project FRBRoo, FRBR-object oriented, which will be described in some detail in the next section of this chapter.

As for the Europeana Data Model (EDM), this constitutes a qualitative leap for aggregation and the provision of access to special collections operating as a top-level ontology for different data models that come from the various communities constituting Europeana, such as museums, archives, audio-visual collections and libraries. EDM adheres to the modelling principles that underpin the approach of the Web of Data (i.e. the semantic Web), and therefore positions Europeana as the main cultural heritage project in this context. The model is based on several key elements:

- Distinction between the intellectual and technical creation, the object this structure is about, and its digital representations. This feature is essential for performing arts resources that are conditioned by the dynamic nature of the event to which these refer, reproduce or promote.

Table 3.2 The CIDOC-CRM model

E1	CRM Entity	
E2	-	Temporal Entity
E4	- -	Period
E5	- - -	Event
E7	- - - -	Activity
E11	- - - - -	Modification
E12	- - - - - -	Production
E13	- - - - -	Attribute Assignment
E65	- - - - -	Creation
E63	- - - -	Beginning of Existence
E12	- - - - -	*Production*
E65	- - - - -	Creation
E64	- - - -	End of Existence
E77	-	Persistent Item
E70	- -	Thing
E72	- - -	Legal Object
E18	- - - -	Physical Thing
E24	- - - - -	Physical Man-Made Thing
E90	- - - -	Symbolic Object
E71	- - -	Man-Made Thing
E24	- - - -	*Physical Man-Made Thing*
E28	- - - -	Conceptual Object
E89	- - - - -	Propositional Object
E30	- - - - - -	Right
E73	- - - - - -	Information Object
E90	- - - - -	*Symbolic Object*
E41	- - - - - -	Appellation
E73	- - - - - -	*Information Object*
E55	- - - - -	Type
E39	- -	Actor
E74	- - -	Group
E52	-	Time-Span
E53	-	Place
E54	-	Dimension
E59	Primitive Value	
E61	-	Time Primitive
E62	-	String

- Distinction of core classes and contextual classes, adapted to object-oriented conceptual model, a main trend in description organization at libraries, archives and museums besides being compliant with the FRBRoo model.
- A common metadata encoding model, which enables a greater reuse and integration of domains represented as collections of performing arts, allowing exchanging resources and linking with other domains.

FRBRoo: a domain ontology for performing arts

The main feature of the current description paradigm shift is the requirement for interoperability and integration of information resources regardless of their original domain. With this purpose, a working group was set up in 2003 for the harmonization of IFLA (International Federation of Library Associations and Institutions) FRBR and CIDOC-CRM models. The main objective was to design a conceptual model to represent the concepts underlying information systems at libraries and museums. In 2008, the first version of Functional Requirements Bibliographic Record-Object Oriented (FRBRoo) was published.

The relevance of this model for the performing arts is evident from the privileged role given to the 'Event' as an entity that connects objects, agents, time periods, and places. This could help to overcome the difficulty of modelling the performance event with traditional descriptive schemes intrinsically bonded to the physical nature of the object thus ignoring the temporal and non-material objects like manifestations of performing arts (Bellini and Nesi 2014).

To briefly introduce FRBRoo, only those classes suitable to describe the performance event and its associated documentation will be extracted. First, the 'Event' class from CIDOC-CRM

Table 3.3 Functional Requirements Bibliographic Record-Object Oriented (FRBRoo) model

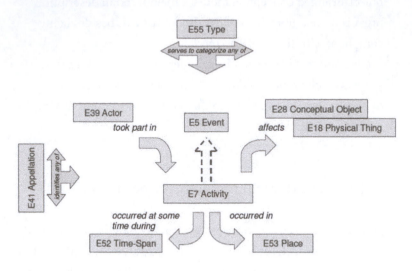

is adopted by FRBRoo to develop a set of classes, subclasses, and properties tailored to the performing arts singularity (Table 3.3).

E7 Activity is the central node from which the rest of the classes and relationships derive. It produces two major classes of resources (conceptual and physical), happening in a particular place (E53 Place) over a period of time (E52 Time-span), and engaging an actor or agent (E39 Actor). E55 Type class serves to categorize instances of each class from a controlled vocabulary, and E41 Appellation class identifies each of those instances.

FRBRoo proposes a new class, F31 Performance, a subclass of E7 Activity that refers to those activities including a series of planned behaviours, addressed to an audience, and that can be performed live or be recorded for later broadcast and distribution. Furthermore, FRBRoo clearly distinguishes between the author's mental conception of the work (F20 Performance Work) and the set of instructions and resources that serve that process (F25 Performance Plan), both

Table 3.4 F31 Performance within FRBRoo

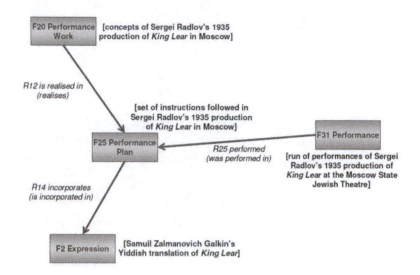

culminating in a concrete expression of that work (F2 Expression) (Table 3.4).

A case study: Teatro Municipal Miguel de Cervantes

The different types of resources held by the archive of the Teatro Municipal Miguel de Cervantes in Malaga, Spain (hereafter TC), are considered here to illustrate further how this model could be applied to an actual collection of performing arts. TC's archival resources have been generated by its performance activity during three decades, and comprise hand programmes, press kits, posters, riders, sheet music, photographs and audio-visual materials, and photographic and audio-visual collections from press conferences, performances, rehearsals, interviews, promotional spots, etc.

Some primary and secondary entities could be drawn from TC's archival collections (Table 3.5). Documentary Resource is the main

Table 3.5 Entity-relationship diagram

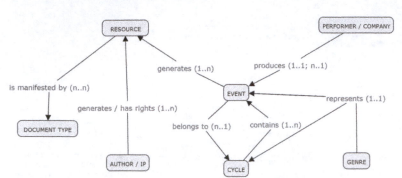

entity represented in a specific type of document and whose instances can be either analogue or digital. The Agents entity includes the performers and, wherever appropriate, the intellectual owners of the documents. Finally, the Event entity can refer to an independent action or a series of activities of a specific subject or individual production. As secondary entities, there is Concept — which designates the genre and subject of the event and the documentary resource respectively — and Place.

This entity-relationship diagram does not express all relationships that could be relevant to the archive, and does not reflect the different uses and the nature of its information resources. In addition, there is no way of introducing the temporality of the scenic event, a link between Agents, Places and Documentary Resources. FRBRoo object-oriented approach facilitates expression of both the temporality and the persistence of the documentary resource, through the use of E77 Persistent Item and E2 Temporal Entity classes.

Persistent Item E77 can take the form of E39 Actor, where performers, players, event participants as well as work creators can be represented. E53 Place and E70 Thing illustrate two types of relations between the scenic event and the persistent item.

Table 3.7 shows the interactions of E70 Thing from subclass E72 Legal Object and E71 Man-Made Thing. Both also serve to distinguish

Table 3.6 Entity-relationship diagram

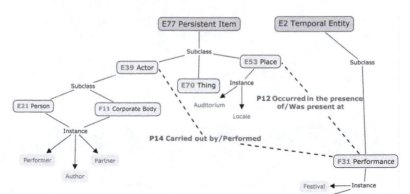

Table 3.7 Entity-relationship diagram

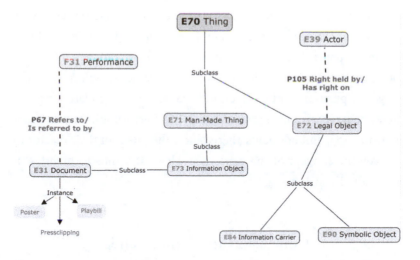

between those information resources aimed at the promotion of the event (E31 Document) from those that are the result of an intellectual expression and have their own cultural value (E90 Symbolic Object).

Table 3.8 depicts the last section ruled by the E90 Symbolic Object class. Thereof it derives a subclass F22 Self-contained Expression

Table 3.8 Entity-relationship diagram

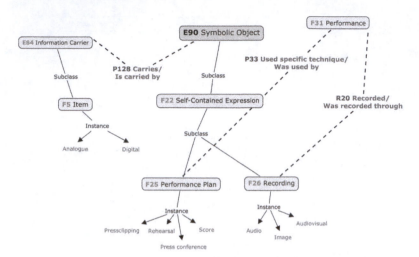

exposing the autonomous nature of the object that represents or reproduces the performance event. It may seem paradoxical, but it is a very appropriate refinement to the characteristics of those documentary resources in the collection, used specifically in the stages of planning and production (F25 Performance Plan), or those documents recording the actual event (F26 Recording). Despite being non-material embodiments, these reflect the intent of their creator to convey the concept of the work as a whole and thus to manifest it through physical media.

Conclusion and future trends

The particularity of live performance as a specific type of cultural object is highlighted by its singular features and specific descriptive needs. This has led to low agreement and heterogeneous description models and procedures within performing arts information collections, which go along the path set by LAM cultural heritage institutions. This chapter has presented an overview of major developments and the change of paradigm of description standardization at these institutions, taking advantage of the web technologies, formats and vocabularies. This trend opens up new opportunities for the inclusion of cultural heritage collections coming from the performing arts.

The use of FRBRoo ontology provides the conceptual basis for defining a semantic structure that is compatible and interoperable with background information from similar institutions. Based on this structure, descriptive schemes and controlled vocabularies can be developed according to the needs of each collection while maintaining a standard conceptual base required for the exchange of information between organizations responsible for managing such collections. The FRBRoo model can support initiatives to go across boundaries and enable the inclusion of performing arts collections in the European cultural heritage ecosystem and beyond.

Intellectual Property Matters for Documenting Performance: Challenges and Current Trends

Jeanine Rizzo

This legal discussion about documenting performance starts off by trying to grasp the golden nugget that is the subject matter of the entire exercise – what is a performance, and what legal protection is afforded to a performance? While discussions as to what constitutes a 'performance' are the subject of other discussions, the focus of this chapter is on the legal treatment not only of the performance itself but also of the documentation of the performance.

Out of all the industrial and intellectual property rights, the most obvious place in which to start when looking for an answer is in the realm of copyright law, which offers protection for the arts. Copyright is also the intellectual property right that forms the subject of truly international agreements. The environment of international legal frameworks is already strong, but the most pertinent in the context of copyright are the Berne Convention (Berne 1887), the TRIPS Agreement (TRIPS 1995) and the WIPO Performances and Phonograms Treaty (WPPT 1996). This, together with EU legislative harmonization, has meant that copyright laws throughout Europe and most of the world have converged and confer copyright on works and reciprocal rights to creators wherever they are located.

Before going further, the other face of the coin is also worth considering here. Copyleft[1]: the free dissemination of content and information for collaboration, via, for example, the use of the Creative Commons licences, is a viable solution when compiling and/or releasing content for public consumption. Following that, the chapter focuses on the protection of the person documenting the performance, the documenter or, in a broader sense, the 'memory keeper'.

A warning is not out of place here: this path of enquiry will see more questions raised than answered. However, the aim of providing this basic legal information here is mainly an attempt to raise awareness of the myriad intellectual property right issues surrounding the processes of documenting performance.

Copyright

Copyright is the legal instrument originally dedicated to protecting, amongst others, aesthetic, or rather, artistic creations. With more traditional art forms, the scope of protectable material falls squarely within the categories of works created and defined by copyright law. Copyright has laid out these categories for quite a while now. This leads to the first question: are these categories still adequate?

Turning our attention towards the categories themselves, as per copyright laws in various jurisdictions, these are usually arranged as follows: literary works, audio-visual works, musical works, artistic works, dramatic works, databases, sound recordings, and typographical arrangement of published editions. Not all countries use the same categories, for example UK law classifies specific types of works as 'dramatic works' while Maltese law does not. Parenthetically, a category directly related to the subject of this book is the UK's Copyright Designs and Patents Act (CDPA) definition of a 'dramatic work' which definition extends to include a work of dance or mime.

Regardless of these differences, it is plays, film scripts, choreography, lyrics, photographs, musical compositions and films which are the performance arts protected by the intellectual property right of copyright. From the above named legislative categories, these can be classified as literary works (plays, film scripts, lyrics and, if recorded in the proper process,[2] choreography[3]), artistic works, musical works, and audio-visual works, and if the law of the country provides for it, as dramatic works. For the sake of ease, these shall, throughout this chapter, be referred to as 'performance'.

We can therefore say that a performance can enjoy some degree of copyright protection as:

A. A literary work – the underlying script, stage directions and notes, and lyrics;
B. An artistic work – the photographs taken of the performance enjoy their own protection; also if any costumes or make up is especially detailed and complex (such as in the Frankenstein case in which the make-up prosthetics were so elaborate and moulded in such a way as to attract copyright protection);
C. An audio-visual work – the video recording of the performance capturing the performance per se;
D. A musical work – with regard to the soundtrack, or in the case that the (majority of the) performance is music based;
E. A dramatic work – for the dramatic work itself, which includes works of dance and mime.

In any case, as seen in the above, there are various forms of copyright protection for performances in terms of international laws.

Any document of the performances is also capable of attracting copyright protection – any write up, criticism or review takes the form of a literary work, the video recording of the performance is an audio-visual work, and whereas a compilation of written pieces, films, audio recordings, photographs and the like would be treated as a database. Moreover, European Union harmonisation efforts have provided a *sui generis* right for databases, the Database Right.

Fixity[4] in copyright

One of the main requirements for the subsistence of copyright in literary, musical or artistic works is the element of fixity. The work must be fixed in a tangible, or otherwise material manner. Therefore, written, drawn or captured on film or digitally. The element of fixity also applies to the category of dramatic works.

This begs the question of how a performance is fixed, or captured. The most obvious answer is having an audio-visual recording of the performance. Scripts and/or scores are also ways to capture performance, in this context. If such documents are not available, would copyright laws cover the work? Performance art pieces *per se* may not be scripted, nor filmed or otherwise recorded, as discussed elsewhere in this book. Copyright law therefore is not completely satisfactory on this point in relation to unscripted or improvised works.

The restrictions of copyright when applied to the performing arts

Art has long been moving away from traditional views of permanence which has been a staple of copyright internationally for these many years. The visual arts have delved into the ephemeral, the everyday, the *objet trouvé* (the ready-made), and other unconventional forms. Likewise, performance arts have long explored unscripted pieces, improvisations, and the impermanent. These works are therefore 'copyright challengers' since they lack sufficient permanence, something which is usually required by copyright laws, and do not fall comfortably within the definitions given in these laws.

As a loose example, which shows that this is a subject that has been around for at least the last couple decades, in the 1997 Creation Records[5] case involving the popular British rock band Oasis, the band argued that the installation or scene created and curated by Noel Gallagher for the cover of their album *Be Here Now* was protected by copyright. The question arose before Mr Justice Lloyd who was faced with the question of which category such a work would fall into. One of the arguments that was proposed was that the scene was a work of artistic craftsmanship, more specifically, a collage, thus falling within the definition of 'artistic work' as per the UK Copyright Act. In a studied and insightful judgement, the judge examined the various elements of what constitutes a work of artistic craftsmanship – since one of the main arguments was that the installation was a work of artistic craftsmanship, more precisely a collage. This led to the judge's discussion that a collage would involve the element of adhesiveness, which was lacking in the scenario presented to him. This type of debate, and the analysis as to the classification of the work in terms of the different categories under each country's copyright laws, can be extended to many works of art, not only contemporary, but also ones dating back decades, and across different art forms.

Returning to performance arts therefore, how can performances be protected by copyright when they are transient? Should they be totally excluded by copyright? Should another right be created? Or should they simply belong to the domain of contract law? The most unsatisfactory reality faced by the latter scenario is that contract law gives no protection against misuse by third parties who are not parties to the contract.

Originality and authorship

Apart from the element of fixity, one of the most fundamental tenets in copyright law is that the work must be original. This does not mean that the work must be unique or novel, but that it must originate from the author.[6] This has in fact been the major argument used by many IP lawyers and authors (and a US federal judge) in stating that the now infamous 'monkey selfie' does not enjoy copyright – because it was taken by a monkey and not by a human.[7]

Apart from that, different jurisdictions have different tests to determine whether there is sufficient 'originality' in a work. Different jurisdictions treat this differently, and have themselves undergone some degree of evolution in the theory of originality. Therefore, we see tests such as the 'sweat of the brow',[8] 'skill, labour and judgement'[9] in the UK, to 'creative spark' in the US, to 'an imprint of the author's personality"[10], and recently the "result of the author's personal intellectual creation."[11] The latter was introduced in the EU's Database Directive,[12] and was confirmed in recent cases by the Courts of Justice of the European Union giving jurists a pan-European standard to use.

Once the hurdle of originality is surpassed, and sufficient creativity is exercised in creating a work, and copyright attaches to the work, the next step is to identify the author. Who does the law consider the author of the work? In most jurisdictions, if the person is considered the author, then that person is the first to enjoy the rights, economic or otherwise, granted by copyright.

However, it is not as easy as the previous sentence may make things seem. Most European jurisdictions historically favour the author. On the other hand, is the work for hire rule, embraced by common law jurisdictions. According to the latter, whoever has engaged another to create a work will enjoy the copyright arising in the work, and the economic rights granted by copyright. The author in such a case, does not, at any moment in this relationship, enjoy the economic rights granted by copyright.

In the European approach, the author is generally held to be the first owner of the economic rights to the copyright in the work. Some exceptions do exist in the case of employment and are catered for in each country's laws.

The economic rights conferred by copyright may, nevertheless, be assigned by written agreement. This is to say that rights can be sold and/or bought, through a formal arrangement between two or more parties, or bequethed through testamentary disposition. Indeed, the principal benefits of copyright are in the so-called 'economic' rights. These are the rights which are enjoyed exclusively by the author or owner of the copyright, and which mainly deal with acts such as the reproduction, public performance, distribution, adaptation, rental and lending of the works protected by copyright.

Performers' rights

Apart from the economic rights granted by copyright, there is another family of ancillary rights: the 'neighbouring' rights, which protect those people who are involved in bringing the work to life, or to fruition. Most jurisdictions, also thanks to the influence of a number of international treaties such as the WPPT[13] and European Union legislation, provide these neighbouring rights to producers, performers and broadcasters. Performers have the exclusive right to authorize and prohibit the doing of a number of acts involving their performances. These include the fixing of their performances (i.e. for the purposes of this book, the creation of documents of the performance); the direct or indirect, temporary or permanent reproduction by any means and in any form of their performances;

the rental and lending of their fixed performances; the distribution of the original performances fixed in phonograms; the making available to the public of their performances; and the broadcasting and communication to the public of their performances. These rights may be administered by collective rights management organizations acting on behalf of performers, producers or broadcasters – such as the PPL[14] in the UK.

Documenting performance

The context presented so far in this chapter is meant to provide an understanding of the legal framework in the environment in which those who document and catalogue performances are working. This is the very foundation from which any process of documenting performance must start, because how can anyone go ahead with performance documentation if there exists, *a priori*, a legal impediment for its creation, storage or preservation?

From a legal standpoint, the first thing that needs to assessed by any person documenting a performance is captured in two basic questions: 'In what way and how would I like to document this performance?' which must quickly be followed by, 'What am I allowed to do?'

What are the ways in which someone documents a performance? By simply cataloguing its existence? By writing a review? By taking photographs of the performance? By taking audio-visual recordings of the performance? By uploading photos or video on to a website, blog, or database?

The examples listed in these questions vary from a degree which does not require consent (cataloguing, writing a review) to one which requires consent (taking a video recording of the performance). Once the person documenting – the documenter – has established the way in which the performance will be documented, it is then necessary to check whether any consent is needed from the performance rights-holder.

If the use planned by the documenter is of the more 'intrusive' type and if the owner of the performance has chosen to avail themselves of their intellectual property rights, then the documenter must obtain consent from the relative person in order to reproduce, use or adapt the work as part of the documentation process. Therefore, if the documenter is cataloguing the performance and would like to use the poster for a performance to upload or copy into a database, the copyright owner for the poster must give their consent for such use. If the documenter wishes to take a video recording of the performance, consent to do so is again needed.

Consent is not necessary if the rights holder allows free use, reproduction or adaptation of the work under Copyleft or any of the creative commons licences. Seeking consent is also unnecessary if the work has passed into the public domain – this would be the case, for instance, with old film footage or photographs. Checking whether a work has passed into the public domain may prove trickier than it first sounds. Under revised copyright law, for example in the EU, copyright subsists for the author's lifetime and for seventy years *post mortem auctoris* (following the author's death). This is not the only rule. With regard to the neighbouring rights, that is rights for producers and performers, copyright lasts fifty years from the date of the performance or of the production, however if the performance is published or communicated to the public, that term lasts seventy years not fifty, from the date of the performance. This is the modern rule, but things were not always this way. The seventy-year term for neighbouring rights is a recent development, one spurred by EU harmonization efforts, and which is a compromise between the previous fifty-year term and the proposed ninety-five year term.

What has happened is that with the evolution of copyright law, the term (i.e. duration) of copyright has also evolved – such as the most recent step regarding neighbouring rights, as outlined here. Whenever the term of copyright is extended, this is usually accompanied by a clause, which extends existing copyright by the term as extended. What may happen, however, is that some works would fall in between terms and would not be eligible for extension – for example, if the term is calculated according to the date of publication or of fixity and this would have run out. This may mean that, for example, some works involving the same performer may have passed into the public domain, while others are still covered by copyright.

Going back to the issue of consent, even though it may be considered as stating the obvious, if consent is needed, then it must be sought and obtained. The process of obtaining consent may be simple or complicated. It is simple if the person owning the rights to the performance is known. On the other hand, most lawyers will advise that one of the most complicated aspects in intellectual property law lies in trying to obtain a licence, owing to the lack of clarity as to the identity of the rights-holder.

While the rights may at first have been easy to track, throughout a work's lifetime there may have been copyright transfers, inheritances, licences and assignments that are granted but which are not searchable since there is no central registry or depository of such information. This is because ever since the Berne Convention, copyright is an automatic right, and requires no registration in order to subsist. Stemming from this, most jurisdictions do not necessitate the registration of such transfers or licences for them to have effect, which leaves us with the current situation in which tracking down the correct rights-holder may seem like a quest – but with no maps involved! This has sparked many debates, even at EU level, in favour of the creation of voluntary copyright databases or registers to facilitate the searches of any person wishing to contact the legitimate rights-holder.

With the lack of a central system, one must be innovative in tracking down the rights-holder. Other sources are consulted, such as searching on a collecting society's database if one is involved, or finding information on posters or performance websites.

Of course, in obtaining consent, the person holding the right/s, which are necessary to the documenter's desired use, must be addressed. The use that is to be made of the document must also be disclosed and discussed. So, if the documenter organizes an archive of all performance reviews, then the rights-holders whose consent is required are the newspapers, journals and, if the case may be, the writers themselves. Once contact is made, the use intended and the format of such use must be cleared, so in the example given here, the documenter can ask them to reproduce the piece as is or to post an electronic link to it, or both. If the documenter is himself the author of the review, then no consent is necessary and the content may be used directly.

Protecting the documenter's work

What remains to be discussed here is the work created by the documenter. In the example given here, the documenter may be the one writing the reviews directly. This would mean that the review is deemed to be a literary work, and therefore would classify for protection as a work of copyright in its own right.

But most importantly, if the documenter has put together an archive of work, what results is a database. Apart from being covered by copyright, a database is protected by the *sui generis* intellectual property right – the Database Right. Whereas the content of the database may be, of itself, covered by copyright, the database itself is also an asset, which attracts protection in and of itself. The *sui generis* database right is a relative newcomer to the intellectual property scene – created in the EU in 1996 via Directive 96/9/EC. This 'new' exclusive right applies to database producers and is valid for fifteen years.

The EU's Database Directive, in its first part protects the investment of time, money and effort, irrespective of whether the database in itself is innovative, and which by reason of its selection or arrangement must constitute the author's own intellectual creation. As discussed earlier, this is the first time in which such a metre is codified: 'the author's own intellectual creation'; the link between the author and the product of their intellect. This part of the directive confers copyright upon the database itself, and not upon its contents. With this right, the author of the database has the exclusive right to a number of acts, such as the reproduction of the database in any means and in any form, in whole or in part, the translation or adaptation of the database, the distribution to the public of the database and the communication, display or performance to the public.

The directive then moves on to create the *sui generis* right itself. This, in essence, is a right granted to the maker of a database that shows that there has been a qualitatively and/or quantitatively substantial investment in the obtaining, verification or presentation of the contents, giving rise to the power to prevent the extraction and/ or re-use of the whole or of a substantial part, evaluated qualitatively and/or quantitatively, of the contents of that database.[15] The term of protection, as already outlined, is of fifteen years.

A closer look at these terms reveals that 'extraction' means the permanent or temporary transfer of all or a substantial part of the contents of a database to another medium by any means or in any form; while 're-use' means any form of making available to the public all or a substantial part of the contents of a database by the distribution of copies, by renting, by on-line or other forms of transmission.

While borrowing heavily from copyright principles, the database right is to be kept firmly separate in the mind of the documenter – it is a separate and useful tool by which to protect the work done.

Finally, the directive is useful in that it gives a wide definition of what constitutes a database. This is actually sometimes regarded as a negative in that the definition is far too expansive in its reach. According to the directive, a 'database' is a collection of independent works, data or other materials arranged in a systematic or methodical way and individually accessible by electronic or other means. For the purposes of this chapter, however, it may be deemed a positive, since different documenters may have different ways in which they bring their work together, or may be bringing different types of work together in a database: such as written reviews, video reviews, photographs, designs/sketches and audio commentary.

The question, however, should be whether documenters wish to have their works protected by the database right, or whether they would like their work to be freely accessible? If so, the Creative Commons licences are a satisfactory instrument with which to safeguard basic rights, such as attribution, while making the work accessible to those wishing to consult it, use it, or develop it further.

Conclusion

With this we wrap up the legal study into the documenter's work. We start with the social obligation, or rather, service, which is being carried out by the documenter. It is thanks to this work that society benefits from the documentation, archiving, and memory of the performances that are being documented. And may we add, the benefit is not just in documenting the performance itself, but in the links to the author, the performers, the producers and all other persons involved in the creation of the performance.

We have therefore journeyed from what it is that the documenter is working with, how that source material is classified and treated, to the treatment of the work carried out by the documenter directly – the obstacles, and more importantly, the rewards.

Expanding Documentation, and Making the Most of 'the Cracks in the Wall'[1]

Annet Dekker, Gabriella Giannachi and
Vivian van Saaze

With the arrival of ephemeral, conceptual, performative, processual, networked and 'mixed reality' works of art, the document, by which we mean the physical or digital remaining trace of a work, has become a focal point of conservation and preservation strategies. The growing popularity of the document resulted in a proliferation, as well as in a dispersion, of documents. Questions, however, need to be raised as to how to value this growing body of work within the museological context. Here, we reflect on three artworks that have, for different reasons, challenged museological documentation and preservation practices regarding documentation, and suggest that a revision of museological processes of documentation, including novel strategies for the creation and management of documents, are necessary to take on board the growing complexity of what in fact may be considered a 'document'.

Problematizing the document

Documentation plays a significant role within the museological context. From the first discussions about the acquisition of an artwork, and throughout its entire existence in a museum, the artwork is subject to various processes of documentation. In most museum practices, the core of documentation strategies is focused on the conservation of the artwork. Other documents, for example, flyers or videos that are produced for publicity and presentation, or ephemera that artists may generate alongside an artwork, are also kept, but these are often regarded as being of secondary importance and stored in 'documentation' or 'acquisition files' rather than in the 'collection archive'. Building on past research (Dekker 2013; Giannachi 2017 and Giannachi et al. 2012a), we show here that secondary and auxiliary documents, as well as artists' overall approaches to documentation, should be considered when thinking through the documentation of performative artworks. Reflecting on the value of documents, including 'unauthorized documents', and expanding on the idea of audience documentation, this chapter also explores the potentiality, as well as challenges, that an upsurge and a dispersion of documentation cause to the museum. Standardized definitions of the 'document' are also questioned, to show that documents may include physical and digital attributes, as well as visual and textual documentation, and that they may, in time, become artworks.

Our first case study, Lynn Hershman Leeson's *Roberta Breitmore*, consists of the manufacture of a performed persona, interpreted by different people, technologies and platforms through an expanding number of documents which are usually identified as artworks. The second case study consists of a number of artworks by Tino Sehgal labelled by the artist as 'constructed situations', that attempt to escape documentation altogether, yet generate what has been regarded as unauthorized or 'illicit documents'. Finally, JODI's *THIS PAGE CONTAINS . . .*, elucidates the challenges posed by a performance that requires the creation of documents for both its physical and digital components. What these artworks have in common is that they generated a diverse body of documents whose status is unstable and, museologically speaking, still to be determined.

Traditionally, documentation is produced by museum professionals, such as curators, conservators and registrars, sometimes in collaboration with the artists. In the case of Hershman Leeson, the documents were generated by the artist over a prolonged period of time; in the case of Sehgal, they were generated by museum visitors and interpreters; and in the case of JODI, they were created by a group of documentalists, consisting of art students, artists and researchers.

In this chapter, we explore how these (artistic) practices reconfigure the relationship between the artwork and the document and thereby challenge museological documentation. In the process, we question to what extent Suzanne Briet's well-known work on documentation (2006 [1951]), in particular her distinction between primary, secondary and auxiliary documents, can shed light on expanding these hierarchies of documentation, and whether her classification still holds today. Elaborating on Briet's analysis, we discuss how these documents should be seen as inter-documents, environments that comprise primary, secondary, auxiliary documents, showing also how they can become, as in Hershman Leeson's case, artworks in their own right. Finally, we show how the valuation and subsequent hierarchy of museum documentation needs to change to reflect the growing complexity of artistic and visitor or audience generated documents. This includes new ways of thinking about what the document and documentation mean, which may also require a reconsideration of their structure and role in the museum.

When the artwork is the document: Lynn Hershman Leeson

The first case study is *Roberta Breitmore* (1972–8).[2] In this artwork, the artist Lynn Hershman Leeson embraced the role of the fictitious persona of Roberta Breitmore for an initial period of six years.

Using surveillance technology (photography and moving image) and developing a graphic novel in collaboration with Spain Rodriguez, Hershman Leeson captured various moments in Roberta's life, creating a set of documents that were then re-formed, often through collage, including text and painting, into individual artworks. Here we see how these documents, both primary and secondary, which were originally conceived of as a testimony to the occurrence of the performance of *Roberta Breitmore*, together with a new set of documents produced in recent times, became both part of, and the totality of, the still evolving artwork known as *Roberta Breitmore*.

The chronology of the documents that form *Roberta Breitmore* reflects their creation, rather than the occurrence of particular events in her 'life'. From these, a number of biographical factors can be deducted that may be interesting so as to interpret the construction of Roberta's persona or role. For example, from *Untitled from Roberta's External Transformation from Roberta (Roberta's Construction Chart)* (1975), we know that Roberta was born on 19 August 1945; she was educated at Kent State University where she majored in Art and Drama; she married Arnold Marx in 1969 and was divorced after three years; and she travelled on a Greyhound bus to San Francisco and checked into room forty-seven at the Hotel Dante on Columbus Avenue. At that time, Roberta was carrying $1,800, which corresponded to her entire life savings. The hotel was also the site of Hershman Leeson's artwork *The Dante Hotel* (1973), an early site-specific piece in which Hershman Leeson rented a room in a run-down hotel on Columbus Avenue in San Francisco where visitors would encounter evidence of its inhabitation by a fictitious character.

Hershman Leeson's live performance started with Roberta's arrival in San Francisco. Here, she underwent a series of external and internal transformations that can be traced through a number of documents. The *Roberta Construction Chart* #1 (1973) shows how Roberta was painted by 'Dior eyestick light', blushed through '"Peach Blush" Cheekcolor by

Revlon', and how her lips were shaped though '"Date Mate" scarlet'. *Untitled from Roberta's External Transformations (From Roberta's Body Language Chart)* (1978) shows that she also had a vocabulary of gestures so that, for example, she would have tried to 'avert attention' by 'avoiding your eyes' and that she sat in a stiff and tense way.

One such transformation was filmed by Hershman Leeson's friend Eleanor Coppola in 1974, with whom she was working on *The Dante Hotel*, and is now often exhibited as a still document dated 1975. After checking into the Hotel Dante, Roberta tried to find a roommate by placing an advert in some local papers, including the *S.F. Progress* (1974) and, later, on *The San Diego Union and Evening Tribune* (1975). Roberta's meetings with potential roommates were documented, for example, in *Roberta and Irwin Meet for the First Time in Union Square Park* (1975). *Roberta Breitmore Blank Check* (1974) shows that she also had a financial existence, while *Untitled from Roberta's Internal Transformations, Language from Roberta (excerpt from Roberta's psychiatric evaluation)* (1978) shows that she suffered from severe alienation and experienced difficulties in distinguishing dreams from reality. Finally, *Untitled from Adventure Series: Meet Mr. America (Roberta contemplating suicide on Golden Gate Bridge)* (1978) shows that, unable to integrate in contemporary society, she contemplated suicide.

Looking at the individual documents, some of them could be described as primary, such as, among others, Roberta's check, her driving licence, a button from her coat, her dress. Others could be described as secondary, like the construction charts and the diary, for example. Finally, there is a growing number of auxiliary documents such as, to some extent, this case study. Brought together, and seen as an inter-document, these documents do not so much construct a persona as an environment. Being part of this environment of the performance, both primary and secondary documents moved beyond being mere representations of a former activity to become part of it. Throughout this process, they also became autonomous artworks.

In line with John Seeley Brown and Paul Duguid (2000), who argue that information is meaningful because it is so within a network, we regard documents as signifying forms that acquire meaning in relation to other documents. Moreover, we agree with Ronald Day's comment '[documents] are meaningful signs in relation to other signs [...] within whose difference from one another and in relation to things and events they gain their identity and their referentiality' (2014: 5). We suggest here that documents are not in opposition to performance, but rather they emerge from and are part of the environment generated by performance. Not only do they acquire meaning in relation to it, they become a sign for it. This phenomenon also explains the potential performativity of performance documentation and a current obsession with replaying and restaging documents. The document is implicated in its past, present and potential future performance.

During her lifetime, *Roberta Breitmore* became a multiple as Hershman Leeson engaged three women, including the art historian Kristine Stiles, to 'be' Roberta. Hershman Leeson recalls that Stiles went out as Roberta, and Hershman Leeson as herself because 'there was a rumour about Roberta' and she wanted people to 'think that she existed' (2015). *So Untitled (Roberta's Signature in Guest Book)* (1975) is in fact Stiles's, and not Hershman Leeson's, signature. All performers wore wigs and costumes identical to the ones worn by Hershman Leeson when performing Roberta, and all underwent a series of transformations: '[e]ach had two home addresses and two jobs – one for Roberta and one for herself – and each corresponded with respondents to the advertisement and went on dates that were obsessively recorded in photographs and audiotapes' (in Tromble and Hershman Leeson 2005: xiii). Finally, Hershman Leeson ceased performing as Roberta, leaving the three hired performers on their own. In 1978, an exhibition of Roberta's artefacts entitled *Lynn Hershman Is Not Roberta Breitmore/Roberta Breitmore Is Not Lynn Hershman* was presented at the M.H. de Young Memorial Museum in

San Francisco during which a Roberta look-alike contest was run that led to an additional multiplication of Robertas accompanied by a further expansion of documents. Noticeably, most studies of this artwork only refer to Hershman Leeson's performance of Roberta and rarely discuss the artwork as a multiple or a remediated artwork.

After being exorcized at the Palazzo dei Diamanti in Ferrara (1978), Roberta was re-mediated as the telerobotic doll *CyberRoberta* (1995–8), who was dressed identically to Roberta, and had a fictional persona that was, as in Hershman Leeson's words, 'designed as an updated Roberta' who not only navigated the internet, but was in herself a creature of the internet, a 'cyberbeing' (1996: 336). Roberta was also brought back in *ReConstructing Roberta* (2005) which shows an image of Hershman Leeson taken in recent years alongside the text 'botox injections three to six months – Cut and Lift, pin back xxxx Liposuction Electric Stimulation Rejouvenation ////'. Additionally, Roberta appeared as a bot in the Second Life remake of *The Dante Hotel,* called *Life^n (Life to the Power of n),* or *Life Squared* (2007–), which turned a number of documents in the Hershman Leeson archive about the homonymous artwork now hosted at Stanford University Libraries into a mixed reality experience where visitors could explore digital reproductions of fragments of the original archive under Roberta's guidance in Second Life (Giannachi and Kaye 2011).[3] When asked why Roberta keeps on reappearing in her artwork, Hershman Leeson commented: Roberta 'just comes back in different forms every now and then. For *CybeRoberta,* it was twenty years later as a surveillance system, which she originally was, but used the technology of that time; for *Life Squared* as an effort for immortality in digital space. She also came back thirty years later and appeared in a plastic surgeon's office'.[4] These re-mediations, produced through the reworking of other documents, testify to the fact that different technologies literally re-formed both the body of the artwork and the environment that is *Roberta Breitmore.*

While the M.H. de Young Memorial Museum in San Francisco did not retain any documentation of its 1978 exhibition, *Roberta Breitmore* is now part of a number of collections, including those at the Museum of Modern Arts, New York (MoMA), the Walker Art Center, the Whitworth Art Gallery, and the Donald Hess Collection. It also featured in a major retrospective about Hershman Leeson's artwork that started at ZKM and then toured Germany and the United Kingdom in 2015. The artworks that form *Roberta Breitmore* are usually shown individually. However, at the ZKM retrospective, a number of them, including dresses, photos, collages of transformations, were exhibited alongside each other, making it possible for visitors to begin to read them as inter-documents. MoMA displayed a number of artworks that are not ordinarily on display on their website,[5] including *Roberta's Room, Baker Acres* (1976), showing Roberta's barren room at Baker Acres, between Baker and Jackson, and *Kristine Stiles as Roberta Breitmore at Gallery Opening* (1976), an artwork that documents the gallery visit cited above, *Untitled (Roberta's Signature in Guest Book)* (1975), which is, however, dated one year earlier. The same is true for the Walker Arts Center, which has a wide collection of artworks that are grouped together online, including *Untitled from Roberta's External Transformation from Roberta (Roberta's Construction Chart)* (1975), subtitled 'an Alchemical Portrait Begun in 1975 by Lynn Hershman', suggesting how *Roberta Breitmore* is related to processes of trans-formation, in the sense that the artwork literally migrates between forms and documents created through them. This online document also offers a 'meta-narrative', including the brief synopsis of Roberta's life that we discussed above.

Most museums do not make public their own interpretation or documentation of the artworks in exhibitions. However, reading their documentation offers an interesting insight into the challenges artworks often produce for museum curators. For example, former Tate curator Kelli Dipple noted in her justification for acquiring the artwork, how each of the 'three complete editions' of the *Roberta*

Breitmore inventory,[6] in addition to one artist's proof set, contained items from her personal rendition of the character, consisting of 'around 300 individual photographs, documents and artefacts'.[7] By documents, Dipple probably meant what, in line with Briet's suggestion, we call secondary documents and by artefacts she probably meant what we call primary documents. In a further e-mail to Frances Morris, she also noted: 'due to the nature of the project I was unable to settle on the best way to annotate the individual vs. collective artwork. I started with the Roberta Construction Chart # 1 vintage print, but found that most explanation of the artwork was indeed an explanation of the entire project of Roberta Breitmore'.[8]

Roberta Breitmore can be described as a body of work, formed by an environment comprising a series of sites, people, documents and objects, which, over the course of Hershman Leeson's live performance, multiplied exponentially, leading to an expansion of documents across a variety of forms and media. These are rarely exhibited together and so audiences usually perceive them as instances of a dispersed artwork rather than as a body of work. Exhibited or interpreted together, as was the case at ZKM, they show a more complex and organic aesthetic vision about the relationship between performance and documentation that allows us to surpass existing debates in the field which identify the two as dichotomous (Phelan 1993a) and rather see them as inter-related (Jones 1997; Clausen 2005; Auslander 2006). However, reading them as inter-related highlights the presence of substantial 'cracks in the wall', as ultimately, despite this expansion of documentation, it is impossible to comprehend, or even grasp, the entirety of *Roberta Breitmore*.

Unauthorized documents: Tino Sehgal

In contrast to such a richly documented artistic practice, is a growing body of artists who challenge existing relationships between the artwork and the document by rejecting any form of documentation of their artworks. Our second case study focuses on one of the most rigorous and consistent examples, Tino Sehgal's attempts to avoid any visual documents and material traces resulting from his 'constructed situations'. His pieces are live encounters, often executed by hired (amateur) actors or dancers, carrying out instructions conceived by the artist and learned through rehearsals. As many of his artworks are now entering museum collections, his particular practice challenges standardized documentation processes which museums rely upon (Laurenson and Van Saaze 2014: 35). As Justin Graham and Jill Sterrett (1997) write: 'to the extent they exist, documentary traces from the past shape the institutional memory of what the work can be'. In the case of Sehgal's artworks, however, instead of relying on materialized memory, such as a score or photographs, knowledge of how to perform his pieces is intended to be transferred from person to person, from body to body. The restriction on the production of all kinds of documents goes as far as to avoid any written set of instructions, written receipts, wall labels and announcements (Richards 2012). With only a few interviews available, several critics have attempted to identify the motivations behind this restriction. According to Arthur Lubow, for example, Sehgal 'makes art that does not require the transformation of any materials. He refuses to add objects to a society that he says is overly encumbered with them' (2010). Another explanation is provided by Dorothea von Hantelmann who argues that for Sehgal the reason for prohibiting any form of documenting lies in preventing 'the translation of situations into a two-dimensional medium, thus preventing documentation from functioning as a kind of surrogate for the artwork. It is of crucial significance whether a situational artwork enters history as a memory or as a document' (2010: 134).

The ban on visual or written documents prevents the existence of a score or inter-document, yet emphasises the pervasiveness of a perceived dichotomy between performance and document as mentioned earlier. This is addressed in one of his pieces, *This is critique* (2008). In this artwork, the museum visitor is spoken to by, what appears to be, a museum guard stating three critiques of the artist's work and initiating a discussion about his approach. One of the criticisms addressed by the interpreter is the artist's refusal to allow photographic and video documents of the artwork.

With respect to the artworks' ephemeral character and the ban on document creation, it is not always clear which forms of material traces are considered to be problematic and which are not (Van Saaze 2015). Some authors even display a certain hesitation to write about his artworks, while others indicate that their writings are inconsistent to Sehgal's practice. Art critic Stéphanie Moisdon notes: 'One cannot write about Tino Sehgal's artworks without committing a first anomaly, by attempting to give them a title, to describe or to list them, that is, to enter into rivalry with the form of the artwork itself, which is the affirmation of what it is' (2003). In a similar vein, one of Sehgal's interpreters, Nico Colón, asks whether he is allowed to reveal his memories: 'I guess as long as I'm not actively working for him, at this moment, I can be free to express myself. So I am morally off the hook. It's *my* experience, after all. The artwork is Sehgal's, but I own my own experience. If *he* owned *my* experience, that would actually bother me' (in Jensen 2013, original emphasis). While visitors, interpreters and museum staff are asked not to take pictures of the artworks, interestingly Sehgal's practice evokes an ever-growing body of visual and written documents outside the confines of the museum. Echoing what Michel Foucault has called 'the incitement to discourse' (1978: 17) – the prohibition of a certain word or practice leading to a proliferation of that same word or practice – his artworks generate a remarkable amount of images. These 'illicit' or unauthorized pictures and videos taken during exhibitions appear online and are shared through social media networking sites.

In addition to this emerging body of visual material, his practice has sparked an immense number of witness reports from members of the audience, as well as from interpreters – all expressing a desire to share something of their experiences and memories. These tertiary documents, however, are not archived by museums as they are largely considered to be materials produced against the artist's wishes or regarded as 'merely interpretation' (Van Saaze 2015). Yet, instead of rejecting them altogether, an emerging challenge would be to consider the potential of such 'unauthorized' documents and the role of members of the audience and interpreters as distributed memory holders enabling future enactments of Sehgal's artworks. Especially considering the vulnerability of institutional memory in the absence of material traces, the visitors' and interpreters' accounts may be of value with regard to the artwork's perpetuation in the longer term. This in turn speaks to larger issues of shifting notions of experts and expertise in a museological context as well as to questions as to what the relationship is between documents produced by artists or professionals and those generated by audiences or even the general public.

Expanding documentation: JODI

The final case study of this chapter consists of a performance by JODI, *THIS PAGE CONTAINS . . .*, which was performed on 1 October 2015 at the Stedelijk Museum in Amsterdam. The Dutch/Belgium duo, Joan Heemskerk and Dirk Paesmans (JODI), are renowned for their subversive acts. Advertised as a performance during which 'the physical and digital worlds are both united and destabilized', JODI lived up to their reputation. With their artworks, JODI invert the visible and invisible in an attempt to come to grips with the computer environment. Their projects vary from net artworks, to game modifications, videos to performances, and the individual artworks are exhibited and performed in various ways over the years. An interesting question emerges, how to document such variable artworks for future reference?

In an attempt to explore different forms and ways of documenting, we asked several 'documentalists' to create a document of JODI's performance at the Stedelijk Museum.[9] The intention was to emphasize the variability in JODI's practice, while at the same time moving beyond traditional documenting practices. The idea to expand on existing documenting practices, derived from a three-year long experiment in creating new types of documents that was initiated by Dekker at the Piet Zwart Institute in Rotterdam.[10] This experiment was developed as part of a course on how to document complex artworks. In the course, the meaning and value of documentation is analyzed by comparing different types of documents; paying particular attention to how different goals affect documentation and how this in turn influences the documents that are created. Attention is also paid to how documents are used by different kinds of institutes, organizations and individuals that produce, collect and manage cultural material. Moreover, the students are asked to create their own documents: the first year MA students need to document the final work of their second year colleagues. While choosing a specific goal – from documents that are used for publicity and presentation, for funding, to those made for re-enactment/preservation – the motivation is to capture the significant properties of the artwork that is documented in whatever form they think is suitable.

The three-year experiment resulted in many different forms and methods, ranging from traditional artists' interviews, photography and video of an installation or performance, to elaborate concise code analysis, an intricate web interface showing screenshots from the artist's online research process via social media platforms, an IKEA-like manual, and a process-based flipbook. Although most students struggled at first to get to the core of their colleagues' artworks, through several talks and assessing the research and its outcomes the students managed to capture what they thought was the essence of the artwork and the intention of its creator. At the same time, while the documents showed what the actual artworks or performances were about, it was often argued – in a positive sense – that some of the results became new artworks.

One of the reasons for seeing these documents as new artworks was perhaps related to the amount of time, once a month during one year, which was spent thinking, talking and reflecting on the assignment and its outcome. Another reason perhaps was that being artists themselves, the documentalists, found it difficult to distance themselves from their own practice as artists. However, instead of pondering over reasons, we asked ourselves whether these documents, rather than being secondary documents, perhaps showed signs of what Briet termed auxiliary documents? Briet mentions that documents are contextual, and rather than delivering remains of an isolated event, they are reflective of the networks in which that object appears. This, according to Briet, 'can in certain cases end in a genuine *creation*, through the juxtaposition, selection, and the comparison of documents, and the production of auxiliary documents' (2006: 16, original emphasis). To overcome the 'artificial' situation of the classroom assignment in which documents were created, and to further explore the distinction between secondary and auxiliary documents we used the performance by JODI as a case to show the multiple ways of creating documents, and in the process, address the meaning and potential (re)use of documents.

As mentioned earlier, a group of seven people was asked to document JODI's performance, which lasted twenty-eight minutes. Beforehand, there was a short brief about the content and set-up of the performance and the various possibilities of documenting the event. The use of the PA system was discussed, along with additional lights, placement of cameras and the possibility of screen-casting the performance from JODI's laptop. In addition, we talked about different forms of documenting and decided that each person, or duo, based on their interests, would focus on one particular form.

The results ranged from a video reinterpretation (Michaela Lakova), a short text description (Hélia Marçal), a written account of the event that combined personal impressions with objective script logs (Lucas Battich), an interview with JODI as part of the creation of a conservation record (Molly Bower and Nina van Doren), and a double screen video capturing the audience perception (Thomas Walskaar), to finding ways to distribute the documents that were created (Julie Boschat Thorez). Except for the latter, all the documents became individual interpretations of the performance, in which some focused on the presentation itself, others on the audience experiencing the performance, or attempting to capture the intentions of the artists. Some of these outcomes could be seen as stand-alone new artworks; for example, Lakova's video was a remix of some of the sounds and the content that were used in the performance, overlaid with a design that is reminiscent of the title sequences. This translation was not a 'faithful' recording of the event and more of a subjective interpretation of what was shown, indeed, in some ways, a new artwork. At the same time, the aesthetics of the original performance were still clearly visible. Likewise, Battich's designed paper publication read like a short novel, alternating between personal observations and exact timings. The precise notation of the timings, the technical environment of how the performance was created and what was shown could be seen as a written score of the performance, potentially to be used to re-perform the performance. Moreover, his personal comments and specific design of the text emphasised exclusivity and uniqueness, which was closer to a new artwork than a document of an existing artwork. Even the more traditional approach taken by Bower and van Doren, following a museum's method of documenting an artwork, in its final design attempts to show the multiple layers of understanding a mediated performance. Working with transparent layers of information, each layer presenting a specific aspect of the performance, they tried to create a non-hierarchical document in which technical and subjective approaches existed simultaneously.

Moving beyond traditional methods of documenting, these documents had in common the quality of possibly being seen as extensions of the original artwork, the performance – which, also, in part, consisted of documents generated through code that were performed to the audience. Suggestive of both secondary and auxiliary documents, and still implicating some primary documents formed by the original code, it is in the multiplicity of documents and their shared environment that, like *Roberta Breitmore*, they become inter-documents.

The idea of the inter-documentary is further emphasized by the document that Boschat Thorez created. Based on the idea that digital artworks are vulnerable over time and that their strength resides in the possibility of their dissemination over the internet, Boschat Thorez explained that 'collaboration and the multiplication of documents over a wide range of hardware and operating systems, belonging to differently skilled people, should also be regarded as a strategy for sustaining memory over time'.[11] For her documentation effort, Boschat Thorez created a digital folder that contained all the (digitized) documents that were made of JODI's performance, including screen captures from the laptop that were sent by JODI after the performance, which she then distributed via various online networks – to be (re)used by anyone. It was an attempt to reflect on the sharing of information far and wide as an alternative preservation method. It could be argued that this is merely a distribution method, and not a document. However, the way the information was selected, packaged, repurposed and contextualized reflect the characteristics of Briet's notion of an auxiliary document. At the same time, shifting the thinking of documentation as a single interpretation, a set of instructions or guidelines, to a conceptual method from which new interpretations can be made, provides new ways to understand the meaning and value of documentation.

Conclusion

In this chapter we have shown that artists creating what could be described as ephemeral, conceptual, performative, processual, networked and 'mixed reality' artworks have expanded our understanding of what a document could be, and so challenged our evaluation of its relationship to an artwork and, in turn, to the documentation processes museums undertake. We have described the practice of Lynn Hershman Leeson, whose artwork *Roberta Breitmore* is usually exhibited as a series of artefacts, and claimed that to understand all the intricacies of the artwork it should perhaps be exhibited as an inter-document or environment. In describing how Hershman Leeson's documents evolved over time, we have seen how they became artworks and so challenged the distinction between primary, secondary and even tertiary documents. We have reflected on Sehgal's refusal to enter practices of material documents, which has inspired questions as to what may or may not be a legitimate relationship between the artist's game plan and documents produced by others. We have also shown, in the case of JODI's artwork *THIS PAGE CONTAINS ...*, that artworks can inspire creative ways of making documents and documentation. Our case studies have shown that Briet's classifications and hierarchies, which were developed for a library context, fall short in an aesthetic and museological context. Through the lens of particular artistic practices, we have demonstrated that documents form part of a complex, dynamic and, above all, expanding environment. This finding challenges museums to revisit their documentation practices and reassess the value of documents and documentation for exhibition and preservation.

Acknowledgements

We gracefully acknowledge the AHRC grant 'Performance at Tate' (AH/M004228/1) which funded research into Lynn Hershman Leeson's *Roberta Breitmore*. We are very grateful to all artists presented in the case studies.

Part Two

Ways of Documenting Performance

The ways we document performance have changed radically over the past hundred years or so. Until the invention of photography, the only two ways to document performance were writing and orality. From the very start of motion picture capture and sound recordings, performances were captured as documents to be accessed at a later date and most often different place. However, throughout most of the twentieth century the means to document performance, other than writing and orality, remained in the hands of those few who could afford the elaborate sound, film or video equipment. With the rise of good quality digital technology that is relatively affordable to many people, it is now safe to assume that millions of people have high-quality sound and video recording devises in their pockets.

Before plunging in to the use of digital technology it is essential to re-evaluate orality as a method for documenting performance. That is why this section of the book opens with Panayiota A. Demetriou's 'Remembering Performance Through Oral History'. Still, the techniques involved in contemporary oral history preservation, frequently also involve recording technology and written transcripts. This points to the fact that there are more elaborate ways to document performance, outside the performance event itself, and these often involve more than just one medium.

In presenting chapters reflecting on the ways performance is documented, I also considered the role of drawing, painting, sketching and other art methods or techniques. However, this book does not contain a chapter that deals directly with this topic. The use of visual art objects is the approach discussed in Lee Campbell's contribution to the special issue of the 2014 *International Journal of Performance Arts and Digital Media* discussing interdisciplinary approaches to documenting performance. Campbell focuses on the relationship between performance documents and visual art objects in response to a philosophical position concerning forms of documenting performance held widely in the relevant works on liveness by Philip Auslander. In that same journal issue, Michael J. Wooley writes about documenting performance art through photography from the perspective of a professional photographer. Here Helen Newall, Amy Skinner and Allan Taylor take a broader approach to photographic documents of performance. In chapter 7, 'Translating Performance: desire, intention and interpretation in photographic documents', they provide ample reflection on the role of photography in the processes for documenting performance.

Although they allude to the ubiquity of digital photography in our time, it is Joanna Bucknall and Kirsty Sedgman who take the readers of this book into the realm of social media and audience members as documenters, especially through live microblogging. The aggregation of various online contributions, sometimes taking place simultaneously during performances, leads not only to casual use of Twitter, Facebook, Instagram, and similar digital text and visual commentary services, but also the possibility to gather such information through services like Storify,[1] which enable the retelling aspects of the audience experience through curated live feeds from the online social media services used during the live performance.

This form of performance document is much more fluid than the subject of the next chapter. Vanessa Bartlett's 'Web Archiving and Participation', takes a closer look at one aspect of the previous chapter further by exploring the state of institutional web archives and the way these relate to informal social memory. Bartlett speculates about the new kinds of historical information that performance scholars may be able to preserve as a result of recent innovations in web archiving. the chapter points to limitations in the current web archiving structures and points out that further innovation is required to maximize the scholarly potential of the material contained within web archives. That innovation should include aspects of what Daniel Wegner calls Transactive Memory (Wegner 1986). In such a system, groups encode, store, and retrieve knowledge collectively. Knowledge stored in each individual's memory combined with 'metamemory' containing information regarding each collaborator's domains of expertise (Wegner 1995). Like metadata, metamemory allows us to know what information is available for retrieval. Ultimately, a transactive memory system provides collaborators with information about the knowledge they have access to within their group or team. Wikipedia and other open knowledge projects are excellent examples of transactive memory systems.

Another point that Bartlett makes in a subtle way is that ultimately it may be that most of the documents of performance that remain from the early digital era will be whatever web archives manage to capture over the years. Indeed, the volatility of documenting digital material arising either directly or indirectly from live performance work is part of the subject of the final chapter in this section.

In 'Documenting Digital Performance Artworks' (chapter 10), Adam Nash and Laurene Vaughan examine the unique qualities of digital live art works in the context of archiving such works. Like the chapter that closes the previous section, they use case studies to interrogate the role and concept of documenting and archiving live performance in the light of these works. They particularly highlight the way contemporary works of digital live art can blur the distinction between artwork, archive and documentation, as real time data sources are used to bring them about in ways that would otherwise be used to preserve aspects of them through a process of documentation. Such works can therefore create a type of automatically generated archive, possibly producing documentation of the work rather than mere documents of it. They propose a new understanding of the concepts and methods of archiving and documentation, echoing the concerns from Rinehart and Ippolito mentioned in the previous section introduction.

Remembering Performance Through the Practice of Oral History

Panayiota A. Demetriou

The relationship between liveness, the process of documenting performance, has been disputed vigorously by performance theorists since the early 1990s. Philip Auslander (1999, 2006) and Rebecca Schneider (2011) have countered the ontology of performance as a disappearance proposed by Phelan (1993). This chapter applies Schneider's (2011) view of how the event exists after it actually happens; how it lives on through its remains, its ephemeral residues and traces that 'are the immaterial [. . .] of live, embodied acts' (p. 102). Auslander's (2006) point of view, which suggests that the important relationship 'is not the one between the document and the performance but the one between the document and its audience' (Auslander 2006: 6), is also an essential aspect of the approach presented here. These two complementary perspectives have been adopted, in order to discuss how the practice of oral history has been used as a method of documenting memories of past performances. Here James Fogerty's (2006) definition of oral history is used to consider oral history as a performance in itself, one that is established through the interaction of an interviewer with a narrator (p. 207). In this manner, this chapter examines how performance events are able to live on through the stories told by their creators and audience members, and how these recorded narrations of oral histories can act as additional documents when remembering performance events and researching theatre and performance.

A project that has used oral history to record and exhibit specific performance histories is used as an example for the application of the selected theoretical framework following Auslander and Schneider. The project *Memory of Theatre* (2012) established a collection of audience stories about the Bristol Old Vic Theatre and used them to create an interactive archive. Through the discussion of this project, it is possible to examine the relationship between archives, memories and the concerns that emerge when attempting to archive such ephemeral, transitory or experiential data and how it has been used further. The chapter will address the following questions: 'How effective is oral history as a method of documenting performance and gathering an understanding of past performances?' and 'What can oral histories contribute to the archive that other documents cannot?'

Memory of Theatre

In 2012, Paul Clarke together with Bristol Old Vic Artistic Director Tom Morris, theatre production company MAYK, and the creative company Pryxis Design produced *Memory of Theatre*, a Heritage Sandbox project funded by REACT knowledge exchange hub for the creative economy. This was an oral history project that surveyed the relationship between archives and memories.

The project used oral history to record the memories of audience members, artists, performers or staff who used or attended the Bristol Old Vic over the past years. Individual participants were asked to give personal impressions based on a memory of attending the theatre: a performance at the Bristol Old Vic, a memory of performing on the Theatre Royal Stage, a recollection of working in the box office, working front of house; or perhaps to recall an event that they experienced whilst in the building beyond the stage. The stories were told and presented in a variety of tenses, to reflect the plurality of individual experiences found in oral histories. Some began by providing a description of how they saw the space in which their memory took place, at that specific moment. They continued by describing how it was in the past and what had happened there and then. Other participants told the story as though it was occurring at the precise moment of the interview. This meant that the use of variation of past, present and future tenses in the recollections would not only preserve the memory leading to a richer experience, but would also conserve the 'now' of when the interview occurred.

This idea hints at the notion of the oral history interview recording as a document and a record of a discussion about the past event, and not as direct evidence or a representation of the event recounted. In this sense, the interview technique operates as the 'artefact of memory' of the specific past event that the narrator is questioned about and the 'process of memory making' (Shopes and Hamilton 2008). Heddon (2014) and Pearson and Shanks (2001) have identified that memories told reveal less information about facts and more about how they are remembered. This echoes Portelli's (1991) view, which suggests that interviews expose unknown events or unknown parts of known events (p. 2). The interviewees' testimonies, inherent with their subjectivity, not only disclose their drive and intention but also their individual beliefs and their reflections. In this sense, the evidence gathered from oral testimonies, similar to the practice of theatre historiography, reveals less about the events that are being told and more about their meanings. This was certainly the case with the narratives collected for *Memory of Theatre*. The collection that included stories of backstage experiences, ghost sightings and audience recollections, elicited, to use Pearson and Shanks's (2001) words, 'other stories, and stories about stories', which catalyzed personal reflection (p. 177).

In the field of Theatre Historiography, the historical 'fact' of theatrical and performance histories is considered within a preoccupation with events, audience reception, the ephemeral and intangible. The study is not about 'what was' but instead 'what might have been' (Davis in Nicholson and Kersaw 2011: 97). The field focuses on the survey of performances that have been previously unknown in history, or it can be used as a device of cross-examination to question the absence of theatre histories in the historical record. In addition to focusing on play texts and viewing these as social documents of the past, Theatre Historiography also explores events and behaviours of the past by using techniques from ethnography; as the history of theatre can be embodied, orally transmitted and documented. However, because of the ephemeral nature of theatre and performance, 'history and historiography must enable both memorialisation and disruption and must embrace oral testimony and embodied history as well as the material object and written text' (Davis in Kershaw and Nicholson 2011: 98). The archival 'disruption' that Davis (2011) underlines in the above quote, occurs when including such modes from the repertoire, which Diana Taylor (2003) argues represent modes of embodied cognition. Taylor (2003) claims that these modes produce types of historical knowledge that are orthodoxly rejected from archival practices, as they counter the archives' origins. This is because archives tend to hold materials that are removed from the direct effect of the event, which as explained is not the case with the oral history interview and conceptually does not apply to the interviews recorded for *Memory of Theatre*.

Each story from *Memory of Theatre* was captured using binaural recording. This approach was taken to reflect the notions of presence and absence when encountering the captured interviews, as binaural recording is used to create a 3-D stereo sound sensation for the listener. It creates the impression of actually being in the room with the narrator. Alongside this, the interviews were taken in-situ. Heike Roms points out that with in-situ interviews, the site acts as a type of mnemonic, prompting 'practitioners and audiences [to] engage

creatively in a return to the original conditions of the performance'
(Shaughnessy 2012: 219). These methods were not only undertaken
to aid the process of remembering by placing the interviewee in the
place of action, but also adopting the approach of binaural recording –
having the memory-giver wear binaural microphones in each ear –
documented along with the telling, the space's acoustic and location
sounds. Hence, both approaches collaboratively reinforced the notion
of locality and in-situ within the project, and created a practical
response to the exploration of the relationship between space/place
and the process of remembering. The use of different voices (visitor,
artist, performer, staff), the variation of tenses in the telling of the
stories, the spatialization/localization of each individual memory and
the specific approach to recording, generated a collision of thoughts
in regard to memory and the theatre as a space of cultural heritage, in
terms of offering an aural representation for the way that human
memory operates – fragmented, subjective and almost mythical.

The collection of these narratives was then embedded onto an
indoor positioning system that operated similarly to a GPS, which
had the ability to detect and locate an individual when inside a
building. With the help of the specific digital technology that was
developed for this project, the stories were given life and cloaked in
the atmosphere of the Bristol Old Vic's auditorium and foyer. This was
accessed using an application for smartphone that transformed it into
a location-triggering device, which allowed the different memories to
be heard via the smartphone, in the place where they happened. At
present the app is not available for commercial use, but it is currently
in further development to make it available more widely. The objective
of presenting three-dimensional sound recordings was to make the
absent storyteller present again for the listener. As Clarke explains on
the project's blog-posts that describe its development, 'the event from
recent history will encounter the theatre's present [...] the now of
the interview will be overlaid with the remembered place and time

of listening for the future participant/audience' (Heritage Sandbox 2012). This emphasizes the idea of the theatre as a space haunted by stories of individuals who worked, performed or visited the site, and thus playing with the notions of presence and absence, and most importantly it underlines the transient manner of performance and its relationship to oral history: as being bedfellows within the repertoire of embodied cognition.

When applying Auslander's (2006) and Schneider's (2011) perspectives to question how performance can live on through its audiences' memories, it is useful to look at Heidi Roms's work on performance art in Wales. Rom's research and practice rely on the practice of oral history to document collective memories of performance art in Wales during the 1960s and 1970s, staging interviews with artists live in front of an audience. In doing this, she argues that the interviewee performs a 'personal narrative' (Roms 2008: xi). Its form is not only influenced by the conditions of the event and the relationship with the interviewer, but it is also impacted, as she maintains, 'by the awareness of the interviewee that he or she speaks through the interviewer to a larger, absent audience' (Roms 2008: xi). Therefore, the present audience represents audiences that tend to be absent, whose encounters with the accounts usually occur through their recordings or via their transcriptions. By inviting audience members to attend the interviews, Roms aimed to demonstrate that 'remembering a performance must be a communal act' (Roms 2008: xi). This provokes a methodological concern that emerges in the context of oral history: whether during the interview, the subject is engaged in a form of performance. Subsequently, does the process of recording transform the content or delivery of the interviewee's story?

Following Goffman's (1959) model on social life being staged, which encouraged notions of role-playing, impression management and benign fabrications, Austin (1975), Turner (1985), Conquergood

(1998), Friedman (2006) and Pollock (2008) have individually perceived the narrative mode as a type of performance, as a form of structured behaviour and a communicative act. Pollock (2008) states that oral histories are 'consequential, in the linguistic sense of performative utterance', in the context of the speech act theory, 'by which saying is doing: telling history makes it; accordingly, the past is always caught in a run on the future' (pp. 1–2). She explains that the process of oral history 'embodies' Conquerwood's (1998) semantic genealogy of performance, a three-tiered development of performance as political intervention: mimesis, poiesis and kinesis. Pollock maintains 'it represents by re-creating historical events in embodied processes of mobilizing new ways of seeing, thinking, feeling, being and doing the world' (Pollock 2008: 1–2). The practice of oral history engages both the interviewer and the interviewee 'as co-performers in an embodied, spatial-temporal, encounter' (in Roms and Edwards 2011: 172). In this sense, as Friedman proposes, oral history is situated between two spatial-temporal dimensions. The first is the embodied social condition that signifies the place where the interview is being held. The second is a public realm to come, for the future listeners, for whom the interview and event that is described is historical. He explains this as the intangible digest of all the prospective sites, through which the listening acts of forthcoming audiences will take place.

Although the interviews for *Memory of Theatre* were not recorded using Roms's live interviewing approach, her perspective of a collective remembrance can also be applied to *Memory of Theatre*, because of the method chosen to disseminate the content documented. The locality app, once made widely accessible, can potentially prompt future theatregoers to contribute their stories to the interactive archive. Therefore, collective remembering, in this instance, can occur through the exchange of memories between absent and present audiences. This is akin to Auslander's claim that:

[T]he crucial relationship is not the one between the document and the performance but the one between the document and its audience. Perhaps the authenticity of the performance document resides in its relationship to its beholder rather than to an ostensibly originary event: perhaps its authority is phenomenological rather than ontological.

2006: 6

In consideration of this, because oral history interviews are made available from their recordings and transcriptions, they do not rely on the presence of a live audience for them to be performative. 'It may well be that our sense of the presence, power, and authenticity of these pieces derives from perceiving the document itself as a performance that directly reflects an artist's aesthetic project or sensibility and for which we are the present audience' (Auslander 2006: 6). This is indicative of the oral history interview being translated from the place of private encounter to the realm of public engagement. Pollock (2009) considers a performance-centred narration of oral history 'as a critical repetition among repetitions ... the teller as authorized by prior tellings; and the interviewer as directly implicated in a narrative environment' that follows, orientates and outlines the interviewer's discussions. She explains that exercising this theory designates the 'interviewer-as-audience member', who then becomes 'the measure of the micropolitics and ethics enacted at the relational nadir of the interview process'. Their account is an instinctive description of premeditated and sumptuous dynamics that embody history in a small scale 'working itself out in narrative interaction, on, through, and by interview participants'.

The aim of *Memory of Theatre*, was to create an interactive archive that invited the engagement of theatregoers to come, towards remembering performances and triggering site-specific experiences, positioning the audiences' memories in-situ, so that future generations would also be able to place their own memories beside the memories collected. The title of the piece was a reference to Italian philosopher Giulio Camillo's (1550) description of the complex memory system *Theatre of Memory*, which Frances Yates discusses in *The Art of Memory* (1966). In this manner, the project *Memory of Theatre* (2012) is an embodied metaphor and a manifestation of these memory devices. It developed a materialized acoustic mnemonic system, not only creating a space for people to remember performance, but also an environment where memories that emerge from the very fabric of the building can be created, with which both present and future audiences can associate their own memories. Simultaneously, the project's conceptualization conceives the theatre as a space that accommodates the memories of its audience.

The methods chosen to record and disseminate content in the project give prominence to the roles of both the documenter and the audience as creators of re-imaginings (Shaughnessy 2012: 219), of performances' pasts. The practical methodologies undertaken empower audiences to engage with performance histories across visceral means. The visceral means that are not encountered through other archival documents, as this type of ephemera produced, as explained above, represents the domain of physical gestures and speech. Such transitory modalities like oral history, narration and performance 'reformulate and expand our understandings of materiality' (Muñoz 1996: 10). The approaches that exist after performances provide a type of evidence, that may not represent the event itself but because they produce traces of lived knowledge, which cannot be fully experienced from engaging purely with archival documents, they are part of a further performance, as suggested by Auslander (2006). When disseminating oral history, it is important to reflect the practice's ethos to disengage with the idea of corroborating evidence for authorized narratives of the past and to involve the audience, enfranchising them so they can participate in the narrative making. This is a component that was demonstrated through the conceptual and creative approach used to exhibit the testimonies in *Memory of Theatre*. The project highlighted the relationship between performance, memory, place, temporality and materiality which made evident the usefulness of encountering ghosts of a performance past and the importance of oral history as an effective tool to capture a plethora of memories about performance. Stories are told in many different linguistic forms. The diversity in ways of telling the told is embraced to convert lived experience into knowledge that can then be shared in a wider community. Variant modes from the repertoire of embodied cognition, like oral history and performance, demonstrate the persistence of culture on structures of semantic praxis – through which 'Homo Narrans' (man as a storyteller), or 'Homo Performans' ('man the self performing animal') (Turner 1987: 81) relives, refabricates, reiterates and recreates culture. As Roland Barthes (1977) suggested, 'Here in the grain of the voice the story comes to life' (p. 179). In this sense, audiences' memories of theatre and performance gain existence and act as additional documents to aid the remembrance of cultural events, through their telling, recording and mediation.

Translating Performance: Desire, Intention and Interpretation in Photographic Documents

Helen Newall, Amy Skinner and Allan Taylor

Since the 1990s, weight has been given to the reception of the photographic document and the phenomenological experience of observing such an artefact.[1] Debates about documenting performance have focused on the document's relationship with its respective audiences, and this mode of investigation has positioned the camera and its operator as an accidental or passive witness receiving a performance happening in front of the lens, and where the photographs produced are positioned as a by-product, supplement or representation of the live moment.[2]

Furthermore, the advent of digital photography and the subsequent decline of analog photography has not only altered image-making processes but is changing the way in which images are received. This chapter therefore interrogates the notion that digital is any less reliable than analog photography by discussing interventions in the phases of capture common to both formats; and by situating these interventions as a palimpsestic feature of photo-documentation. These interventions comprise: the subject in front of the camera; the photographer and the camera itself; and the spectator or academic scholar examining, receiving and making meaning out of visual information. The construction and editing of photography by subject and photographer is considered in terms of intention; and the authors also consider the notion that if the act of photography, and its resulting images, have their own visual language, then the creation of a performance image can be considered a form of transcription[3] which has implications for how images are read (and particularly the lack of universality in readings).

How the subject intervenes

Multiple photographs of a single event taken by different photographers reveal, as Ritchin notes, that 'reality itself has no single truth' (2009: 147). Such postmodern constructivist doubt might appear useful when photographs are commonly perceived as 'perfect analogons' of their subjects (Snyder and Allen, in Lister 1995: 10): visual literacy theories have long reinforced the necessity of perceptual scepticism (Sturken and Cartwright 2003). Nevertheless, in an era characterized by what Mitchell has termed 'an ontological aneurism – a blowout in the barrier separating visual fact and fantasy' (1994b: 188), any doubt in the integrity of photographic images seems to have shifted from the photograph *per se* to the digital photograph, most especially since the advent of Photoshop. Analog photography appears less manipulated – the process of sunlight reflecting from an object, travelling through a lens, reacting with chemicals in film emulsion seems uninterruptable and incorruptible, and the darkroom a mysterious space in which a latent image was revealed. The computer, however, is an interface in which a digital image is coded and constructed. Photography's new 'truth myth' would have us believe that analog technology was thus more reliable than its digital successor. But as Lister notes, '[c]ultural theorists have become (often disingenuously) preoccupied with the "loss of the real"' (1995: 1), when there was, perhaps, no 'real' to lose.

That this dichotomy between analog and digital technologies is false (in Lister's phrase, 1995: 8), is evident only one year after the official French announcement of photography's invention: in 1840, Hippolyte Bayard staged three photographs of the same subject, all called *Le Noyé* or *Self Portrait as a Drowned Man*, and which quite possibly constitute the first photographic hoax. Complete with caption claiming the subject to be a suicide, they are Bayard's protest at not being officially recognized as one of photography's principal inventors (those named in the French announcement being Daguerre and Niépce).

Bayard's many self-portraits indicate an awareness of the self-constructive possibilities of photography (and perhaps its defiance of time and death). But besides being the first hoax, *Le Noyé* with the capture of 'the self-styled body perform[ing] for the camera' (Levin 2015: 328) also offers an early – if not the earliest – example of photographic performativity, for, as Batchen remarks, the composition is calculated, with objects placed carefully within the frame and the subject's pose parodying David's painting *Death of Marat* (1999: 157–73). Batchen also notes that to replicate the painting via an inverting direct positive print process, Bayard would have had to consciously reverse his pose (166). *Le Noyé* thus documents the photograph's subject tampering with 'reality' in a calculated performance where the emphasis looks to the aesthetic effect of the end result rather than back at the documentary authenticity of the originating scene.

Le Noyé brings to mind Goffman's description of the presentation of self, where individuals request 'observers to take seriously the impression that is fostered before them. They are asked to believe that … matters are what they appear to be' (Goffman 1959: 28), and sometimes audiences are aware of the contract, and sometimes they are not. At face value, Bayard's photograph shouts his anger: 'You have metaphorically killed me!' A deeper reading, however, is invited by the circumstances leading to its creation, as Sapir comments:

This historical context suggests that the self-portrait can be read as a crossroads at which issues of recognition, authorship, display, visibility, invisibility, truth and illusion meet and play off of one another . . . As such it can be seen as an early critique of the dominant ocularcentric scopic regime of post-Enlightenment modernity, which assumed a transparent relationship between photography and truth.

Sapir 1994: 619–20

Le Noyé is thus an example of the subject's own complicity with the analog camera to affect a viewer's perception, and make a point: ultimately, photographs are taken, and performances made, 'for the benefit of other people' in Goffman's phrase, and photographs facilitate their seeing such performances from a spatial and temporal distance.

Bayard was deploying what Goffman terms a subject's 'cynical' ability to perform, where a player is 'not taken in at all by his own routine' (Goffman 1959: 30). What of subjects who are not consciously performing? Barthes writes of being photographed: '. . . once I feel myself observed by the lens, everything changes' (1959: 10). So, despite a subject's best intentions, the camera can incite a 'performance', and there might be at play an observer effect where the presence of the camera is disruptive and influential. Like an auto-ethnographer, in the act of documentation the camera, whether analog or digital, can become implicated in the process.

Bayard's practice anticipates Baudelaire's scepticism in 1859 when he denounced those credulous enough to believe in photography's 'guarantee of exactitude' (Kriebel 2007: 7), a reproach which itself foreshadows recent criticism of digital pixels being imperceptibly intercepted. *Le Noyé* thus offers what Barthes and Kuhn deem to be information, but it does not document a drowning, but a performance of a drowning, and certainly the rage of a slighted man. In this it demonstrates photography's facility to be conceptual, and thus more complex than the mirror held up to nature that at its inception some were lauding it to be: the camera documents, but not always what, as photographers, as subjects, we assume it is documenting, and regardless of camera, darkroom or computer intervention, the intention of both subject and photographer involved in each image, and which we now discuss, is paramount.

Bayard's performance to camera was never intended to be seen live: it was staged wholly for the photograph. So what of the documenting of performances where the photography parallels the live event? When Amelia Jones offers her idea of 'presence-in-absentia' (1997), she supposes the intention in documentation is to provide an indexical access point to the past in order for a spectator in the present to be taken back to that moment, and she is unapologetic about not having experienced directly the performances she goes on to discuss: 'while the experience of viewing a photograph and reading a text is clearly different from that of sitting in a small room watching an artist perform, neither has a privileged relationship to the historical "truth" of the performance' (Jones 1997: 11). The idea parallels Auslander, who in elucidating the performativity of performance documents, motions that these documents are created during the event to be seen as performances in their own right. Citing Gina Pane and Chris Burden, he states that, 'the events were staged to be documented at least as much as to be seen by an audience' (Auslander 2006: 3). Furthermore, he adds: 'The act of documenting an event as a performance is what constitutes it as such' (2006: 6). Auslander infers, but doesn't fully explore, the methods behind the concept that there is an *intention* on the part of the artist and the photographer to create a performance that is received in a different temporal space. The suggestion is that before the photograph is even created, the act of documenting anticipates how future spectators will reconstruct or retrieve the information that lies in the visual document at a future time, which poses processual questions to those documenting about how such documents might be constructed.

A conflict also exists between the prominence of the performer in the analysis of such documents and the relative anonymity of the photographer who has a complicit part to play in this act of performance/document. In Auslander's example of Yves Klein's *Leap Into The Void*, Klein was undoubtedly the artistic director of the final composition. But this image is in fact a photomontage and thus dependent on the darkroom skills of its photographers. As with Bayard's image, it is also a picture of something which did not occur: the documentation of the creation of this artwork might actually be said to consist of both this and the second image, seen less often, of Klein's friends holding the tarpaulin beneath him as he leaps. And yet, perhaps the finished image *is* a document, but of a leap from the window Klein claimed he made, without a tarpaulin, earlier that year. There is no proof he made this first leap: it is undocumented. And what of the role of Harry Shunk and Janos Kender, the Hungarian photographers who took the images for him? There are clearly implications in collaboration and impact in the photographer–artist relationship.

Likewise, whether or not the artist is aware of being documented, more academic awareness of intention as a part of the process of documentation is required, for even the act of clicking the shutter on a camera has intention. There are then two questions: why was this particular photograph created, and what did its photographer intend?

But we must also consider selection and what is intended here: who decided which shots represent the performance work? A photographer might select with aesthetic compositional considerations of what makes a good performance photograph; whereas a director, or choreographer, might choose those images which record what they consider key performance points. A performer, however, might select for a portfolio to further a career. In such selections of shots, human agency foregrounds some images over others, thereby erasing an unselected subset from the archive memory. Photographs constituting documents might be supplanted by an entirely different intention behind their selection leading to an incongruence in the reading of such a document.

Grant (2002) discusses such issues in her paper 'Private Performances', in which she uses Mendieta and Abramovic to illustrate the heavy editorial control some artists employ to ensure the art represented is as they intended. Such editing strategies have been exposed via photographers such as Hannah Starkey and Hellen van Meene, 'in whose work the authenticity and authority of the photograph has been radically eroded and problematized' (Grant 2002: 34). She goes on:

> Through this newer generation of photographic practitioners, the editing process present in the performance documentations of Abramovic, Pane and Mendieta is revealed as a strategic, sophisticated and often overlooked tactic, staged in order to maintain the complexity of these images and descriptions.
>
> ibid.

Such elements of editing and exhibition clearly embedded into documentation constitute what intentists refer to as 'Palimpsestism'[4] – the trail of the creative journey leading from intention to the finished vehicle, where the resolved work is clearly distinguishable from the work in progress. Nemiroff discusses this as a form of layering:

> The textual elements [of the photograph], whether visual or verbal, are most often doubled so that one text is read through another or in juxtaposition to another. Thus, material borrowed from or patterned on popular culture sources is given a new, or supplementary, meaning in the context of their art.
>
> Nemiroff 2005: 47

Thus the photograph becomes several texts written on top of one another until they appear to the audience as one translucent image with many different things to read and multiple entry points to interpretation. The individual selects the relevant entry point, reads the most pertinent texts and assimilates them accordingly to produce their meaning. A photograph can thus be many narratives, but artist and/or photographer intention, constructed via context, manifesto, or complementary writing, is a significant and authoritative voice in the weave.

How the photographer and the camera intervene

In repositioning the photographer as being as important as the artist or work being documented, the debate should perhaps draw on the school of intentism as defined by Pelosi:

> [Intentists] believe that their artwork is able to convey their artistic intention to their intended audience ... As a movement it both recognizes and celebrates the relationship between an artist's creation and its creator.
>
> Pelosi 2009: 3

That is to say that though we learn from interpretation and reception of such documents, if the author of these documents is put back into the picture, then an awareness of the impact that inception, creation and process can have becomes possible. When the knowledge that a performance has the potential to be documented exists, there is then an intentional editing and presentation process before the document is exhibited to its wider audience.

If the relationship between artist and photographer is complex, then the relationship between the photographer and camera is equally so, for the camera has *sight* of the performance it documents; it is the *site* where the performance is photographically constructed and collated; and ultimately, in the resulting images, it *cites* the performances of others. But it is, as Flusser writes, an apparatus 'programmed' by functions decided by its inventors at spatial and temporal distances. It is also a complicated apparatus around which there is often a cult of gadgetry: 'every photograph,' Flusser writes, 'is a realization of one of the possibilities contained within the program of the camera' (2000: 26), and '[e]very single photograph is the result, at one and the same time, of co-operation and of conflict between camera and photographer' (2000: 47). In manual mode, the photographer makes decisions about depth of field, shutter speed and aperture. In auto mode, the camera is making these pre-programmed decisions: the jpeg is the result of algorithms processing a photograph on your behalf: 'straight out of camera' is a false concept. Those decoding photographs must therefore ask:

> 'How far have photographers succeeded in subordinating the camera's programs to their own intentions?' And, vice versa: 'How far has the camera succeeded in redirecting the photographer's intentions back to the interests of the camera program . . .?'
>
> Flusser 2000: 47

Ultimately, photographers can only capture what their cameras can photograph, and state of the art technology can still fail. As Jess Allen notes: 'no matter how sophisticated the documentation strategies that digital technology currently offers, they still privilege that which *can* be documented over the less tangible information gained from live interaction' (Allen 2010: 67). The first war images were, for example, static landscapes rather than action shots, because cameras at that time required lengthy exposures. The first theatre images were similarly defined by the limits of contemporaneous camera technology. Taken not on theatre stages amid the action of rehearsal or performance, these were staged in photographic studios before painted backcloths appropriate to the play, lit by skylights, using the photographer's own props and furniture. The performers posed statically as characters, and were sometimes costumed in clothing borrowed from the studio (Shields: online). But these were publicity photographs taken to sell tickets rather than document performance.

By the early 1900s, the desire for such photographs had increased while exposure times had reduced. Nevertheless, images of Pavlova by Herman Mishkin still involved wires and contraptions to stabilize her while she held poses *en pointe* long enough for Mishkin to expose the glass plates (Mitchell 1999: 70). However, as Senelick notes: 'a given pose is caught but remains segregated from what went before or came after. The image segments a discrete emotional climax, distilling and fixing it in the process' (Senelick 1997: 256). This is true of any photograph capturing either a posed moment, or one captured in the flow of a scene. They are, in Senelick's terminology, crystallized out of context (256). Thus, as photographer Jack Mitchell notes, these images 'reveal much about each dancer – except how they appeared in motion' (1999: 70).

In the end, these early images constitute performances of performance, and in Postlewait's terms they are: 'unreliable testimony because both their final cause or aim (publicity shot) and their formal cause (aesthetic principles of portrait) subvert their documentary potential' (2009: 245). But for the most part they are the only extant photo-documentation: any faulty information comes from faulty positioning of images which were primarily about selling celebrity and tickets, and in this sense they *are* documentation of how early the Faustian pact between the famous and the camera began.[5]

The intervention of the spectator

We now turn our gaze to the spectator, the academic in the archive, viewing images. For such academics, the advent of digital photography and the increasing online presence of performance archives have, in combination, led to an historiographical cognitive schism in the study of performance history concerning 'not only the methods that define and guide the practice of historical study and writing but also the self-reflexive mind-set that leads us to investigate the processes and aims of historical understanding' (Postlewait 2009: 2). This collision between objective methodologies and their application by subjective mind-sets is sited within the academic. But the academic's scope concerns equally fragmented objects of enquiry: for in an era such as ours of unprecedented access to photographic material, performance photographs are both historiographically valuable and problematic documents, and, as Grant has already stated, academics often find themselves dealing not with original performances, but with their traces. As Sallenave observes, 'our memories of theatre are frequently memories of photographs of theatre' (in McAuley 2008: 9).

The shift from analog to digital photography marks a significant watershed in performance historiography. The development of a new mode of photographic production brings a concurrent change in photographic currency: photographs are differently perceived because they are differently produced.

This is particularly apparent in the relationship between photography and temporality. For Barthes, writing before the advent of digital photography, temporality is key in the negotiation of the relationship between the referent and the reception of the photographic image. The photograph is 'a new form of hallucination: false on the level of perception, true on the level of time: a temporal hallucination, so to speak, a modest, shared hallucination (on the one hand "it is not there," on the other "but it has indeed been")' (Barthes 1981: 115). Barthes's 'temporal hallucination' in fact embodies the multiple temporalities found in the photographic image, a collapse of the moments of production and reception, as he explores in his observations of Salzmann's photographs of Bethlehem: 'Nothing but stony ground, olive trees; but three tenses dizzy my consciousness: my present, the time of Jesus, and that of the photographer, all under this instance of "reality"' (1980: 97).

The photographic image, outside of the mechanisms of production involving film emulsion or pixels, is suffused by temporal structures. Engagement with these structures is clearly inflected by the context in which the photograph is viewed: Barthes's *Camera Lucida* revolves around the evocative power of a shared time and the tension embedded in the distance between image production and reception. In collapsing this distance, the digital era has bought about shifts in temporal understanding towards new models of 'sharing', temporalities of 'immediacy', 'acceleration' and instantaneity (*The Experience of Time in Modern Culture*, University of Warwick).[6] If, as Bluedorn notes, 'time is used to generate meaning' (2002: 42), then changes in contemporary understandings of time alter potential engagements with the temporality of the photograph, and particularly of the historical photograph.

The close relationship between temporality and culture (as advocated, for example, by Ricoeur 1984), suggests that different temporal structures can complicate the understanding of a photograph passing from one temporal context to another. Familiarity with the overt formal photographic structures (how the image appears to look, and its constructed transparency, the so-called 'truth myth') can disguise this potentially significant moment of alienation. As such, the shift from analog image-making and Barthes's sharing, towards digital photography and the instantaneity of digital culture, can be seen as a moment of schism: for how photographic practice functioned at the moment of the image's creation is not the same as how it functions in the contemporary moment of reception, and, as the digital revolution accelerates, photography's 'truth myth' shifts with it, acquiring hitherto unanticipated nuances which we will now discuss.

Photography and its intentional gaps

Mitchell says of the relationship between language and the image that 'pictures want equal rights with language, not to be turned into language ... To be seen as complex individuals occupying multiple subject positions and identities' (2005: 38). If it is then considered that performance, and its documentation via photography, have an equivalent status to language, then Derrida's idea of *différance* (1988)[7] can be used to interrogate why it is employed to document performance. Derrida describes the relationship between speech and thought as much more closely related: speech happens as though we are hearing our own thoughts again in a more simultaneous or instantaneous matter. Writing, however, happens as a much more considered process and therefore has a much further distance from the original thought. Nonetheless, it is constructed in the knowledge that when it is read, it will be enacted once again in the minds of those who read it.

In the same way, thought and performance acts have a much more simultaneous relationship, but it is then 'written' by photography, which isolates it from the event and distances it to a point ready to be received – ready to be performed – at a later moment. In both cases, what occurs is a 'deferred performance': a way of transcribing the act or utterance so that when it is seen again, it can be enacted once more. This is the intentional gap, or 'double now' that Phelan notes, echoing Barthes's multiple temporalities (Phelan 2010).

If looked at as intentional practice, it is reasonable to assume that this gap is anticipated by its creator and used purposefully. The 'performative power' of the photograph relies on these gaps and is discussed by Baetans (2009) as lacunae or 'missing text'. Explaining that the photograph 'shows' rather than 'tells', this mechanism of 'showing' allows an audience to fill in the blanks and come up with individual connections to, and performance of, the still image. He writes:

What needs to be stressed is the position that 'lacunae' (vacancies, blanks, uncertainties) have acquired within the narrative impulse, becoming a foundation of narrative reading. Put simply, the more any one medium [for example, film] attempts to explain, justify, unfold or conclude its own narrative, the more its narrative power diminishes.

Baetans 2009: 146

When set into juxtaposition with photography, film dictates to the viewer exactly how the narrative arc plays out. In the still image, ranges of responses are possible and – in fact – invited. The artist makes these gaps by layering several texts: the performance act, the setting and the pose. This, again, is palimpsestism – a trail that academics in the archive need to unravel. Of course, this brings into question the transcription process: if what is written by photography is not consistently read in the same way, how do we resolve this transcription–interpretation relationship? In response, it is perhaps useful to suggest a new model for photographic documentation, substituting ideas of performance documentation, with those of performance translation. The researcher can turn the photographic document into a process of documentation through conscious engagement with the image. In the archive, for example, this engagement can include metadata (such as company records, or the name of the photographer). The model of translation contributes to this process and, in some instances, actively creates the meta-context for the engagement with performance photographs.

The photograph as object of translation

More than a simple re-naming, this new terminology implies a different conceptual relationship between the photograph and the researcher: one of active interpretation and reading which brings the moment of photographic creation into the moment of reception. Translation principles, in fact, underwrite two aspects of photographic historiography in performance: firstly, the photograph itself functions as a translation of the performance event; secondly, the researcher reading the photograph also engages in his or her own process of performance translation. It is this processual act that allows the photograph to perform the function of documentation.

For the performance scholar, the attraction of the photograph is not necessarily its preservation of the performance moment, but what Reason calls its 'transformational truth' (2008: 7), the re-working of the event into a different temporal and spatial frame: photographs of performances are a meeting point of the different visual languages associated with different creative media. By inflecting Reason's use of 'transformation' to the very specific transformative process of translation, salient qualities of the translated text can be applied to photographic documentation, in particular, the consciousness of process and resulting multiplicity embodied in the translated object.

The process of linguistic translation holds in tension the relationship between a text's producing and receiving cultures.[8] The extent to which the producing culture is linguistically embedded in the translated text is addressed by David Bellos:

> If a detective novel set in Paris makes its characters speak and think in entirely fluent English – even while they plod along the Boulevard Saint-Germain, drink Pernod and scoff a *jarret de porc aux lentilles* – then something must be wrong. What's the bonus in having a French detective novel for bedtime reading unless there's something French about it?
>
> 2011: 41

In other words, the translated text mediates between two languages and cultures. As Bellos notes, the pleasure in the French detective story is, in part, its 'Frenchness' – and the language of the translation mediates that Frenchness to the receiving culture. It is the tension between the familiar and the strange, the sense of located and embedded otherness that allows the translated text to function as a (conscious act of) translation. There is something provocative in this foreignness that shifts the reader's perception.

This question of a conscious negotiation of two contexts can equally be applied to the photograph, which becomes an object of mediation. The photograph collapses its own visual language with that of the performance. As with the translated text, it is only when both of these (visual) languages are acknowledged that the photograph 'makes sense', and becomes useful in the process of performance documentation. The translator makes a series of choices that construct the reception of the text (such as those referenced by Bellos); similar choices are apparent in photographic practice. The photographer frames, excludes and directs the eye: like the translator, the photographer's role is primarily that of mediation, transforming the language of performance into the language of photography.

Photographic reception as translation

In addition to its mediation between different media – the 'languages' of performance and photography – the photographic object is also the product of a specific cultural and visual moment. How a photograph is understood is a balance of familiarity and difference: the photograph is the connection point between here and now, and then and there (Barthes's multiple photographic tenses). If photography asks for equivalency to language, then it responds just as much to context as its counterpart, in the same way that an art form like painting does. As such, the photograph is not transparent: not only in the sense that it is not a transparent representation of 'truth', but in the sense that it is not temporally or spatially universal. Where photographic practice can be attributed to a specific (and often well-known) photographic artist, the need to acknowledge a wider aesthetic influence on the construction of the image is readily apparent. However, much historical photography is unattributable, distancing the image from the cultural-aesthetic conditions of its production. As such, it is not only necessary to develop an understanding of the intentions of an individual photographer, but also of the context in which that photographer's practice was developed. Photographs are not just received: they are read.

The visual culture from which the photograph emerges is an essential frame of reference for understanding the images. This extends beyond observations around the intended use of the photograph – for advertising or documentation purposes, for example – to the specific qualities of certain photographic moments. These moments are born out of both developments in visual culture and in advancing photographic technologies: in the early twentieth century, photo secession increased photographic pictorialism, early mass-use cameras flattened perspective or caused a halation effect, surrounding objects with a halo of light (both features put to specific artistic use by Picasso), 1920s Russian experiments in photomontage suggested photography as an interrogative and fragmented formal process.[9] Each moment inflects the construction of the photographic image – and images of theatre and performance are not immune to this influence. To use a photograph for the purposes of historiography requires the researcher to consider not only the broad differences between the photograph and performance space, but also the specific inflections of photographic practice at different historical moments. In other words, a photographic language must be identified and contextualized. The photograph must be translated.

Motion, flux and the need for consciousness

Barthes's understanding of photography as a temporal phenomenon highlights the relationship between movement and photographic practice. The question of capturing movement is at the heart of photography, and the suspension of movement in the photograph creates images that are static, but not still, radiating motion from the captured instant, what Hart Crane calls 'the moment made eternal' (in Sontag 1979: 65): photographs are objects in motion. Nowhere is this more obvious than in their usage by performance scholars. Beyond the photograph's engagement with motion associated with the performance event, Barthes's articulation of the image in 'three tenses' implies a potential sense of flux embedded in photographic reception. The image is constantly changing; re-read in light of developing understandings of its context of creation and its context of reception. This sounds obvious, but it implies that images require translation both in and out of contexts. The journey from photo-making to photo-using is a vital one in understanding photographic reception, and when photographs are used as documentation, they become a bridge between the producing and receiving cultures. This raises a fundamental question around photographic translation: what is being translated? Is the photograph a translation of a visual experience of a performance, and thus rooted in an image, or is it the embodiment of a theatrical idea and process? If it is the latter, this implies a shift in emphasis from image to idea, changing our relationship with the object from what it represents to what it contains.

This shift allows for an engagement with photographic documentation that takes into account not just the content of the documented performance, but also the purpose of the act of performance analysis within the context of the receiving culture. The significance of the dual cultures of the translated text is perhaps most apparent in the debate on the purpose of translation. Sirkku Aaltonen frames the two reflexive models of translation as the window and the mirror (2000: 1). Both analogies are problematic, and serve primarily to highlight the egocentric function of much translation practice, framed as a reflection on the self of the receiving culture far more than on the other of the producing culture.

The window/mirror analogies are reflections on the purpose of linguistic translation that can equally be applied to the historiographic use of photography as a process of documentation: to what extent are observations made based on photographs of historical practice shaped by the concerns of contemporary performance, and to what extent does this inflect the analysis of the historical with a contemporary agenda?

As such, the application of translation theory to photography allows us to question the documentary purposes of these 'translated objects' and the narratives that they prompt us to create. As developments in photographic technologies reframe cultural understandings of the photograph, images increasingly become accessible through online archiving, and shifts in temporal-cultural models alter our relationship with the images that the camera can produce, a consciousness in the use of the process of documentation through photography becomes more and more essential. Above all, translation as a model allows us to see how the historiographic potential of the performance photograph must be handled with increasing care.

Documents are thus as unfixed as the status of the photograph itself, and depend on questions an interlocutor asks of them in an act of translation: the implications for the performance scholar in dealing with palimpsestic texts and photographic transcriptions of performance are thus vast and complex.

Documenting Audience Experience: Social Media as Lively Stratification

Joanna Bucknall and Kirsty Sedgman

Over the course of this chapter we will propose the documentation of live performance as a process of stratification. The live event becomes the nexus for an array of circulating discourse, from reviews to programmes to interviews. Forming layers of strata, the 'fossils' that are left behind perform a cultural legacy after the originating live performance has staged its disappearance. The twenty-first century's upsurge in online technology presents new opportunities for the constellation of fossils to be organized in a lively stratum: one that resists the usual petrification engendered by this process. From Twitter to Instagram, and from blogs to Facebook, users frequently use online platforms as experience repositories. Ephemeral moments can be captured in snapshots, to be revisited and re-experienced later. We will assert that, through the liminal, palimpsestic qualities of new and social media, the fossils left by the originating live performance event can operate as relational discursive fields.

However, such discourse is in turn left open for co-option, with cultural practitioners and institutions increasingly shrewd in their efforts to use the traces of audience responses that are made visible through tweets, photographs, videos and reviews. By using web-based services such as RSS feeds and Storify to collate various social media posts, practitioners are able to re-petrify certain aspects of this potentially lively discourse by selectively collating chosen responses together with their own documents. Operating as a new kind of online archive, these digital corpora are positioned as the 'official' record of what a live performance achieved. The consequence of this has been that, by producing what are often shrines to success, creators tend to exclude dissenting voices. This chapter considers the tensions between official narratives and lively discourses in audiences' social media use.

Documenting 'liveness'

The process of making live performance produces a range of ephemera, documents and artefacts. It is usually the outward-facing publicity and marketing materials that first become a visible part of the stratification process. The live performance is then available to a limited number of audience members, whose expectations and experiences of the event will often be mediated by their exposure to these 'prefigurative materials' (Barker 2004: 5). In turn, audiences will produce a variety of documents including reviews, video footage, photos and other artefacts. To some extent, these diverse documents all operate simultaneously while the live performance is *still* live: before it becomes inaccessible as a performance event. Each layer of stratification impacts on the next; this can therefore be understood as a processual, iterative relationship. What we call 'fossils' are all those pieces of discursive evidence that are produced in and around the performance process, and that will almost always outlast it. However, while these objects leave evidence of the original live event, they can never actually *be it*:

> Lodged in the earth's outermost layer, ephemeral scratch on a mineral skin, life plays cards with a handful of elements – builds molecular extravaganzas of carbon and hydrogen, oxygen, nitrogen, sulphur, or precious phosphorus, and forms the pieces to the parts that, assembled, define it. When the game is over, the cards reshuffled, the parts dismantled – membranes ruptured, shells

dissolved, bones ground to dust – a few of those organic molecules remain in the sediments and rocks, bearing witness to the distant moments of their creation.

Gaines et al. 2009: 3

While live event and documentation authorize and valorize the presence of each other, documents are what survive as petrified fossils, and continually perform an authorizing function on behalf of the disappeared event. This has been addressed by Philip Auslander, who argues that it is the documentation of a live performance event that goes on to perform its legacy. While the original live performance can of course be understood as cultural practice, its visibility persists *through* its documentation. By this process, the fossils produced by the live event become petrified into stratified layers, which maintain a presence within cultural memory beyond the disappearance of the original:

> The documentation of the performance event provides both a record of it through which it can be reconstructed (though, as Kathy O'Dell points out, the reconstruction is bound to be fragmentary and incomplete) and evidence that it actually occurred. The connection between performance and document is thus thought to be ontological, with the event preceding and authorizing its documentation.
>
> 2006: 1

Documentation can therefore be understood to actually *perform* the legacy of the cultural practice in place of the disappeared original.

Experiencing disappearance

Experiencing a live performance event is to pay witness to its disappearance. This is why the documentation question is so central to debates about legacy, heritage and dissemination: because as

Auslander describes, performance's value lives on purely in how it is remembered. Matthew Reason explains that, 'given the ephemeral nature of live performance, except by being there in person it is only through its documentations [...] that it is possible to know, question or see performance at all' (2006: 2).

Although live performance generates a variety of forms of documentary evidence (video footage, scripts, programmes, reviews, reports, blogs, publicity material, press releases and so on), all these things are 'other' to the original: they are not and can never be the actual live event, which is extinguished at the moment of its making. While these ancillary items are indeed indicative of the event, produced in and by the originating conditions of the performance process, they can never stand in its place. This is also true of the experience of performance, which is a naturally lively procedure, intangible and impossible to fully capture (Phelan 1993: 147), and containing the capacity to evolve over time. While the similarly lively process of performance making begins to petrify at the moment the event ends, the *experience* of participating will continue to evolve as long as its original performers and audiences survive. Reason identifies tensions between a scholarly and practical 'investment in the undissolvable experience of doing and being' – an urge to avoid reducing complex phenomenological responses down to simplified markers of experience – and the conflicting 'need to extract and externalise this knowledge, particularly in the form of documentations that can endure' (2006: 3). In 'honour[ing] the idea that only a limited number of people in a specific time/space' (Phelan 1993: 149) can be privy to each ephemeral event, live performance has become especially vulnerable to what we term 'experiential fossilization': a process of petrification led by makers that seeks to assert authorial control over this essential liveliness.

Many performance theorists believe that experiences become calcified the moment they are articulated. For example, Patrice Pavis warns that the act of converting phenomenological reactions into words results in 'fixing' the memory of that experience forever (2006), while Eugenio Barba states that 'the memory of experience lived as theatre, once translated into sentences that last, risks becoming petrified into pages that cannot be penetrated' (2005: 11). However, Reason argues that our conception of 'experience' requires further analysis. Because the in-the-moment experience of live performance is encountered at its own vanishing point, the acts of reflection and discussion that take place after the event has ended are frequently dismissed as a 'pale, wasted and distorted reflection' (2010: 26). Reason suggests persuasively that the process of post-performance contemplation might instead be understood as 'a *connected but different* experience in its own right' (ibid.). These multiple experiences may remain relatively fixed and stable, as the individual audience member effectively makes up their mind about an event, or they may continue to evolve through ongoing reflection. Either way, all experiences contain within them an enduring *capacity* for change.

This chapter contends that is through the process of documentation that diverse experiences become petrified, as an 'official' narrative is produced that asserts a performance's achievements. As described, this is because documents, in all their varied forms, present the only way that an art experience can be disseminated beyond the relative few in attendance. While individual audience members carry with them their own personal memories, unless their recollections are shared more widely this embodied knowledge becomes lost to cultural memory. As the documentation of performance has in the past been largely the responsibility of its makers, it has tended to concern itself with recording the dramaturgy of cultural practices: more often than not, production has been privileged over reception. Where audiences' experiences have been preserved, this tends to be driven by expert voices and led by specific marketing imperatives designed to produce a particular – and a particularly *positive* – cultural legacy.

Experiential divergence and cultural legacy

As well as essentially ontological, the documentation of performance is also a discursive process and therefore ideological, bound up with operations of power and knowledge. Following Foucault, this invites us to ask three broad questions. Who is speaking? From what site are they speaking? What is their relational position? It is out of this 'organisation of the field of statements' that knowledge emerges and circulates as discourse (1972: 38). Importantly, Foucault reminds us of the necessity of exploring how the subject position of the individual or institution responsible for documentation may impact on the artefacts that are preserved. This requires us to examine documenters' actions as part of a dynamic relational discourse: a 'field of enunciation' whose 'rules of formation' ensure a regularity of style (1972: 38).

In the case of live performance, it is professional commentators who have historically controlled the formation of cultural discourse. In her influential *Theatre and Audience*, Helen Freshwater asks why those people who make and study live events tend to 'prefer discussing their own responses, or relaying the opinions of reviewers, to asking "ordinary" audience members – with no professional stake in the theatre – what they make of a performance?' (2009: 3–4). This has further been considered in a recent special issue of the international audience research journal *Participations*, which collectively investigates how certain voices are silenced while others are amplified by cultural operations of power (Reason et al. 2015). It is often the case that only those people in possession of a particular kind of knowledge – Bourdieu's cultural capital – are believed to produce legitimate responses by conforming to the discursive rules of formation. These cultural conspirators are therefore those whose experiences tend to be added to the official strata, and who have also historically been more able than others to access what Foucault calls 'procedures of intervention', which refers to the means by which this knowledge is disseminated and received. It is these enunciations that go on to produce the cultural legacy of a performance.

The proliferation of new media has produced fresh opportunities for people without traditional media connections to produce active contributions within an increasingly globalized discourse. However, Lynne Conner demonstrates how, when it comes to the arts, in many respects the field of enunciation remains largely in the control of professional cultural conspirators. Disheartened by over a century of 'hierarchical interpretative gatekeeping' (2013: 3), audiences 'rarely (if ever) feel knowledgeable or empowered enough to debate the meaning or value of an arts event (unless we are arts professionals and then we feel perhaps too empowered)' (ibid.: 4). This means that if audiences themselves do become documenters – such as through submitting an online review, or by taking part in post-show discussions – they are often dismissed as amateurs, their responses taken less seriously than others.

To ground this theoretical argument in a concrete example, it is revealing to consider the launch of Andrew Lloyd Webber's ill-fated musical *Love Never Dies*, the sequel to *Phantom of the Opera*. First previewed on 22 February 2010, the show was deemed by *The Times* to be 'the most pre-emptively vilified show yet. Vicious verdicts began popping up online immediately after previews [...] [and] have kept coming' (Hoyle 2010a, np). By 5 March the discussion board of theatre news website 'What's On Stage' featured sixty-two pages of comments viewed over 70,000 times (ibid.). This was largely driven by the indignation of so-called 'phans', who were unhappy about how their beloved *Phantom* universe had been continued. Their torrent of discursive activity attracted the ire of Lloyd Webber himself, who denounced the ability of audiences to control the online narrative, calling this new development 'dangerous': 'It's a very worrying situation for anybody now who's opening any kind of play or musical' (quoted Hoyle 2010b, np). While the reviews of professional critics automatically possess 'an authority that makes them more than just one audience member's opinion, although unhappy artists may well dismiss them as such' (Reason 2006: 191–2), what was at stake here was the worry that *amateur* people are increasingly afforded the opportunity – and the confidence – to add their miscellaneous voices into the mix. As Lloyd Webber complained: 'What's happening is that this small number of people have now got this marketplace where they can be the Benedict Nightingale [*The Times*'s veteran chief theatre critic] of the day' (ibid.).

Although practitioners are increasingly eager to encourage audiences to advocate on their behalf for the value of their work, this enthusiasm frequently extends only to those who articulate strongly positive reactions (Belfiore and Bennett 2008). Katya Johanson and Hilary Glow (2015) call this the 'virtuous circle', whereby discursive processes implicitly discourage audiences from publically airing negative reactions. This must be situated within the context of the continued diminishment of public funding for the arts, with theatre companies pressed to revivify cultural interest by making audience enthusiasm visible. Within these narratives, divergent voices are increasingly denounced as inherently threatening to the cultural industries themselves (Sedgman 2016). This sense of peril becomes even more acute in the light of research by the Society of London Theatre, which found that 65 per cent of the people surveyed relied on social media when deciding what to attend (Gardner 2010). This concern extends beyond the arts to encompass a more comprehensive shift in consumer power relations: 'These days one witty Tweet, one clever blog post, one devastating video – forwarded to hundreds of friends at the click of a mouse – can snowball and kill a product or damage a company's share price' (Weber 2010: np). However, Reason argues persuasively that the connection between 'the passing of topical judgements' and their 'direct and current impact [...] is especially tense within live performance' (2006: 190), where the work is brought into being in and through its reception. At worst, then, audiences may find themselves silenced, invisible, their reactions omitted from the official performance documentation: either because their responses have been delegitimized by others, or because they have managed *to disconfirm themselves* (Sedgman 2016). In the case of *Love Never Dies*, there are signs that many audiences felt empowered to engage in contrary discourse because of their shared identities as heavily invested fans of *Phantom*. This phenomenon was actually derided by Lloyd Webber, who called his own devoted audiences 'sad' (Hoyle 2010b). Furthermore, reading the forum comments, what is particularly striking is how audiences themselves often participate in efforts to delegitimize the responses of their peers, by suggesting that a lack of professional implication leaves certain audiences implicitly disqualified from leaving feedback: 'Typical response from a know nothing, do nothing whose opinion therefore means nothing' (West End Whingers 2010, np). This case study therefore presents an especially concentrated instance of tensions between the essential liveliness of the digital domain, and the communal drive to legitimize certain responses while dismissing others.

This chapter resists suggesting that such participants and their recollections are not a valuable resource. In fact, quite the opposite: as we have already argued, the act of remembering or sharing a reaction to a personal experience is a lively process, and an experience in and of itself. The question, then, is how to access, document, and disseminate this information? This task has begun to be undertaken by the niche but burgeoning field of audience research, which seeks to understand the actual lived experience of live performance works, and all 'the wide, complicated, rich, messy, fascinating processes that actual audience members go through in understanding, valuing, responding to and finding meaning in theatre' (Sedgman 2016: 166). Rather than privileging expert voices and rendering other audiences mute or invisible, this research works to map the complexity of audiences' reactions from diverse subject positions, and to consider how people adopt certain orientations and draw on different value judgements to make sense of a performance. Without such attention, the exclusion of experience creates a layer of stratification that is unsympathetic to audiences, and misrepresentative of the complex nature of the originating live event.

The stratification of social media

The social media phenomenon, according to Jan H. Kietzmann et al., is 'an altogether new communication landscape': a 'rich and diverse ecology' (2011) that allows individuals' reactions to be distributed widely and immediately. Sites such as Twitter, Instagram and Facebook, along with thousands of additional social platforms, allow for the ongoing compilation of a range of different media: including audio files, images, video footage, hyperlinks and other resources. Read together in relation to theatre, these offer new opportunities for audiences to document their own experiences.

It is important to make clear that we do not confuse the discursive markers of experience with the act of experiencing. Talking about a performance is not the same thing as living through it: the indexical may never become the aesthetic. However, we do wish to draw attention to the blurry line between these two categories. Following Merleau-Ponty, Panayiota Chrysochou explains that while the act of 'seeing' becomes a 'bodily experience that is inscribed on the flesh' (2014: 643), it is also inextricably linked to questions of representation. Experiences are both embodied and inscribed within a 'viewing subject', who can iterate, in the "here and now," [...] what he sees to another outside himself, the not-I that serves to moor the subject's scopic vision to the realm of concrete experience' (ibid). This is also considered by John Dewey, who according to S. Morris Eames proposes that while '[m]an's "primary experience" is immediate and automatic', a reactionary response to *being* in the world and its sensory stimuli, this experience is always-already mediated by the conscious subject's efforts to *make sense of* the world (1964: 410). This means, Eames suggests, that 'qualities taken alone and without connection or relation to other qualities are meaningless. If such disconnected qualities do occur, they are simply "had" or "felt"' (ibid.). By advocating that 'the actual operative presence of *connections* (which formulated are *relational*) in the subject-matter of direct experience' must be understood as 'an intrinsic part of my idea of experience', Dewey distinguishes between two distinct experiential levels: primary and secondary (ibid.). In other words, as Reason has argued, audiences do not simply experience (primary) events in the moment of an encounter. Their (secondary) experiences will necessarily linger and evolve, as audiences continue to make sense of them through time (2010). New media platforms are one way by which this sense-making process might be brought into focus.

This is significant because it suggests that the documentary objects we discuss in this chapter are not lively in and of themselves. Like fossils, these serve as fragmentary evidence: they are the 'ontological "anchor" of [an event's] indexicality' (Jones 1997: 212). For example, a recorded statement taken from an audience member at a post-show discussion becomes fossilized at the moment of its utterance. It is out there in the ether, ripe either to be petrified within the official strata (e.g. co-opted for marketing material), or to be ignored or dismissed. This therefore offers a snapshot of a single moment in time: an experience at the point of its capture, necessarily constrained by the limits of discourse. Though it may be able to capture aspects of liveliness by indicating something of the *process* of the live performance encounter (Sedgman 2016), the transcript of such a conversation is certainly not itself a lively document. Instead, it is through their *relational positions* that fossils become lively.

To put it differently, they are made lively – or, conversely, encouraged to petrify – in and through the stratification process, whereby an event's cultural legacy is performed beyond its disappearance. While in traditional media discursive utterances become petrified at the moment of distribution, new and social media forms contain the capacity to operate as a lively palimpsest, whereby the audience's subjective document can be continually updated and overwritten. Indeed, in some respects, social media enables the experience of liveness to travel outside the confines of physical co-presence. This has been addressed by Lucy Bennett (2013), who shows how live tweeting allows dispersed audiences to feel part of the event. Furthermore, the liminality of social media places the user's experience at the heart of contemporary documentation, and lends diverse responses a validating voice. In this manner, alternative perspectives are beginning to be identified as an integral part of performance epistemology. In the concluding section, this chapter considers the operation of lively stratification by describing the experience of live tweeting a performance event.

Live tweeting and blogging: a #lively #resistance

Initially heralded as 'a sort of adrenalized Facebook' (van Dijck, quoted McGeeney 2015: 311), Twitter is 'a micro-blogging site that enables users to send 140-character messages. These are referred to as "tweets". Users can deploy and search for particular topics by using the hashtag sign (#), followed by key words or phrases' (ibid.). These can be viewed in real time, offering viewers the sense that a conversation is unfolding in the moment. The practice of 'live tweeting' refers to the act of tweeting in simultaneous response to a live event or activity. Live tweeting has the capacity to reach a wider audience than the originating event can directly engage, and can therefore provide insight into – and broader access to – exclusive aspects of these live experiences. As its moniker suggests, 'live tweeting' seeks to validate the temporary liveness of an activity: an act in which the tweeter is positioned as a privileged participant. Each user's Twitter feed becomes an immediate, direct discursive record, capturing localized enunciations of the audience experience during the act of their experiencing.

As this chapter has already explained, discourse is reliant upon context. In this case, the live Twitter feed produces a discourse that is indexical to a constantly disappearing origin. However, this is only generated by and through tweeters' participation in the originating activity: tweeting is both an *act* that is committed, and a direct and immediate *document* of reflection; an enunciation of participants' embodied experience authorized by their role as an audience member, the tweets they produce generate a dynamic discourse that evidences, documents, and reflects upon the event from a subjective perspective: one that, moreover, is inflected by each person's orientation as a social media user. This is recognized by McGeeney, who writes about being

> aware of the temporal affordances of Twitter – alert to its speed, pace and duration. I experience Twitter as instantaneous, fast and ephemeral. As my tweets are retweeted by colleagues, I am aware of the easy movement of data online, yet as my tweets are subsequently curated, archived and reused I am aware of the indexicality of this data; the time /date stamp that leaves a trace of movement across time and the durability of this fast-moving data that persists even though it is no longer visible on my Twitter feed or screen.
>
> 2015: 311–12

As this suggests, in the moment of its production, live tweeting both supports and resists traditional power structures. As a mode of documenting performance, this practice has the possibility of challenging authoritative voices and resisting petrification. Its immediate and direct nature, at least in the moment, has the ability to evade capture. In seconds, the tweeter can enunciate and disseminate experiential reflections, unleashing their views on a potentially global audience, and avoiding interference by official narratives in the immediate present. Tweets therefore are both inherently lively in their moment of utterance and contain lasting possibilities for liveliness, taking on additional dynamic roles as they are retweeted, recited, and rewritten: a palimpsest of reaction and reflection.

However, Twitter is not immune to institutional control. Most performance companies now have their own Twitter accounts, usually boasting many thousands of followers, and tend to pick and choose only the most agreeable posts to retweet, comment upon, favourite, or share. Furthermore, organizing devices such as RSS software and Storify allow practitioners to collate positive reactions from a range of online media accounts, bringing together admiring tweets with tributary reviews into an online extravaganza of praise. Through such means, traditional lines of influence remain to some extent intact. Nonetheless, functions such as the hashtag allow tweets to have a relational life beyond these authorized accounts. Hence, Twitter frequently becomes the hub for rebellious flurries of activity that resist official narratives. This means that divergent voices can more easily be identified for those who choose to seek them out. To illustrate this argument, our writing now switches to first person singular to describe a concrete experience of live tweeting undertaken by one of its authors, Joanna Bucknall.

From 25 June to 4 July 2015, Forced Entertainment live streamed their new series of performances, *Complete Works*. The video was streamed from a performance in front of a co-present audience at the Berliner Festspiele in Germany. I was not able to attend as a 'live' audience member, but I did log in to watch the performances streamed every night for a week from the TV in my 'snug'. It is worth noting that if I had been at the actual event in Germany, sitting amongst the other bodies, it is very likely that I would *not* have engaged in the act of live tweeting: deeply conscious of the effect this would have had on my fellow spectators and of course on the performer, who was in quite close proximity to the audience. Accessing the live event remotely in this way empowered me to feel comfortable engaging in the act of live tweeting. Through my mediated access, I was experiencing the event as it staged its own disappearance in the same way as the audience bodies present in the room – albeit remotely. This was my first experience of live tweeting, and I explicitly engaged in the act as a theatre scholar interested in this mode of lively performance document creation. It was, for me, an act of research.

As such, I took up the role of 'reflective participant'. Although the term 'reflective practitioner' is commonly used in Practice as Research (PaR), the 'reflective participant' is a phrase I have coined to describe the activity of experiential, embodied research activities such as: attending performances, rehearsals, and any other event linked to the making processes of other theatre practitioners. By participating in these theatrical experiences, I enter not only as a member of the public and as part of the general audience, but as a researcher and maker myself. In doing so, I am aware of bringing a certain agenda to my attendance. In this instance the act of live tweeting was not only a direct, immediate reflection of my experience of the event, but was driven by the motivation to explore a research methodology. I did not, however, disclose my intentions on Twitter, as I felt this would have impacted upon the processes by which my voice became validated. As we have already suggested, knowledgeable voices are frequently privileged over that of the 'general Twitter public', and so in failing to disclose my potential expertise I hoped that my tweets might perform as an amateur voice.

Each time I had a thought, emotion or reflection, I enunciated this through a tweet. Sometimes this included an image; sometimes not.

These were often immediately retweeted and shared by other live tweeters, as well as by Forced Entertainment themselves. At the time of writing this chapter (early 2016) it is still possible to see the full range of activity on Forced Entertainment's Twitter feed, as they have not altered or deleted any of the activity produced by the live streaming. I also entered into direct discourse with other live tweeters if they engaged directly with my own tweets, or if their tweets elicited a response that impacted upon my own experience. This immediately developed a direct dialogue between participants across the globe; at times the conversation included live tweeters from locations as far-flung as Australia and Tokyo. Because the dialogue was performed in cyberspace, my responses had a direct impact on other tweeters' experience of the performance. For example, on occasions a fellow tweeter asked me to fill in a piece of information they had missed, such as to advise on what prop had been used to represent a character. As Kelsey and Bennett recognize, such models take the form of 'dynamic structures' that are 'constantly constructed and reconstructed by different participants in discursive events or exchanges' and alter depending on their interpretation (2014: 40).

While the live tweeting of Forced Entertainment's performance largely attracted professionally implicated commentators – people such as critics, academics, and/or fellow makers, who posted from expert subject positions – this was undoubtedly not the company's intention. Importantly, Forced Entertainment made no effort to collate or control the direction of this discourse. The conversations collected under the hashtag #completeworks might therefore be understood as a layer of lively and resistant stratum, providing access to audiences' immediate, direct, and uncensored reflections on their experience of the performance. This is relatively unusual: Freshwater positions Forced Entertainment as a rare example of a company that encourages audiences to 'talk freely and publically about their experiences' (2009: 72–73), with maker–audience relationships on the whole still predominantly characterized by frustration and suspicion rather than openness and trust (ibid.: 72).

Conclusion

This chapter has proposed that the palimpsestic nature of social media offers an ontologically-resistant potential space in which theatre can collectively be debated and discussed. However, as the example of *Love Never Dies* demonstrates, online platforms are not entirely ideologically emancipated. As Conner explains, '[i]nformation channelling (gathering, sorting, dissemination) has always been the route to power, but social media platforms have adjusted the nature of that power structure' (2013: 79). The key word here is 'adjusting': because while they have opened up new possibilities for disruption, social media sites are still not free from 'legitimated' voices that continue to assert an uneven level of influence. To some extent, performance makers are collectively able to position petrified strata as the 'official' record of what a live performance achieved, while ignoring those online postings that don't fit their chosen narrative.

What the cultural industries need is for more theatre companies to oppose this authoritative petrification and embrace the *true* liveliness of performance experience. As another example we might therefore turn to Tim Crouch, whose works make a point of asking what authority might look like both in theatre and beyond. His performances reject the petrification of experience inherent within the traditional contract, which tends to encourage audiences 'to relinquish self-agency to the virtuosic cast, the "visionary" director, the glamour, the romance. I do not believe our current theatre deserves such mindless devotion. It feels to me like subjugation' (2011: 422). This chapter has begun to demonstrate the operation of ongoing frictions between lively stratification on the part of audiences, who are increasingly free to make their own resistant forms of documentation, and the efforts of theatre makers to petrify these into a solid, official narrative. By embracing experiential divergence, it might be possible instead to reverse these traditional power dynamics and encourage audiences to take ownership over their participation: to respond spontaneously, dynamically, and without restriction, as their responses form and reform over time.

Web Archiving and Participation: The Future History of Performance?

Vanessa Bartlett

Web archiving is the process of capturing portions of the internet, from single web pages to entire sites, for future use. This chapter explores how this archival form might make a contribution to the processes of documenting performance. As contemporary experiences of performance become subject to increasing mediation on the web, including venue websites detailing forthcoming programmes, Facebook invites listing event attendees and post show blog reviews circulated via various social media, there appears to be an urgent need for critical appraisal of the historical and scholarly value of this born digital material.

The analysis of the importance of innovation in web archiving will go beyond technological advancement as an end in itself here, addressing questions of participation and authorship. The problem of custodianship has a long history in archival scholarship (Freshwater 2003: 734) and the act of archiving the web, a medium that comes with its own integral debates about authorial control (Garde-Hanson 2009: 137) amplifies many of these issues. The concern here is not just with *how* web archiving changes the way that histories are recorded, but with the authorial implications of *who* authors this developing archival mode. As part of this approach, informal archival media such as social networking sites form as significant a source as official web archives held at national libraries.

The main reference point in this chapter is Richard Rinehart and Jon Ippolito's book *Re-collection: Art, New Media and Social Memory*, which develops a useful critique of the role of formally curated archival repositories in the digital sphere. Their thesis is that preservation of digital media should engage users as active participants rather than passive cultural consumers, 'spreading memory around in order to protect it' (Rinehart and Ippolito 2014: 111). Inherently this spreading process involves increased collaboration between libraries, amateur archivists and other organizations, a practice that I will argue is best embodied in the field of web archiving by the Internet Archive (IA).[1] Although Rinehart and Ippolito's book is written primarily as a contribution to the field of archiving new media art, its arguments resonate with the current status of the field of web archiving.

This chapter builds upon previous research undertaken in 2014 about the Live Art Collection of The UK Web Archive (Bartlett 2014) and responds to a wider range of web archives and digital tools. As in this previous work, the emergent nature of the technologies involved means that more questions are posed than it is ultimately possible to answer in this context. Hopefully, however, this will provoke debate about the possible adoption of web archiving technologies in the performance sector and ways that this might increase participation and diversity in collections. Focused primarily on archival content rather than technical execution (for the pragmatics of web archiving see Julien Masanès' book *Web Archiving*), this chapter is an exploration of archival contents and approaches that web archiving may bring to future histories of performance.

Web archiving and performance

Performance scholars have historically described their craft as study of the ephemeral, unmediated event augmented through archives of printed paper or hand-written documents such as photographs, diary entries, posters and ticket stubs. However, in the digital age, many scholars have exploded the apparent ontological oppositions between performance and mediation, asserting that recorded or digital media itself is a constituent part of the history of performance (Auslander 1999; Bay-Cheng 2012). Nestled in this existing discourse between performance and digital technology, this article understands web-based documents of performance not as ontologically separate from the live event, but as a constituent part of the audience's experience of the work. This stance is influenced by Sarah Bay-Cheng's (2012) framing of performance as a network of linked media events and by Rinehart and Ippolito's (2014) work on variable media. Bay-Cheng (2012) in particular has made a compelling case for the ways that digital technology has become tied to our experience of performance and of performance history:

> Digital access to documentation via computers (searching library databases, viewing digitized documents, scanning photographs, and most significant, sharing these within digital networks) affects the ways in which we approach and organize performance history . . . At the same time, our participation within digital media – through social networking sites, blogs, and phone-based communication – constitute forms of performance.
>
> 2012: 32

The use of web pages as archival objects is of particular importance in any effort to take ongoing discourses around digital humanities and performance in a new direction. It is important to clarify that the practice of web archiving covered here is different to the process of digitizing existing archives of performance and making them available on a website. In the field of performance there are multiple examples of this latter form of interface, including the Digital Dance Archives[2] in the UK and Realtime Dance[3] in Australia. These archives use the web as a platform for making archival material accessible to a wider audience and have already been the subject of many valuable scholarly texts.[4]

The IA was the first ever web archiving initiative, founded by internet entrepreneur Brewster Kahle in 1996. The core of the IA is the Wayback Machine, which offers online access to bulk harvests of individual sites, including many of the world's most significant theatre and performance websites. Held in its digital coffers are recurrent copies of sites from New York's PS122[5] starting at 1996, Sydney's Performance Space[6] starting at 2001 and eighteen-year-old copies of websites from significant companies such as Franklin Furnace. The information contained in these sites ranges from simple show listings, to the remnants of early dance and performance webcasts[7] and blog posts detailing artists' responses to contemporary artistic production and current affairs.[8] The IA also runs Archive-it, a subscription service that allows schools, universities and other organizations to create their own collections of web pages. As the most longitudinal and multifaceted web archive available, the IA will be my foremost case study throughout the first part of this chapter.

While the bulk of the analysis provided in this chapter is based on information found on individual web pages, the potential of web archiving for generating quantitative data about performance is also explored. This is informed by existing digital humanities projects such as Analytical Access to the Domain Dark Archive,[9] which uses web archives to produce and analyze longitudinal research data from detected patterns in extensive bodies of text.

Mapping the field: web archiving and performance

Social memory or 'the long-term memory of civilization' (Rinehart and Ippolito 2014: 14) is collective remembering related to political, social and cultural events. It is the connecting thread that allows cultural identity to persist between generations. For Rinehart and Ippolito social memory can be broken into two categories: formal and informal, both of which have dedicated groups that play a role in their preservation. Formal social memory described by Rinehart and Ippolito is 'canonical' and is stored by institutions such as 'museums, libraries, and archives'. Conversely, informal social memory is defined in terms of 'folklaw' and 'popular forms of remembering' and is driven by widespread community participation (Rinehart and Ippolito 2014: 15). Rinehart and Ippolito's vision for the future of digital archivization stresses an expansion of formal institutional practices to embrace the kinds of community and collaborative processes that would traditionally have been associated with informal social memory. This merging of practices, which I will argue is best exemplified in the IA, is part of a wider necessity within the web archiving field for collaboration and cross-pollination.

Formal social memory

As part of this mapping of the area of web archiving, formal social memory is collected in this field by interfaces held at major national libraries. These include examples such as the UK Web Archive[10] managed by the British Library, PANDORA at the National Library of Australia[11] and web collections archived by the Library of Congress in the US.[12] These archives organize materials deemed to be of national importance into collections selected by specialist curators and researchers. For example, the interface of the British Library's UK Web Archive presents a taxonomy of links organized under headings such as 'medicine and health', 'education and research' and 'arts and humanities'. Users click through to pages that present multiple copies of individual websites captured with varying frequency. The archive is driven by a Collection Development Policy (2013), which specifies that the websites must:

- reflect the diversity of lives, interests and activities throughout the United Kingdom;
- contain research value or are of research interest;
- feature political, cultural social and economic events of national interest; and
- demonstrate innovative use of the web.

In acknowledgement of the fact that this selective approach to web archiving 'inevitably misses important resources and takes them out of context of the web pages to which they are linked' (National Library of Australia Policy and Practice Statement 2015) several of these national collections have begun to engage in annual online harvests of their respective country's entire national domain. At the British Library, work is underway to make this body of information searchable and accessible to researchers, although the scale of collection and usability of any resulting interface poses ongoing challenges (Jackson 2015). At present, these bulk harvests are not a publically accessible part of the UK Web Archive's web interface. UK regulations passed on legal deposit materials in 2013 dictate that this material should only be made accessible on one computer at a time at each of the Legal Deposit Libraries (The British Library n.d.). This mode of display is different to the IA and its Wayback Machine, which makes its entire web crawls available online.

While important contributors to web archiving discourse such as Julien Masanès have proposed that archival gatekeepers are not necessary in a virtual space with no physical limitations (Masanès 2009: 19), these sites of formal social memory often still rely upon specialist practitioners to determine the significance of archival material. Previous research work in this area has suggested that there is a tendency in institutions archiving arts and humanities to impose outdated archival practices on developing digital technologies (Bartlett 2014: 100). In Reinhart and Ippolito's words, 'today's institutions, no matter how digitized, remain hamstrung by their own history as centralized repositories' (Rinehart and Ippolito 2014: 79).

Informal social memory

In web archiving, informal social memory is represented by certain types of social media sites, wikis such as Wikipedia and popular video repositories like YouTube. While these sites are unstable as web archiving interfaces and have limitations that cannot be overlooked, they are a useful paradigm for imagining the kinds of content that Rinehart and Ippolito's ethos might admit into web archives of performance. They are highly participatory, user friendly and have been claimed by some scholars to be 'capable of posing serious challenges to the hegemony of the historical imagination that has dominated Western thought in the last century' (Garde-Hanson 2009: 135).

Rinehart and Ippolito evoke a computer metaphor of a 'network system' to describe the contemporary properties of digital informal social memory. In chapter eight of *Re-collection* the authors describe the amateur efforts of computer enthusiasts to preserve out of date video games using software hacks that are circulated and modified between members of the community. They explain how prominent sites such as Emulator Zone[13] become central access points where users upload their home-brewed software, creating a crowd-sourced archive of informally held and non-copyrighted video game history. Crucially this form of recollection is 'distributed' rather than generated out of central repositories of knowledge such as libraries or museums (Rinehart and Ippolito 2014: 15).

As an example from the field of performance, a search for the term 'Performance Art' within Facebook creates an aggregate of historical narratives about performance pulled through from Wikipedia (a crowd sourced repository) plus a selection of photographic posts from the user's Facebook 'friends' that have been tagged or captioned with the words 'performance art'. Facebook automatically generates pages such as this one based on what users have previously viewed. On my Facebook profile this produces a digital photograph advertising a forthcoming performance event at Sandrabh, a volunteer-led arts space in India, plus an image of a gathering of female performance artists after a show at Chelsea Theatre. The page also contains links to major institutions associated with performance and to a cluster of individuals who have included the phrase 'performance art' in their work information or interests. Following these links to personal and event pages creates a trail of primary evidence about who attended what events and who works and socializes together. While it is possible to trace similar links across traditional paper archives, the relationships evidenced by Facebook pages make this process far more expedient. However, Facebook pages like this one differ from an archive as they are generated by algorithms rather than holding a collection of documents deliberately set aside for permanent preservation.

In her writing on pervasive performance Elena Pérez has pinpointed the growing significance of archiving audience experience in a technological age and the role that social media plays in this process. Her experimental research seeks to document audience involvement in her works using a blogging platform and other social networking sites such as Facebook. The work responds to what she refers to as 'a paradigm change from documenting "objects" . . . to documenting "experiences"' (Pérez 2014: 78) and results in the creation of documents that she frames as an archive. Echoing Bay-Cheng's assertions that digital augmentation has become integral to the experience of performance (increasingly we experience culture via social media), she suggests that this form of documenting can capture 'a sense of liveness that cannot be matched' (Pérez 2014:

78). Pérez goes so far as to suggest that this process of crowd-sourcing documents for a performance archive in this way reflects a 'democratic culture and an empowerment of the cultural agent' (Pérez 2014: 77), a perspective that resonates with Rinehart and Ippolito's recommendation for the archive as 'public playlist remixed by curator and public alike' (Rinehart and Ippolito 2014: 111).

Pérez's notion of Facebook as democratic archive is highly seductive, but also problematic. If a user clicks to say they are attending an event, there is no guarantee that they actually arrived. Users who may have no awareness of themselves as web archivists fill these sites with performance documents such as audience commentary, photographs and videos, yet this population of amateur archivists can also be responsible for removal of material and a loss to the archive. According to the estimates of Luke McKernan, Lead Curator, News and Moving Image at the British Library, as many as one quarter of the videos uploaded to YouTube might potentially be removed within eight years of posting, creating an interface that he suggests should be treated more as a gallery than a stable archive (McKernan 2016). While the IA is taking regular snapshots of YouTube,[14] the videos themselves are not present in the collection. Furthermore, each individual's view of Facebook is customized by the presence of algorithms driven by criteria controlled by Facebook itself. Facebook's emphasis on user-driven and crowd sourced content may appear to offer a participatory interface, but Garde-Hansen has pointed out that corporate collectivism and ideologies abound in this online space (Garde-Hanson 2009), ultimately controlling what users do and don't see. Quoting Derridian paradigms of archival control, she reminds us that archival technologies always impact on interpretations of content: 'the technical structure of the *archiving* archive also determines the structure of the *archivable* content even in its very coming into existence and in its relationship to the future' (Derrida 1996, cited in Garde-Hanson 2009: 137).

It is important to stress that Rinehart and Ippolito's recommendations for an open and flexible archive propose a series of interlinked databases rather than an interface that is specifically modelled on social networking sites. What is useful in thinking about social media as document repository for performance archives, is the potential diversity of media and content generated by an interface to which many users are able to contribute.

Mixing formal and informal social memory: the Internet Archive

While the distinction between formal and informal social memory is useful for organizing this exploratory study of web archiving practice, it also comes with limitations. Faced with the restrictive values of institutions representing formal social memory and the fragility of interfaces holding informal social memory, it is necessary to consider a meeting point between the two forms. Reinhart and Ippolito suggest that new approaches to archiving in the digital sphere should in fact borrow tactics 'from both "high" and "low" culture and both formal and informal social memory' (Rinehart and Ippolito 2014: 16) in order to create a system that archives most effectively for the digital sector. The web archive that best begins to blur definitions of formal and informal social memory in this way is the IA. Initially the sister site of Alexa Internet,[15] a company that provides commercial web traffic data and analytics, now owned by Amazon.com, this site aims to capture as much of the web as technology will allow, resulting in an assembly of more than 452 billion web pages. As web archiving legislation has evolved and institutions of formal memory have gained legal rights to archive websites, this collection process has increasingly been undertaken in formal collaboration with national collections such as PANDORA and the National Library of Australia (The National Library of Australia n.d.).

For staff working on the IA its transition from 'experimental project into established institution' occurred in 2000 when it embarked on its first collaborative partnership with the Library of Congress (Kimpton and Ubois 2009: 206). This collaboration was driven by recognition that a variety of approaches are required in order to capture the full scale and breadth of the World Wide Web. Abbie Grotke, web archiving team lead at the Library of Congress, has suggested 'a hybrid approach is needed to ensure that a representative sample of the web is preserved, including the complementary approaches of broad crawls such as the Internet Archive does, paired with deep, curated collections by theme or by site, tackled by other cultural heritage organizations' (Grotke 2011: n.p.).

While this relationship with larger libraries might suggest that the IA occupies the territory of formal social memory, the IA is notably more informal in its archival gatekeeping than most large libraries and archives. In 2006, when the IA launched a web archiving service to help other organizations build their own collections within the archive, it created a unique platform that could delegate archival control to a much larger pool of partners than had previously been possible. Archive-it provides a subscription facility for museums, educational institutions and other bureaucratic and amateur associations to function as archivists, sometimes as part of specialist education initiatives such as the K12 Web Archiving Programme.[16] Organizations pay a fee and are given their own login interface, where they can create collections that meet with their own archival needs. While the paying mechanism makes this interface less accessible than other informal social memory repositories referenced here, there are no strict criteria about the types of organizations that can use the service. Searching within the Archive-it database for the term 'performance' yields a variety of collecting organizations including colleges, universities and one K12 high school that has created a collection largely made up of students' personal sites. Under the 'collections' tab organizations such as the Hemispheric Institute and Salt Lake County Center for the Arts have created small, self-referential collections that often contain no more than versions of their own organization's website. These results are scattered between other performance-related collections, which pertain to subject areas such as information technology and government performance.

The IA offers many of the functions of formal social memory, such as an in house team of archivists who curate collections in response to one off special events.[17] However, invoking the term 'research value' (which we have seen is central to the collection development policy of formal archival institutions) highlights a characteristic of the IA that is more closely associated with informal social memory. 'Partners' using Archive-it have a large degree of freedom to determine 'research value' in their own collections, including the possibility to create a collection that refers only to their own web output. In the past, the IA has attracted critique from the libraries and archives sector for its 'limited notion of collection development' and lack of 'judgment on the veracity, quality, or appropriateness of the content being archived'. The core of these critiques, that the IA is 'not a library' (Edwards 2004: 5) reflects an attitude held by mainstream collecting organizations that Rinehart and Ippolito might describe as a 'fixation with fixity' (Rinehart and Ippolito 2014: 95), an ongoing emphasis on maintaining traditional archival structures. While Archive-it creates an opportunity for taxonomy within the IA, the act of collection is overall highly dispersed between participating communities. Archive-it, like the IA's other interface the Wayback Machine, appears to favour accumulation of large numbers of sites as opposed to a defined collection development policy.

Writing on the UK Web Archive blog site, Peter Spooner has explored the UK Web Archive's options for working with partners on the creation of special collections. Logically he points out that individual archivists from within the library team cannot manage expansive special collections alone, so collaboration with partner researchers is required. He conjectures over the level of control given to these partner researchers, suggesting various levels of jurisdiction including the possibility that the library's in house archivists act as technical support. In this scenario it is hinted that collections may become repetitive and unruly, as 'each researcher is likely to have slightly different interests or questions in mind' (Spooner 2015) Having already taken the risk of delegating collections to partner researchers, the IA has opted for the sprawling, collaboration based approach that the UK Web Archive is only able to speculate upon at present.

In *Re-collection* Rinehart and Ippolito site the Open Library, a crowd sourced online library also sponsored by the IA's founder Brewster Kahle as an exemplary distributed database that embodies their own ideal for an open museum. Kahle's success in pioneering these kinds of participatory archives perhaps reflects a difference in the levels of archival freedom enjoyed by public institutions and privately funded experimental initiatives. As we will see in the following section the British Library does have a remit to pursue innovative practices, yet the pace of these tends to be slower and less public facing than the work undertaken by Kahle and his team.

Web archiving and big data – a participatory method?

One of the key arenas in which web archiving may innovate in future arts and humanities practices is the use of distant reading as a means of analyzing longitudinal bodies of data. This process broadly moves interpretation away from individual texts or artworks towards understanding trends that manifest over time through the processes of aggregation and cross referencing. Also known as 'big data,' quantitative analysis of database information has emerged as a key concern in the digital humanities sector – inspiring excitement, controversy and a confusing cacophony of both utopian and dystopian zeal (Boyd and Crawford 2012)

In the field of web archiving, implementation of these techniques is best exemplified by the research project Analytical Access to the Domain Dark Archive (AADDA), funded by the JISC and led by the Institute of Historical Research in partnership with the British Library and the University of Cambridge. AADDA developed new forms of access to bulk harvests of websites captured between 1996 and 2010 but not yet available on the UK Web Archive interface. This work is at the innovative edge of archiving services that the British Library and its partners seek to provide, although it is interesting to note that it is aimed primarily at researchers as users and contributors, locating it securely in the domain of formal social memory.

Participating researchers in AADDA have included Martin Gorsky who used the dataset to interpret changes to the representation of public health policy after the Health and Social Care Act of 2012. The methodology for this study included creating a database that recorded links, keywords and themes, and then undertaking discourse analysis 'to identify recurrent tropes germane to the questions of public health vision' (Gorsky 2015: 601). Strikingly, one of the methodical conclusions of this study was the extent to which websites are amenable to the process of historical research: 'Although generated by diverse individuals in different locations, it is possible to observe common languages circulating through the sites, whose very succinctness makes them easy to identify' (Gorsky 2015: 601). Gorsky's study suggests that the text contained in web archives may be particularly suitable for big data processes.

Following similar procedures as part of AADDA, Helen Taylor used sentiment analysis to research public reception of performance poet Adrian Henri. She suggests that this process revealed fascinating non-academic, crowd sourced histories of the 1960s underground, where 'Henri and the Merseybeat poets appear as far more important than in "official" criticism' (Taylor 2013). However, the conclusions in her report express more about her methodological frustrations with the dataset than they do about public perceptions of Henri's work. Her major assertion is that sentiment analysis (in this case simple formulations of positive or negative attitudes towards Henri) can be misread by the technology, leading to incorrect analysis of parts of the data set. She asserts that researchers must 'dig down' to the actual websites themselves, to ensure that close reading of the relevant text supports the interpretation given by the technology. Her frustrations appear to have been somewhat alleviated in a subsequent report written for Big UK Domain Data for the Arts and Humanities in 2015, where she suggests that innovations around the database have enabled researchers to search for more specific queries, obtaining increasingly accurate results (Taylor 2013). While further outcomes from this project are pending, one implication of Taylor and her colleagues' work is that innovation improves only as the technology becomes more sophisticated – an assertion that holds for much of the emergent digital humanities sector.

Marrying the ethics and aesthetics of performance research with distant reading of data is a problematic task for a researcher interested in textual meaning. As Christof Schöch has pointed out, for many arts and humanities researchers: 'the apparent empiricism of data-driven research in the humanities seems at odds with principles of humanistic inquiry, such as context-dependent interpretation and the inevitable "situated-ness" of the researchers and their aims' (2013: 3).

Performance scholars often mount a charge of statistical oversimplification in response to data processing that turns individual authors into lines on a chart. However, for Franco Moretti distant reading derives from a 'Marxist formation' (Moretti 2007: 2), and is primarily a means of expansion of artistic and literary studies to include a greater diversity of participation – a prospect that should be appealing to anyone interested in historical diversity. Addressing specifically the value of distant reading in the study of literature (Moretti's own field) he stresses the impossibility of understanding the breadth of literary production – or world literature, as he would like it to be known – through reading a limited number of celebrated novels (although this is the way that we have officially approached humanities scholarship for hundreds of years). Instead, he calls for a focus on 'the system in its entirety' creating 'units that are much smaller or much larger than the text: devices, themes, tropes? or genres and systems' (Moretti 2000: 57). As Rinehart and Ippolito call for broader, participatory methods of admitting content into the archive, Moretti advocates an approach to historical research that focuses less on individual authors and on a wider bracket of historical processes and trends.

While the above formulation presents a neat fit for my exploration of archives and participation, it should also be treated with caution. From a purely pragmatic perspective the kinds of qualitative data that are processed through distant reading demand high levels of archival and data expertise that can only be managed by the most formally trained researchers (justification perhaps for AADDA's focus on researchers as their key audience). Moreover, the ethical questions charged against big data appear in certain cases to be legitimate and well founded. Tracking the relationship between ethics and access, Danah Boyd and Kate Crawford have highlighted moral problems presented by a 2008 study that accidently made the private data of 1,700 Facebook users publicly accessible, concluding that 'very little is understood about the ethical implications underpinning the Big Data phenomenon' (Boyd and Crawford 2012: 672). As copyright and data privacy laws become increasingly flexible, many artists and performers might question their capacity for 'none participation' or 'opting out' of the models of web archiving performance that data harvesting proposes.

Andrew Jackson (2015), Web Archiving Technical Lead at the British Library, has described his work on AADDA and the subsequent project Big UK Domain Data for the Arts and Humanities as an attempt to unify: 'the modern notion of "distant reading" of texts with the more traditional "close reading" approach, by encouraging individual items to be discovered via (or contra to) the prevailing trends, while also attempting to embed and present those individual resources in their broader context'.

It appears that while distant reading and data collection propose potentials for widening the range of historical voices included in archival data (as in Taylor's encounter with non-academic documents on the history of Adrian Henri), the technical and ethical challenges posed by this technique should inspire a degree of caution. The pace of invention at the British Library is likely to be gradual, as researchers such as Jackson attempt to marry innovation with the politics and processes of formal social memory institutions. It may therefore take years for these techniques to become fully integrated in performance research. In the meantime, I return to the spirit of *Re-collection* and the authors' suggestion that massively distributed archival databases are 'worth imagining and may be even within the realm of the possible' (Rinehart and Ippolito 2014: 112). While we still have much to learn about the practical possibilities of data analysis and web archiving, the opportunity for expanding our perceptions of performance history using these techniques is worth engaging with, in ways that are both imaginative and pragmatically driven by research outcomes.

Conclusion

This chapter is written with the intention of provoking debate about the value of web archiving for documenting performance. It offers a number of case studies: the UK Web Archive, the IA and social media such as Facebook, which have exhibited various degrees of sophistication in their ability to increase participation in the production of performance history. This chapter has suggested that a willingness to mix elements of formal and informal social memory is an extremely valuable attribute for an archive that intends to increase participation in authoring histories of performance.

While formal memory institutions such as the British Library might appear somewhat maligned by the calls for access and innovation put forward by this article, its involvement in projects such as AADDA serve as a reminder of its important role in research driven aspects of innovative archival practice. As archival technologies become increasingly sophisticated, a range of approaches will be required to implement them to greatest effect. I hope that an ethos of participation and collaboration can influence all agents of formal and informal social memory involved in this process.

10

Documenting Digital Performance Artworks

Adam Nash and Laurene Vaughan

In this chapter we examine the consequences, for the concepts of archiving and documenting performance artworks, brought forth by digital art works that use real time digital data as a constitutive or major part of their construction and execution. We use case studies of the three works that made up the exhibition *Everything is Data* in Singapore in 2015[1]: *The Mood of the Planet* by digital art pioneer Vibeke Sorensen, which mines global social network data in real time to drive multiple LED lights within monumental stacks of crushed glass; *Man A* by Gibson/Martelli, which uses 'augmented reality' to drive motion-captured dance sequences in interaction with a large physical object; and *Out of Space* by Adam Nash and Stefan Greuter, which uses real time motion capture combined with an immersive virtual reality headset to build an immersive abstract audiovisual environment. We interrogate the role and concept of archiving in the light of these works that radically blur the distinction between artwork, archive and documentation. Because such works use real time data sources to build themselves, they therefore might be seen as a kind of 'real time archive' or documentation themselves. Boris Groys (2008) considers such works as primarily performances since they are based on algorithms that must be enacted in real time at the time they are encountered, and can never be said to exist as a single work. Rather, the works can be enacted, or instanced, in widely varied circumstances on different platforms. Using theories from both performance and practice theory (Auslander 2008; Schatzki 2002; Schechner 2003) and digital game archiving (Swalwell, 2013; deVries et al., 2013; Stuckey et al., 2014; Harvey, 2011), we work through the implications of attempts to both document and archive such real time, data-based artworks. In conclusion, we find that a new understanding of the concepts and methods of archive and documentation are required to appropriately conserve these works for the future, and present examples of such approaches.

Live performance in the digital era

What does it mean, in the digital era, for a performance to be 'live'? Indeed, how can we define 'performance' in the digital era? The digital represents the apotheosis of Marshall McLuhan's container concept, where every new medium contains all prior media as content. The digital takes this concept to its extreme, subsuming all media into a virtualized process that recreates media in real time (Clemens and Nash 2015). The digital therefore represents some sigificant problems for our understanding of 'performance' and 'liveness', since it is possible to see the digital itself as a 'live performance' each time a process is enacted. These problems in turn affect our understanding of the documentation of performance.

The version of live performance that the digital inaugurates may, in practical terms, perhaps be treated phenomenologically and accepted for its empirical utility in the case of, say, digital video used to document a live dance performance in the conventional sense of documenting a work. But when considering performances that involve or rely on digital processes to enact the performance work, the digital process becomes the crucial defining factor in the notion of documenting or archiving the work. As we shall see, the digital process also calls into question the status of all previous understandings of document and archive.

Everything is data

Here, we examine three such works, all presented in an exhibition called *Everything Is Data* at Gallery A of the School of Art, Design and Media at the National Technological University of Singapore in 2015. The works were *The Mood of the Planet* by Danish/American artist Vibeke Sorensen, *Man A* by British artists Gibson/Martelli and *Out of Space* by Australian artist Adam Nash and Australian/German games researcher Stefan Greuter. The exhibition was curated by Australian designer Laurene Vaughan.[2]

Much has been discussed about the implications of so-called mediation for the concepts of 'liveness' and 'performance' (Auslander 2008; Bolter and Grusin 2000), but such discussions rely on an essentially pre-digital acceptance of the concept of 'media'. This attitude often sets the 'screen' in opposition to live performance, conflating different kinds of screen and eliding any considerations of live performance as a technology of reproduction that is already mediated, mediating and mediatizing (Auslander 2008: 2). Such a view traditionally sets the concepts of 'live' and 'recorded' in mutually exclusive opposition, enabling an uncomplicated understanding of what constitutes documenting and archiving. In this understanding, to document is to create an impoverished record of a performance, missing the crucial element of liveness that defines the performance.

Similarly, Auslander describes an attitude that, even while acknowledging both McLuhan's concept of the simulating function of new media and Bolter and Grusin's specifying of that concept in the early twenty-first century, insists that theatre and television compete with each other without really offering any proof and, worse, precludes any possibility of other relationships in which these two forms may participate. Such an enforced dichotomy precludes any considerations that could come to bear on discussions of liveness, such as the audience as performer, the real time transmission of an atmosphere of liveness and the assemblage of mechanical, electronic and social processes that ultimately comprise any performance experience, whether live in person, transmitted live, ascynchronously live or putatively not live at all.

Of ultimate relevance here is the fact that the attitude Auslander describes is unable to conceive of a live performance that is immanently digital. Boris Groys recognizes this when he acknowledges all digital images as performances. What he means by this is that a digital image can not really be said to exist as an image until the time it is called up from data stored on a hard drive and modulated into a display register, i.e., displayed on a screen as a collection of red, green and blue pixels (Groys 2008: 84; Clemens and Nash 2015). For this modulation into the display register to occur, a series of actions are initiated based on an associated alogrithm that is used to 'read' the digital file and display it to the screen. This series of actions, implicitly equated with the performance of a musical score, is what Groys considers a performance, performed anew every time the image is displayed on a screen. At this point Groys becomes distracted by considerations of original and copy, showing an inability to think beyond images. At the same time, Groys implicitly acknowledges the fundamental leveling nature of the digital that renders meaningless both any thought of the distinction between images and other sense phenomena and any meaningful distinction between original and copy. The distinction between original and copy is not relevant to those concerned with performance and liveness, since no individual performance can be said to be a copy of another peformance. At the same time, on the grounds of geospatial, social or temporal elements, every performance can be said to be original, even though it is the same work being performed. It is this formulation that, as intimated earlier, causes problems for concepts of documenting performance, since every performance is unique in one sense and generic in another, a formulation that is also true of the digital. Some concrete examples will help to examine further the implications and processes involved.

The Mood of the Planet

Vibeke Sorensen's work *The Mood of the Planet* provides a particularly relevant example of the problems and paradoxes involved in documenting digital works that are presented in physical settings. The core idea that drives the work and its reception also presents the core problem when attempting documentation of the work. Sorensen's idea is to monitor popular web-based social networks such as Facebook, Twitter and Instagram for occurrences of words that express emotions. This data is then modulated into a display interface in the form of a large rectangular arch made of clear acrylic plastic filled with thousands of small chunks of crushed glass and coloured LED (light emitting diode) lights. The arch was installed in a darkened, mirrored room so that the visitors had the experience of walking through an infinite periodic tunnel. In the words of the artist herself: 'The "arch" or "doorway" is iconic and references developmental transformation, the metaphoric passing from one state to another, of growth and change that is analogous to the transformative effect that global communications technologies have upon our collective human condition' (Sorensen, 2015).

It is clear from this description that there are two crucial elements that ostensibly render the work, an intrinsically *live* work that is more or less impossible to document usefully or faithfully. The two elements are, first, the emotional keywords being expressed by social network users across the planet at the moment an individual experiences the work and, second, those very individual visitors who experience the work as it is situated in the gallery. It might be said that any artistic experience that involves an individual physically attending that experience – whether a live performance, a film, a painting or any other kind of artwork – will be unique to that individual. Each individual will experience the work slightly differently from anyone else. Their experience will be informed by their disposition, which in turn is informed by what might be called the emotional timbre of the world. Such unique experience therefore renders relatively useless any attempt to document any artwork or, inversely, renders every individual who experienced the work a living document of that artwork. This might contribute little to our understanding of the documenting of digital work, were it not for the fact that Sorensen's piece is *literally* constituted by the emotional timbre of the world as expressed on global social networks at the moment the individual experiences it, thereby codifying both the momentary uniqueness of any experience of the artwork and the impossibility to adequately document it. This realization radically extends Auslander's assertion that 'the relationship between live and mediatized forms and the meaning of liveness be understood as historical and contingent rather than determined by immutable differences' (2008: 8).

A new approach to documenting and archiving such a work is clearly called for. The consideration of such approaches is concerned with the 'question of the future of the specter or the specter of the future, or the future *as specter*', as Derrida (1995: 84) reminds us; meaning that we really are dealing with a phantom. As we saw earlier, the digital complicates this spectral phantom even further by necessitating a new performance at every access of the archived version. As is often the case with the digital, this realization shines a retroactive light on the nascent qualities of the very idea of documenting and archiving in the pre-digital era, calling on us to acknowledge the performative nature of the archive in its very conception. Acknowledging the spectral nature of the exercise also allows us to understand any document or archive of the work as its own entity, independent of the work it is documenting.

How would a new approach to the concept and practice of documenting and archiving actually work in this context? Clearly, conventional forms of documenting and archiving, such as video, photography and audio recording of the work will be deficient, because the individual experience itself will be lost through lack of peripheral vision, lack of audible stereo positioning, lack of visual resolution due to darkness, etc. At the same time, such attempts are capturing useful documents would be able to capture and preserve certain important aspects of the construction and procedural experience of the work. Depending on the viewpoint of capture, certain aspects of the individual experience of the work may also be recorded. So conventional documenting approaches offer two potential aspects: a somewhat objective view of an individual experiencing the work, and a more subjective view from the individual themselves whilst experiencing the work.

Much of the whole work is lost if only these two aspects are used. This is what Melanie Swalwell and Helen Stuckey try to address with their concept of discursive archiving. Speaking specifically about the archiving of digital computer games, but of enormous relevance to this discussion, they describe Lowood's question of whether digital games are 'artefacts or activity' (Stuckey et al. 2015: 10) and their attempt to reveal the answer as 'both', by proposing and building an archive that can 'support multiple narratives' (ibid.). Crucial to their formulation is the importance of the memories, stories and impressions of the players of the games to the concept of the documenting and archiving of those games. This allows for a more 'open and non-hierarchical' (ibid.) sense of the archive, which enables 'fragmentary and plural interpretations' (ibid.). We can apply the same principle to those who experience Sorensen's work, and this will help provide another dimension to its documenting and archiving.

This gets us so far in terms of documenting and archiving the experience of the work from the point of view of a visitor or putative objective observer. This might be called external documenting. But what about the experience of performing the work? This might be called internal documenting. Performance theorist Richard Schechner (2003: 300) maintains that there is a 'great big gap between what a performance is to people inside and what it is to people outside [the performance]', but is this a relevant consideration in the case of digital, interactive works? Who or what is the performer in such works, and how might their experience be documented or archived? The next two works in the *Everything Is Data* exhibition help think this through.

Man A and *Out of Space*

Man A by Gibson/Martelli is a work combining an irregularly shaped polygon constructed of cardboard (approximately 2 × 2 × 2 metres in size) decorated with geometric patterns inspired by World War I era dazzle camouflague and serving as the trigger for augmented reality animations of motion captured dancers similarly geometrically rendered with dazzle-style patterns. The animations are viewed on a smartphone which is pointed at the large cardboard polygon. *Out of Space* by Adam Nash and Stefan Greuter was an abstract audiovisual virtual reality work using a head-mounted Oculus Rift display for visual 'immersion' of the user, and motion capture to track the physical movements of the user, which are mapped in real time into movements in the virtual reality space, allowing the user to use body movements to *play* the virtual reality space as a combination of game and visual/musical instrument.

Both of these performative works call into question the status or identity of the performer, and in doing so, offer potential new approaches to documenting and archiving the work from the point of view of the performer. While *Man A* uses dancers as conventional performers in one sense, theirs is both already a documented performance, in that it has been motion captured, and also a performance contingent on the specificities of each individual accessing the work in the gallery via their smartphone. Similarly, the visitor in the gallery experiencing the work is a performer of the work in the sense that the experience of the whole work – the interaction of the motion-captured animations with the cardboard sculpture and the user's phone – is entirely dependent on the actions of the visitor and the essential realization of the work. Indeed, the movements of the visitors pointing and moving their phones around the sculpture form an important movement motif of the work.

The visitor to *Out of Space*, on the other hand, becomes the player of the work, quite literally performing it through their physical actions. It is a single-user work because only one person can don the head-mounted display at a time, but other gallery visitors can see the resulting performance displayed on a large two-dimensional screen behind the user. This creates a real time, ephemeral kind of external documenting that also forms an aspect of the experience of the work. Other forms of external documenting, as discussed earlier, can also be applied to these player/performers, and we may adapt some of them for internal documenting too. These would include video, audio and photography from the players' viewpoint, post-facto written or spoken personal impressions of the players, and even such impressions collected whilst playing the work.

Having described a process of assembling a collection of discursive documenting approaches to create an archive that is its own dynamic entity rather than any kind of impoverished copy, there is one more crucial element remaining.

All three of the works discussed rely on digital programs to bring the idea into existence. These programs are created by the artists through programming, also known as coding. As discussed earlier, *de*coding these programs can be considered performative. Accordingly, digital code occupies a uniquely indeterminate ontological status, in that it is both specific and generic. It is specific because it is unique to the situation being coded, for example the storage and triggering of the motion-captured dancers in *Man A*, or the modulation of social network emotional keywords into red/green/blue values in *The Mood of the Planet*. It is generic because it is stored as an indeterminate collection of magnetic polarities on a disk and it can be modulated into any display register in an arbitrary number of ways. Similarly, documenting or archiving the programs and the code used to create them involves both internal and external documenting at the same time. As well as the executable program, the code itself needs to be archived, along with descriptions of the equipment used to realize the work. Such descriptions can be written as comments (i.e., non-executable code designed to be read by people rather than computers). Descriptions like these are needed because technical specifications change quickly, and what could once run on common computer equipment may be unusable just a few years later. This is where the generic nature of the digital becomes apparent, allowing the preservation of the code used to construct the program, which can later be used, or referred to, to rebuild the program using appropriate contemporary technology platforms. This is the process that, for example, allows so-called emulation of digital games originally built to run on now-obsolete hardware. It would also be prudent to keep a paper copy of the code to insure against disk degradation or failure (Pogue, 2009).

Conclusion

To summarize, we have drawn upon the theories and practice of Stuckey and Swallwell, Auslander, Schechner and others to identify the need for discursive documenting and archiving to create archive entities that are dynamically independent of their originating works rather than an impoverished copy. Such discursiveness requires a more open and less heirarchical approach than has been hitherto conventional in the field of archiving. Discursive documenting means assembling a collection of a range of elements from different sources. External documenting comprises records (video, audio, photography, written, drawn, spoken) of people experiencing the work, taken from outside their point of view or from outside the work, with 'outside' being defined non-precisely and discursively. Internal documenting is comprised of records from the point of view of the experience of performing the work, or from within the work itself. Digital works are defined ontologically as performances that internally document themselves in their very creation. Artworks that use digital media in their execution, such as the three works exhibited in the *Everything is Data* exhibition in 2015, enliven the gallery visitor from being a viewer into a performer and thus every individual experience of the work can be considered as uniques performances of the same work and requiring the kind of discursive approach to documenting and archiving that we have described.

In conclusion, three short but important points. First, the purpose of documenting or archiving a work needs to be defined in order to know what elements to include. Second, much of the internal and external documenting of digital works needs to be considered by the artist/s while creating the work. Finally, the role of imagination comes into play as an important post-facto 'voice' in the discursive archive. This is implied by the opening up to a concept of the archive as a dynamic entity, because all people engaging with the archive will need to use imagination to bring the work to life. But we must not consider this as being 'condemned to imagination!', as Augusto Boal (2006: 62) rues of the fragmentary nature of documentary evidence of early Greek theatre. Rather, we should embrace imagination as an important aspect of the discursive, dynamic documenting and archiving of performative digital artworks.

Part Three

From Documents to Documenting

The word documentation is used widely among performance practitioners and scholars as a synonym for documents or the basic processes of documenting. However, there is a very significant difference to be made between documents as objects and the many processes of documenting performance for the eventual creation of performance documentation. The use of the term documentation in this book has been carefully limited to the ultimate result of a process of creating, collecting, processing and preserving documents to provide long-term access to documentation. In this section of the book, this distinction becomes most evident, particularly because each of the chapters presented here focuses on a particular example of documentation that contains the other parts that lead to the creation of documentation, rather than taking mere documents as documentation, which will somehow automatically be accessible in the future divorced from their original context and removed from any efforts to ensure their preservation and dissemination.

The first chapter in this section tackles a rather exceptional example of documentation. In Paradocumentation and NT Live's 'CumberHamlet' (chapter 11), Daisy Abbott and Claire Read look into the phenomenon of high-definition limited-access broadcasts of live performance from the National Theatre in London through a study of Shakespeare's *Hamlet* (2015) starring Benedict Cumberbatch in the title role. This type of spectacle is not restricted to the NT programme but stretches far beyond the UK to New York's Metropolitan Opera and Moscow's Bolshoi Ballet, among others. By bringing in so-called encore presentations of these live broadcasts to cinemas around the world (replays pre-recorded live performance), the authors of this chapter add a further layer of complexity to the argument against the loose use of the term documentation as a synonym for documents. Not unlike the argument made by Adam Nash and Laurene Vaughan in chapter 10, in such cases, the work itself, or at least a significant aspect of the work itself, becomes the document that is automatically archived for later access in a systematic manner. This documentation is able to give the impression that the work is being viewed for the first time, if the suspension of disbelief goes as far as assuming that the live action on the screen is happening in the physical space of the theatre at the same time as the audience sits in the cinema watching it.

To ensure that this book provides a broader approach to the documentation of performances based on Shakespeare's plays, in the next chapter Alvin Lim describes the Asian Shakespeare Intercultural Archive, which is a multilingual online archive in English, Mandarin, Japanese and Korean. This project aims to collect and present video recordings and related documents from productions of Shakespeare's plays in a number of East Asian countries. Interestingly, Lim manages to use the story of the Danish prince, especially his relationship with his murdered father, as a way to highlight aspects of what Derrida calls hauntology within the archive, without citing Derrida or hauntology directly. Although Derrida goes on to discuss the nature and function of archives in *Archive Fever* (1996), the notion of hauntology first appeared in *Specters of Marx* (1994), arguing for the idea that being does not entail presence. This is what is at the heart of the relationship between the value of a document arising from a performance and the performance itself that, as performance essentialists would have it, defies being captured beyond the ephemeral moment in which it is first produced.

Miguel Escobar Varela rides on this understanding in his chapter, 'From Copper-Plate Inscriptions to Interactive Websites: Documenting Javanese Wayang Theatre'. He explores the affordances of different media towards the creation of particular types of document and the subsequent documentation of Javanese puppet performance forms known as *wayang*. Some of the concerns he raises about the Contemporary Wayang Archive are also present in the following chapter on the Western Australian New Music Archive by Cat Hope, Adam Trainer and Lelia Green. In their case, the reader of this book will likely go away with two critical thoughts. The first is that there are various ways to connect an interested community to the documenting processes involved in preserving performance work that is meaningful to them. The other is that institutions need to ensure sustainable longevity for digital preservation and online archival projects. There are far too many projects that suffer from lack of the sort of expertise that specialists from the digital humanities can provide. Eventually they succumb to outdated technology or the lack of appropriate long-term preservation plans.

Lauren Vaughan's critique of the Circus Oz Living Archive (chapter 15) engages with both these concerns. Audience engagement is a rather crucial element for many archives of performance. The reasons for this are at least threefold. Audiences can contribute directly to giving context to the documentation of particular performances. They are also likely to be the primary users of the documentation contained within any particular archive that is of interest to them, and their interest in the archived documents will potentially give good reason for planners and policy makers to endow archives to develop and preserve performance documentation for generations to come, ensuring that the memory of particular works is kept alive through collective memory projects and community engagement schemes that are at the heart of successful large archives, beyond the realm of performance.

11

Paradocumentation and NT Live's 'CumberHamlet'

Daisy Abbott and Claire Read

Live broadcasts of theatrical events result in complex documentation processes for performance at the points of production, consumption, interpretation and further production. Following a model created by Met Opera Live in New York, since 2009 NT Live has streamed live performances to cinemas around the world.[1] The increasing popularity of live broadcasts offers brand new possibilities for documenting performance, not only for theatres but for audiences. Acknowledging the temporal, spatial and conceptual distances between the theatre production of a particular play and discrete audiences enabled via the NT Live streaming, this chapter focuses in particular on the concept of 'paradocumentation,' asserting a notion of unity between performances and their documents, borne in part from the technology of NT Live. In the context of NT Live screenings, documents are produced by both official and non-official sources before, during and after a live-streamed performance; for example, the leaflets and online articles promoting the performance, programmes distributed in theatre and cinema venues for audiences, reviews from critics, and unofficial documents created by audience members. Considering the single 'live' performance and its documentation via live streaming as the primary 'text' of a play, other types of documents can function as pre-text, post-text and con-text. Building upon the concept of 'paradata', defined as data that 'document(s) the process of interpretation' (Bentkowska-Kafel, Denard and Baker 2012: 1), these non-core documents of the play that include audience reaction to the primary 'text' will hereafter be referred to as 'paradocumentation', echoing a holisitic approach to experiencing, interpreting, and creating records of a live-streamed play, advancing and extending the life of a single performance.

Hamlet at the Barbican Centre in 2015 played eighty times to sold out audiences, and was the fastest selling London theatre show in history; yet 'in an era of NT Live, it's the cinema that is King', with 87 per cent of cinemas live streaming the performance from 15 October.[2] This production of *Hamlet* starred Benedict Cumberbatch as the Prince of Denmark, broadcast four years after his NT Live streaming debut in *Frankenstein* (2011). In an interview with Cumberbatch, broadcast immediately before *Hamlet* was live streamed in cinemas, Melvyn Bragg asserted that Hamlet was 'fading' (NT Live screening, 15 October 2015). This chapter argues that the portrayal of *Hamlet*, popularized particularly by the lead actor, reaches new audiences and ignites new passion for the original play text, whilst simultaneously reinventing itself. An analysis of *Hamlet* identifies key features of the Barbican Centre and NT Live production with particular attention to the merging of performance and its documents. The latter part of the chapter expands upon the notion of paradocumentation, with an exploration of data gleaned from an audience survey (n=183), and analyzes and suggests patterns of evidence for audience-created paradocumentation.

National Theatre Live

NT Live's cinema audiences experience additional material compared with theatre audiences. In addition to adverts for upcoming NT Live performances and introductions to the specific performance being aired, rehearsal notes are often shown, mirroring in this regard the typical inserts of a theatre production's programme. *Hamlet*'s rehearsal photographs, depicting actors working on scenes from the upcoming performance, formed part of the core text, playing on a loop whilst the countdown to the performance began. The scenes, whilst currently unknown to cinema audiences, were evidenced as performance shots of *Hamlet*, as Cumberbatch was centred within to ground and create visual attachments for the audience. Creating thereby a metaphorical anchor between times, NT Live displayed past pictures of a future tense; the rehearsal shots, taken chronologically before the performance, nevertheless display the very scenes that the cinema audience are keen to witness, and indeed will, within the next few hours. In this way, the documents of the performance extend to before, during and after the production: whilst the performance itself logically plays before the documents of the performance are gathered, teaser material such as production photographs complicates this path of display, affecting the causal relationship assumed between performance and documents. Moreover, as the Encore screenings depict the same rehearsal shots before their showing of *Hamlet*, at a later date than the NT Live screening on 15 October, the logical sequencing of rehearsal to production to documentation is further altered: the rehearsal shots appear to occur *after* the performance has in reality aired *live*. The notion of the post and after life of performance, working as an extension of the performance via the use of documents, reinforces the concept of paradocumentation, where the essence of documentation is divided between times to reflect its confusing state of identity borne from live-streamed performances.

During the pre-production material, Morgan Quaintance, art commentator as well as broadcaster for NT Live's *Hamlet*, confirmed that the Barbican Centre's theatre was playing to a full auditorium. To compensate for the lack of seats due to the extremely high demand, the Barbican Centre's cinemas live streamed the production, which was running simultaneously in the same building in the theatre above. The Barbican's advertising highlights the uniqueness of the situation, stating: 'Due to unprecedented demand, we are screening this very special NT Live production of *Hamlet* in cinemas 1, 2 and 3; giving you a chance to see this sold-out show live'.[3] Considering the use of the word 'live', the Barbican Centre split its liveness into two categories: live theatre and live cinema. Philip Auslander considers liveness as a condition brought about only by the emergence of its counterpart, the mediatized, noting that the 'first citation of the word "live" comes from the *BBC Yearbook* for 1934 and iterates the complaint "that recorded material was too liberally used" on the radio' (Auslander 2008: 59). That the distinguishing factor between the two states of display lies in their mode rather than their content, Auslander asserts that the labelling of the live was secondary to the labelling of the mediatized, set in opposition tautologically rather than ontologically; a terminological and binaristic separation, rather than a realistic difference (Auslander 2008: 59). Accordingly, the notion of the live as one of co-temporality and co-presence has altered dramatically and expanded to include technological advances such as live streaming, identified as an example of digital liveness (Auslander 2012: 3). As such, the Barbican Centre's unique position when showing *Hamlet* forced a splitting of the live in not only practical but also in theoretical terms, divided between theatre audiences and cinema audiences, demonstrating a traditional, theatrical 'live' as well as 'live' digital display.[4]

The Barbican Centre's splitting of live performance creates further theoretical queries. Considering the binary nature of performance (either 'theatrical' or 'digital') the causal relationship previously identified is problematized in relation to NT Live's *Hamlet*. In a more explicit way than with other NT Live performances, where the live cinema audiences are estranged and distanced from the theatrical bodies onstage, Cumberbatch spewed and spat Shakespeare for over three hours to a live theatre audience, with a live cinema audience watching his cinematic double a few floors below; a co-temporal and co-physical presence, if not for a few staircases, curtains, and a Cumberbatch in the flesh.[5] Whilst there can be no doubt of where the 'original' Cumberbatch performed, the live cinema audiences no doubt sought a live experience to mirror the experience of those in the theatre, perceiving Cumberbatch as 'live' via technology. If we are to consider both theatre and cinema Cumberbatch as 'live', a similar sentiment to Auslander's, as analyzed earlier, provides the only logical conclusion: if liveness was borne from the mediatized, then the understanding of the 'live' Cumberbatch is concluded only because of its technological counterpart. That the technological Cumberbatch is also termed as 'live', any distinction between the two Cumberbatches can be seen as merely terminological; one Cumberbatch is *alive*, playing to a theatre audience, whilst the other is (digitally) *live*, playing to a cinema audience. Regarding both portrayals of *Hamlet*, the cinematic version is logically the replicated version, with Cumberbatch's body and thus 'original' depicting *Hamlet* to the theatre audience upstairs at the Barbican Centre. In this scenario, the digital double is a document of Cumberbatch, thus marking the cinematic version of *Hamlet* as a represented version of the performance. Considering Auslander's notion of digital liveness, however, and given the nature of the cinematic version so aptly termed as NT Live, the cinematic document can be seen as a live performance of *Hamlet* in its own right. Whilst arguably still a document of the version of Cumberbatch's *Hamlet* presented in the theatre, the application of the term paradocumentation aims to resolve this theoretical circling of states. Brought about via technology, as with Auslander's concept of liveness emerging due to the mediatized, paradocumentation accounts for the various attempts to document this performance, as a necessity for live streaming as well as official documentation and unofficial records and interpretations. Whilst the cinematic version of the performance may be seen as a document, in reality played seconds behind the theatre due to streaming delays, its live performative qualities, and significantly its labelling as *live*, mark it as a hybrid working between performance and performance document. The notion of paradocumentation, encompassing various elements of the theatrical and performative, can be discussed with regard to Cumberbatch's depiction of Hamlet in a larger context too.

The deposits of *Hamlet*

During the interview between Benedict Cumberbatch and Melvyn Bragg, aired as part of the pre-production material, the latter questioned Cumberbatch on the deposits left by *Hamlet*. The idea of 'deposits' conjures ideas of a metaphorical archive, filled with detritus from texts, plays and material relating to the 'original' text. Over 400 years after the play was first performed, William Shakespeare's *Hamlet* portrays a young Prince left bereft and bitter after the sudden passing of his father and remarriage of his mother to his uncle. Desperate to prove his uncle guilty of his father's murder, Hamlet is haunted by the ghost of his father. Within the text and played out for audiences since, the remains of the King resonate and act as deposits thus reminders of Hamlet's turmoil. A key scene in depicting Hamlet's angst and his turbulent family relations involves a theatrical technique of staging a play within a play. Reinforcing the Queen's haste in mourning and remarrying, and thereby demonstrating Hamlet's despair at the Queen's decisions, the First Player recites a monologue from Hecuba telling of her sorrow upon losing her own King Priam. Using other texts to emphasize his own, this citation from Shakespeare effectively enables a document to (re)perform through its inclusion in *Hamlet*. Shakespeare's citation is further to this, reused and represented, as many of the 'problem' plays include quotations from Hecuba. Involving a cycling between documents in performances, Shakespeare's *Hamlet* contains deposits of the King of Denmark's death through his ghostly return appearances onstage. The Queen's lack of remorse is depicted in contrast to Queen Hecuba's, as well as further reminders of Shakespeare's own work through the repeated use of Hecuba in his writing. A tapestry of citations, the metaphorical archive contains deposits *of* deposits.

The iconic image of the skull figures significantly in the metaphorical archive. A prop that cites past and future *Hamlet* productions, held by famous leading actors such as Laurence Olivier, Jude Law, Ben Whishaw and Michael Sheen, the skull carries significance not only in terms of performance but also its documentation of each actor's handling of the role, or handling of the skull.[6] Indeed, David Tennant, playing the role for the Royal Shakespeare Company in 2008, worked with the skull of André Tchaíkowsky, who donated his body to science upon his death in 1982, with the exception of his skull, that was donated to the Company for theatrical use. Whilst the skull had been used during rehearsals, other actors had failed to take the skull into performance. Tennant, who used the skull throughout the rehearsal process, continued to act with the skull onstage for twenty-two performances of *Hamlet* (2008).[7] Although the prop was watched without turning a head (it was felt that to reveal to audiences that Tennant was acting with a real skull would alter the focus of the performance creating a false sense of spectacle),[8] the significance of the image cannot be understated. Creating a palimpsestic quality, the prop used whilst awaiting permission for Tchaíkowsky's skull was that used by Edmund Kean in his 1813 production of *Hamlet*. Reportedly, a 'piece of theatre history happened that night on the Stratford stage as David Tennant, a twenty-first century Hamlet, stared into the empty eye sockets that a nineteenth century Hamlet had used. For those of us watching, a little shiver of connection occurred.'[9] Rehearsal detritus such as notes, stage bibles and props cease their primary use after a play has run, transforming into documents of the process of creating a performance. That the skull of Tchaíkowsky emerged from rehearsals to the stage alters its function as well as its state: a skull of a deceased theatre fan is resurrected through its use in live performances. As media displayed Cumberbatch holding the skull from Shakespeare's grave scene throughout the advertising and review process thus joining other star actors in undertaking the role and using the skull,[10] Cumberbatch in turn becomes another deposit of the archive.

The director of NT Live's *Hamlet*, Lyndsey Turner, created an imagistic setting for the Prince's tale, echoing the idea that the text is a moveable performance in and of itself, rather than a document of scripture. As Cumberbatch himself was praised for 'ringing the changes,'[11] so Turner's direction with set and detritus onstage affected the atmosphere, time and theatrical world of the performance. Modern citations used throughout enabled attachment, whilst possibly distancing audiences through their interwoven use: Hamlet, amongst soldier costumes and hoodies, Adidas sports shoes and a David Bowie T-shirt; a gramophone is spun, playing Frank Sinatra, shortly after the audience has been submerged in the dulcet tones of Nat King Cole singing *Nature Boy*. Moving from the 1930s and 1940s to the 1970s and 1980s seamlessly, the text itself is grounded in Shakespeare's verse and prose. In a bold directorial decision, Turner's Ophelia documents the events onstage using a camera. The actress is seen carrying the camera throughout the first half of the production, gathering pictures and moments enthusiastically. Turner's interval, occurring after the death of Ophelia's father onstage, marks the deterioration in Ophelia's mental state. Rushing around busily at the beginning of the second half, Ophelia noisily drags a large trunk down the full flight of stairs to eventually reveal to all its contents: the collection of photographs that she has created, stored and loved. In a moment of reflection before her inevitable suicide, the documents work to create a pause in the play. As if collecting their own deposits onstage, Turner and her cast are cited and reflected in Ophelia's own performance of memories. Turner's decision to impose relatively modern documentary techniques onto Shakespeare's text creates further juxtaposition between performance and documents, interrupting the production of *Hamlet* with the document that depicted Ophelia's demise.

Encores

Along with the Barbican Centre's live stream of the production in three of its own cinemas, running simultaneously with the theatre above, cinemas around the UK and the world streamed Cumberbatch's performance of *Hamlet*. For several months after the live screening, Encore screenings were still being advertised at independent cinema venues in several countries, including Ireland, the Netherlands, Denmark, Germany, the USA, Singapore, Hong Kong, China, Korea and Japan.[12] Such demand for the production echoes the popularity of not only Cumberbatch and *Hamlet*, but also the concept of live streaming, enabling an attachment to the production, despite the distance or temporal disjuncture between the cinema audience and the theatre audience. Following the live-streamed performance, Cumberbatch thanked the audience and reminded the extended audience viewing the performance in cinemas, 'you're all in this theatre with us' (NT Live screening, 15 October 2015). In an attempt to unify the liveness of the theatre and cinema audiences, Cumberbatch's sentiments arguably isolated the Encore viewers. Audiences watching the production as an NT Encore showing, weeks or even months after the live streaming in October, were certainly aware that they were not in the theatre with Cumberbatch and his cast owing to their location and knowledge that the run of the production finished soon after the live-streamed performance. Martin Barker, who surveyed audiences when watching live-streamed performances in 2011 at the early stages of NT Live's development, argues that some sense of liveness is crucial to live-streamed audiences (Barker, 2013: 64). Given the nature of the Encore performances, and the content of *Hamlet*, surrounded by death and decay throughout, this feeling of liveness clearly emanates from another source.

Paradoxically, the feeling of liveness that reinvigorates the ghosts of *Hamlet*, transcending distance and time, occurs through the creation of documents. The text of Shakespeare, adapted anew by director Turner, alters the writing from a document to a working script: a performance in its own right. Melvyn Bragg notes in his interview with Cumberbatch, 'such is his [Cumberbatch's] profile, the actor has drawn new audiences to the play from his legions of fans across the world' (NT Live, *Hamlet*, 15 October 2015). The same text has extended its life into other performances and works of art, inspiring poems and paintings over centuries of interest. The stimuli for various performances, director Katie Mitchell (*Ophelias Zimmer* 2016; *Five Truths* 2012), director and playwright Heiner Müller (*Hamletmachine* 1977), and playwright Tom Stoppard (*Rosencrantz and Guildenstern Are Dead* 1966), are amongst others who have extended the life of *Hamlet* through their performance work. Most notably perhaps, the Wooster Group attempted to reverse the recorded version of John Gielgud's *Hamlet* from 1964. Starring Richard Burton, Gielgud's *Hamlet* was filmed from seventeen cameras angles and edited into a film to be shown at over 1,000 cinemas simultaneously. A precursor for live streaming, the Wooster Group's production dances with the digital Burton – another ghost of Hamlet.[13] In the case of NT Live and their production of *Hamlet*, the performance itself becomes a key 'text', performed 'live' to separate audiences in separate locations. Enabling representations of the same performance through the Encore screenings, the 'text' or document of the performance becomes performance anew; the live reference point for *that* audience, in *that* location, at *that* time. The notion of paradocumentation encompasses this cycling of performance and documents, theoretically enabling documentation to divide its state and thus functionality between a deposit of performance, and a deliverer of performance again.

Pre-, post-, and con-text: framing the survey

A pre-text is typically the foundation of the performance, for example, the play script (including dialogue and stage directions). It is generally recognized that 'drama [pre-text], as fixed and recordable, is the part of theatre most accessible to examination and analysis' (Fortier 2002: 12). However, in the case of a live broadcast event, taking place towards the end of a theatrical run, many other examples of paradocumentation feed into, and form part of, the pre-text to the cinematic event. These include NT Live marketing materials (e.g. teaser text, posters, film-like trailers, social media activity) which form part of the conventional marketing strategies of the theatre industry – and, as can be seen, adopting new strategies typically used more in the film industry. 'Teaser' materials also notably include many examples of paradocumentation surrounding the process of creating the live broadcast, for example, interviews with the play's actors, designers and director, footage from rehearsals as in the case of *Hamlet*, or information about the technical setup of the upcoming cinema events. This type of material is more akin to the 'extras' found on film DVDs than the typical apparatus of theatre marketing, however NT Live is increasingly using such documents of theatrical and technical processes as part of pre-texts advertising live broadcast events.

Much of the official pre-text can also be remixed and adapted by non-official sources, particularly by fan communities (as previously presented in Abbott 2015). Non-official pre-texts for live broadcasts include multimedia mash-ups, original or adapted artwork, and social media discussions around the logistics of the broadcast and access to tickets. Of course, as the live broadcast event is itself a separate event screened at a later date, many other forms of paradocumentation which would normally be considered as part of the post-text of a theatre show (for example, reviews and reactions) actually are incorporated into the pre-text and context for the cinema event. This applies to NT Live official materials but more so to online communities who tend to be particularly active in writing, reading and sharing reviews of the (live) play and their personal experiences.

A live cinema broadcast of a theatre play has a particularly complex 'performance text'. It includes not only the filmed record of the play itself but also all the supplementary materials presented onscreen before the play starts and during the interval. Pre-recorded material can include the mentioned advertising (typically for other NT Live productions or other theatrical shows), interpretative material about the play (e.g. production photographs, textual information about actors or venues, or short documentaries), and more typical cinema content (such as announcements or adverts). Although pre-recorded, this material is experienced live by the cinema audience alongside and as part of the performance text. Additional material broadcast to cinema audiences includes live footage of the theatre audience taking their seats and live announcements or interviews that take place on stage before the play starts or during the interval. Clearly, paradocumentation broadcast as part of an NT Live event functions as a part of the performance text itself, creating a hybrid form that nevertheless goes on to inspire further paradocumentation.

A performance of a play continues to have influence and meaning after its enactment, producing a range of post-texts such as newspaper or online reviews, discussion and analysis both formal (e.g. published articles) and informal (for example on social media). Engagement with and production of post-texts varies widely from community to community: the theatre industry relies upon 'buzz' to engage with its audiences; scholarly articles engage academic communities; and a range of post-texts are both produced and consumed by different fan or enthusiast communities. These can include sharing of personal experiences, creative works inspired by the performance event, and even direct recording of the play. In fact, the frequent act of filming the performance itself led Cumberbatch to appeal directly to his fans requesting that they do not engage in this particular form of document-making (*Evening Standard*, 2015). As already noted, in any repeating performance post-texts from one performance can become pre-texts for subsequent events, creating a complex system of interaction with different forms of paradocumentation at different times.

To discover more about engagement with (and creation of) official and unofficial documents, three cinemas showing NT Live's *Hamlet* were selected for audience surveys: Richmond's Curzon (approximately twelve miles from the Barbican); Warwick Arts Centre (a more distant UK venue); and Spazju Kreattiv at St James Cavalier in Valletta, Malta (international venue). Both Warwick Arts Centre and Spazju Kreattiv live streamed on 15 October 2015, as did Richmond's Curzon, but also independently showed Encore performances, with Warwick Arts Centre replaying *Hamlet* a month later on 15 November, and Spazju Kreattiv replaying on the 15 November as well as a week prior on 7 November.[14]

Engaging with pre-broadcast paradocumentation

Audience engagement with paradocumentation begins at the point they learn about the performance. Across the six performances, NT Live *Hamlet* audiences demonstrated the importance of personal and social contacts, with word of mouth being the most common means of finding out about the live broadcast. The other major factor in learning of the broadcast was publicity from or at the cinema venue (including the cinema's website) – this is perhaps surprising; 27 per cent of audiences indicated this was how they learned about the broadcast, compared to only 11 per cent who learned of it from the National Theatre or the theatrical venue's (the Barbican) marketing efforts. Eleven per cent found out from print media, compared to 19 per cent who found out from other websites (free-text responses indicated that this tended to be from actively searching online or arts event aggregator sites) and relatively low proportions (under 10 per cent) learned of the event from the cinema trailer and/or television and radio. This data highlights the importance of local-level marketing and promotion to spread awareness of NT Live events.

Conversely, once aware of the live broadcast, active engagement with paradocumentation is focused around 'top-down' sources, with 62 per cent of the audience having read a review of the production from an 'official' source such as a national newspaper (or website thereof). Engagement with NT Live's own paradocumentation via their website is somewhat less common with 20 per cent having visited NT Live's website to view the trailer and 11 per cent seeking

Table 11.1 'How did you hear about the performance?'

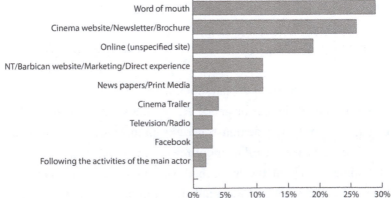

Table 11.2 Engagement with pre-text paradocumentation

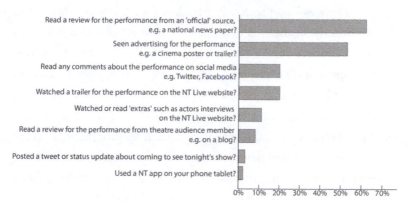

out extra material such as production and rehearsal photographs, interviews with Benedict Cumberbatch, venue information and FAQs (NT Live, 2015). Only 3 per cent had used the National Theatre app (National Theatre, 2015) – which includes information about NT Live in general and fifty seminal productions (i.e. it is not focused only on *Hamlet*). Engagement with non-official sources of paradocumentation was lower: 20 per cent had read comments about the production or its live broadcast on social media, with 4 per cent having contributed their own comment, tweet or status update to the discussion. Eight per cent of survey respondents had read an 'unofficial' review from an audience member who had attended the show in person at the theatre.

Engaging with paradocumentation during the broadcast

Audiences were surveyed on their use of digital technology during the live broadcast of *Hamlet*. The aim of these questions was to ascertain which forms of paradocumentation were actively sought out by audiences – as previously noted, NT Live broadcasts include various material in addition to the play itself, much of which functions as paradocumentation. This material forms part of the core broadcast and is assumed for the purposes of this survey to have been consumed by all audience members, therefore the survey concentrates on voluntarily seeking out additional documents. There are also non-digital examples of paradocumentation such as programmes which may be consulted by audience members during a broadcast, however programmes were not consistently available at all six broadcasts surveyed, therefore the focus here is on digital methods.

Overall, paradocumentation activity during the broadcast is very low. Eight per cent of respondents said they had used a mobile device to search for more information about the performance and 4 per cent had posted a tweet or status about their attendance. Only seven respondents said they had taken a photograph of themselves, their friends or the screen during the broadcast. It is unclear whether the above activities took place while the play itself was being broadcast or during the pre-show or interval content broadcast alongside it.

Table 11.3 Engagement with paradocumentation during performance

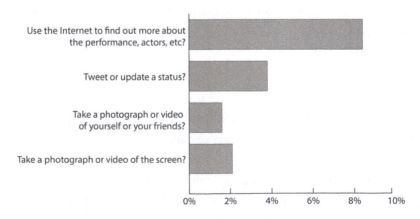

Engaging with post-broadcast documentation

The two most common (intended) post-text paradocumentations are to seek out further information on the internet and/or to keep a physical programme as a souvenir. The first is a logical first step to enhancing knowledge and enjoyment of the performance and is likely to lead to other activities. A physical reminder of the event in the form of a programme was desired by 22 per cent of respondents (and where a programme was not available some respondents commented that they wished it had been). The importance of physical items is also evident in the 14 per cent who said they would consider buying NT Live official merchandize after watching the broadcast. Social media paradocumentations appear to be less desired with 14 per cent of the audience intending to post a short-form status about having attended the event and 5 per cent intending to write a longer review or comment. Less than 5 per cent intended to share photos of the event. Three per cent of the audience stated their intention to become a producer of their own creative works, based on or inspired by the broadcast.

Table 11.4 Engagement with post-text paradocumentation

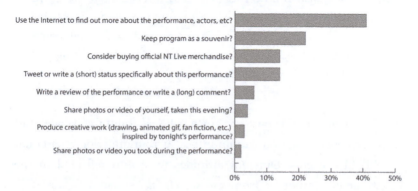

Comparison of audience groups

Previous research indicates that different types of audience member engage with paradocumentation in quite different ways, with widely varying desires for what they want to see documented (and why), and attitudes towards documenting performance in general. For example, the paradocumentation most used and desired by performing arts academics (Abbott and Beer 2006: 30–1) is markedly different from the 'prosumer' role taken on by many fans of particular actors in their engagement with NT Live paradocumentation (Jenkins 2006; Abbott 2015).

These different expectations can create tensions between audience groups and between NT Live themselves as the provider of the live broadcast and the audiences who want to consume this cultural product in more forms than it is currently provided. These issues are highlighted in the fascinating discussions leading on from a movement to gain on-demand access to a previous NT Live production starring Cumberbatch as mentioned, *Frankenstein*, first broadcast in 2011. NT Live addressed the demand directly with a statement via their Tumblr page stating:

> We appreciate there is a huge amount of interest in making the broadcast available on DVD but currently this is not the wish of the artists involved. [. . .] If you are a fan of anyone involved in the creation of *Frankenstein* or the National Theatre, we would ask that you respect their wishes and decision, and hope that you will continue to support National Theatre Live in your local cinema.
>
> National Theatre Live, 2012

The comments on this post reveal a great deal about the debates and disagreements within fan communities surrounding documentation of NT Live events. Different attitudes were also reflected in the questionnaire responses from the six *Hamlet* broadcasts surveyed.

Several respondents wrote unprompted comments on the questionnaire to make their attitudes clear; for example, when asked in neutral terms to indicate if they had taken photographs or video of the screen during the performance, outraged notes added to the margins of the questionnaire included 'No!', 'No but some bitch did', and 'WHAT? SURELY NOT LEGAL?' [original emphasis].

Further insight into the engagement of different groups with paradocumentation can be gained from a comparison of two groups with two distinct reasons for attending the NT Live broadcast. The survey requested a text response to the question: 'What are your primary reasons for coming to this performance today?' Data were categorized according to answers, which specifically mentioned the following reasons.

The two primary reasons are not surprising: to see *Hamlet* and to see Benedict Cumberbatch playing the lead role. However, data indicates that Cumberbatch was actually more of an incentive to attend (34 per cent) than the play itself (29 per cent). The inherent nature and logistics of an NT Live broadcast also provided a significant draw with

Table 11.5 Main reason(s) for attending (categorized from free-text responses)

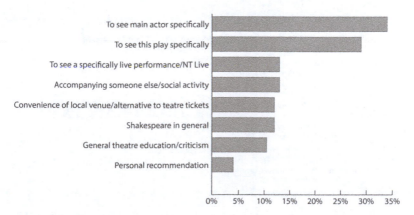

13 per cent of respondents indicating that the liveness of the broadcast was in itself a reason to attend, and 13 per cent also indicating that their local venue was a convenient (or only) way to experience a surrogate for attending the play in person. (This group was largely made up of respondents from the London cinema for which attending the Barbican in person is a more realistic prospect. Responses typically fell into two categories: 'couldn't get theatre tickets' and 'saves me going into town'.) General reasons such as love of Shakespeare or theatre education are also evident, as are social reasons for attending.

Survey responses show that the two most common reasons, whilst not mutually exclusive, identify two distinct groups of audience members with limited overlap (only 11 out of 183 indicated both reasons): fans of *Hamlet* and fans of Cumberbatch. A comparison of these two groups in terms of their engagement with paradocumentation shows that Cumberbatch fans have consistently higher engagement levels in almost every category across pre-, during-, and post-broadcast activities (Tables 11.6–11.8). The difference is significant

Table 11.6 Comparison of engagement of pre-text predocumentation between different enthusiast communities

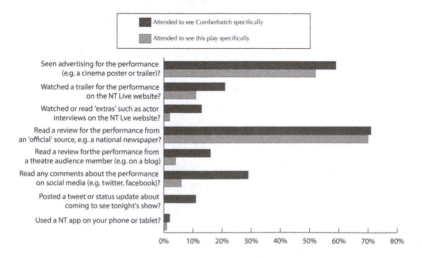

Table 11.7 Comparison of engagement with paradocumentation during the performance between different enthusiast communities

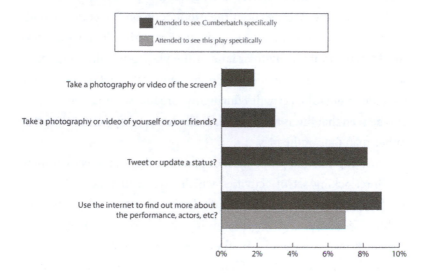

Table 11.8 Comparison of engagement with post-text documentation between different enthusiast communities

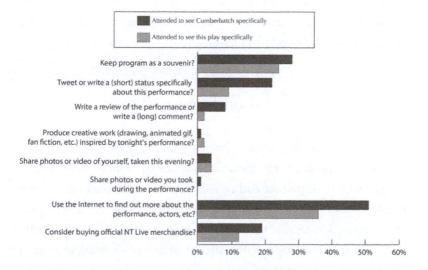

(>10 per cent) in seeking out paradocumentation provided by NT Live via their website before attending the performance and in both reading and writing about the production on social media both before and after attending the broadcast. Cumberbatch fans were also considerably more likely than fans of the play to use the internet to seek out further information after the show. Whilst the figures for paradocumentation activities during the broadcast remain low, it can also be seen that this is almost entirely undertaken by fans of the actor rather than fans of the play.

Consumption and production of paradocumentation is a complex and interlocking set of activities which extend in time well before and after an NT Live broadcast. Audiences engage with a range of technologies and delivery methods for paradocumentation and are far from homogenous in their desire for different forms and methods of documentation of such an event, as well as their attitudes towards what is both acceptable and appropriate. Whilst the cinema audience in general remains primarily a consumer rather than a producer of paradocumentation, this varies between groups and the same complexities apply to the organizations who act as the primary producers of paradocumentation, and indeed the cultural industries surrounding a theatrical production and its live broadcast.

Conclusion

The aim of this chapter has been to consider the possibility of a broader approach to document creation, which theoretically merges with performance and creates in turn performance anew. The practical examples previously discussed such as the rehearsal shots of a production shown before NT Live screenings and eventually represented potentially months after their initial showing at Encore performances, demonstrate the validity of the theory. Assigning the term 'documentation' to material that reasserts itself as a performance, given the determined labelling of the Encore screenings as (still) NT Live, troubles the meaning and essence of documentation. The solution is to divide and analyze its parts (pre, post and con-text) that work together as a whole (para). These terms and this approach more appropriately describes the state of documentation in relation to performance.

As with the changing nature of live streaming and technology, attempting to survey cinema audiences from every venue's screening of *Hamlet* would be an impressive, if not impossible undertaking. Indeed, the Barbican Centre itself declined any opportunity to interview the audiences watching *Hamlet* at their own cinemas and theatre venue (email correspondence, C. Read, 23 September 2015). The survey collected, with a total of 183 responses, represents a proportion of the cinema audiences present at six screenings of *Hamlet*, but is by no means a complete sample. Whilst the survey is a beginning step, it is a valid and useful one in demonstrating the application of a theory that aims to demonstrate the changing nature of performance and processes for documenting it that have evolved from live streaming. The results clearly demonstrate interaction with document creation at all stages of the performance process, even significantly engaging viewers who are distanced by space and time from the initial 'live' event. The idea of the star actor pulling audiences to theatre to see his portrayal of *Hamlet* has arguably advanced the pull of live streaming, with more audience members attending *Hamlet* to watch Cumberbatch than those who attended because of the significance of the play. Whilst denying the gravity of the play would be misguided, the social media relabeling of the performance as 'Cumberhamlet'[15] demonstrates the importance of the actor in attracting audiences to the production. It can be concluded that *Hamlet* is not fading from audiences: it is being represented, relived and redefined, even re-documented, through live streamed performance.

Thinking Virtually in a Distracted Globe: Archiving Shakespeare in Asia

Alvin Eng Hui Lim

Hamlet My father – methinks I see my father–
Horatio Where, my lord?
Hamlet In my mind's eye, Horatio.
Horatio I saw him once; he was a goodly king.
Hamlet He was a man, take him for all in all:
  I shall not look upon his like again.
Horatio My lord, I think I saw him yesternight.
Hamlet Saw? who?
Horatio My lord, the king your father.

Hamlet 1.2.183–9[1]

A theatre archivist who provides online access to a performance recording facilitates a remembrance of a past performance. At the same time, the theatre archive may provide the means to watch a performance anew, albeit a recording, that becomes a sort of haunting of the original production. In this sense, the role of a theatre archivist is similar to Horatio's role in *Hamlet*, who saw King Hamlet when he was alive and when he appeared as a ghost, and must find a way to present that experience to Hamlet. This chapter is about the development of an archive interface for viewers of the Asian Shakespeare Intercultural Archive (A|S|I|A)[2] to 'see' Hamlet again as well as the acts that remain unseen but make possible the persistent hauntings of *Hamlet*.

A|S|I|A Web is a multilingual website with four parallel interfaces in English, Mandarin (中文), Japanese (日本語) and Korean (한국어). It provides streaming videos of full production recordings, presented together with scripts and translations mostly in these four languages. A|S|I|A also functions as a scholarly apparatus with a searchable database developed concurrently in English, Mandarin and Japanese. By the end of 2015, the archive had already accumulated fifty-two productions in sixteen languages, prepared by a team of sixty editors, translators and scholars. As a result, the website's design is contingent on the production, selection, collection and archiving of materials and information.

When Horatio first meets Hamlet, he does not immediately reveal his haunting encounter with King Hamlet's ghost. There is a deliberate pause, perhaps a moment of hesitation as suggested by the semicolon in 'I saw him once; he was a goodly king'. Horatio clearly distinguishes seeing the living King Hamlet and King Hamlet as a ghost, both of whom are given a significant measure of attention and dramatic action in the play when Hamlet himself 'sees' his father again as a ghost. Street Theatre Troupe's *Hamlet* (Korea, 2009), Ryutopia Noh-theatre Shakespeare's *Hamlet* (Japan, 2007) and TheatreWorks and Face to Face's *Search: Hamlet* (Singapore/Denmark, 2002), from A|S|I|A Web provide appropriate context for a discussion of the passage from live performance to digital recordings of the three *Hamlet* productions as documented online. The viewing experience is inevitably altered when *Hamlet* moves from the theatre to the digital medium, but the ghosts of Hamlet are multiplied by the increased availability of those hauntings across media and beyond the live event.

Hamlets' ghosts on the video player

The video player on A|S|I|A Web can also be seen as a new site of *Hamlet*'s 'haunting'. The black and light grey interface is part of a

Figure 12.1 A screen capture from A|S|I|A Web of the ghost scene in Ryutopia Noh-theatre Shakespeare's *Hamlet* (2007)

stylized environment. The A|S|I|A team has built an environment that demands a particular navigational behaviour that may be unfamiliar to first-time users. At the same time, some things are determined by the technology employed in the project, such as the aspect ratio, the streaming speed and a rectangular-shaped screen. The concept of clicks and the icons (play, pause and 'X' = 'to close') all refer to existing online conventions and codes. Nevertheless, it is still an unfamiliar environment that needs a little getting used to. Each video begins with a black display as a precursor to the actual performance, as any internet connection requires a little time to link to the server that hosts the video. Both the video and the text can only emerge after a streaming connection is established. Thus, the processes behind its appearance disappear with the playback.

The video player is a host for and shell of many kinds of ghosts – the performances, the Hamlets, the actors playing as Hamlet the ghost, and the performance texts. To some, creating a video player may be a straightforward answer to their dissemination. However, considered as a whole, the video player becomes the recorded productions' site-specificity. For example, having three *Hamlet* productions in the archive presents a researcher with a chance to compare the three productions. The growth of networks and the sheer number of people they connect to position the internet as another performance site. Networks do not only consist of people, they consist of information, institutions and invisible and automated robots (or bots) that process artificial thoughts and shape behaviour. It is within this universe that the three *Hamlet* productions re-perform collectively. Hence, how we perceive these documented productions of *Hamlet* online differs from how we physically participate in a *Hamlet* production in its original physical location.

Similarly, theatre has always depended on networks – local and global, mediated and translated. Hamlet depended on his messengers to describe their encounter with his father's ghost. Theatre may seem to resist digital recording because it is a form that hinges on the liveness of physical bodies, but there are ghosts and hauntings that an audience may refer to when they watch a live performance. A theatre-goer's memories of certain actors, words or theatre spaces, and reference points of other *Hamlet* productions (be it in terms of film, television or stage) may conjure up 'ghosts' which may affect their viewing experience of a current performance. As Marvin Carlson puts it, 'every play is a memory play' and theatre is 'the repository of cultural memory [...] it is also subject to continual adjustment and modification as the memory is recalled in new circumstances and contexts' (2003: 2).

Similarly, in the new circumstance and context of the World Wide Web, internet users and theatre audiences share some of the same 'haunting' conditions as audiences of a live theatre performance— they consciously or unconsciously add on to or fill in the gaps of details, logic and emotions in a performance with other sources of information, or they reconstruct the scene with their own memories. However, there is no pause button to stop the performance and toggle the screen to do a search online. A user can also be distracted by and immediately respond to a message or notification from a social media networking site. The attention given to the performance is predicated by the context of the performance and its framing.

As users watch the recordings of various productions of *Hamlet* on A|S|I|A, they encounter not only the images of the castle walls and actors, but also the texture of the keyboard, the clicking of the mouse, and the surface of their computer. They also interact with the codes—the playback, pause and close buttons. In a theatre space, members of the audience may encounter and react to other audience members and bodies on stage. They may also be aware of the comfort level of their seat, and whether or not they have a good view of the stage. Thus, mediation plays a crucial part in both the recorded and live performance, and suggests the constant negotiations we make as viewers with memory and our embodied states. Similarly, when Horatio retells his encounter of old Hamlet's facial expressions, he functions as an intermediary, connecting King Hamlet to Hamlet and the audience. Extending this analogy to digital mediation, his role as an intermediary and a storyteller echoes the digital archive, now charged with the responsibility of retelling these past ghosts that are still haunting Hamlet.

Restaging *Hamlet*

Later, when pressed further by Hamlet to describe the ghost, Horatio relates the silent presence of the ghost: 'it lifted up its head and did address / Itself to motion like as it would speak' (Act 1.2.215). Hamlet is not satisfied with his response and probes his guards and Horatio with more detailed questions such as 'saw you not his face?' (line 228). Horatio is then compelled to give a more emotional and intuitive response and he describes the ghost's face as 'a countenance more in sorrow than in anger' (line 230. This sorrowful-looking king is different from the 'goodly' king that Horatio remembers – 'goodly' gives one the positive impression of a lively, warm and smiling king – and the drastic distinction between the king's expressions must be haunting to him and to Hamlet too.

It is important to note that while *Hamlet* begins with the two guards and Horatio meeting the ghost of King Hamlet, it is only later in Scene 4 that Hamlet finally meets him too. Pre-empted and perhaps influenced by the messengers' and Horatio's disturbing accounts, and haunted by his own private fears and thoughts, Hamlet approaches his own father armed with a sword, as if to confront him directly.

Such re-tellings and re-framings of Horatio's encounters with the ghost occur in a different way on the digital archive – the environment has been built with a particular design and conception in mind and would in some way influence and frame one's anticipation of Hamlet's ghosts, just as Horatio's moved from the belatedly familiar 'goodly' king to the hauntingly unfamiliar sorrowful king. Before the user encounters the 'ghost' for himself or herself, the design of the video player or its 'countenance' encourages, supports and approves its re-viewing; but it is perfectly plausible that it discourages, veils and distorts the ghosts too.

A large part of this 'countenance' is made up of a display of translated scripts. On A|S|I|A Web, each recording of a production is accompanied by a production script, which is translated into three or four languages. Each production script is divided into blocks of text that appear in the video gallery. Each choice of language any individual user makes on the site acts as a new framing device and performs a different cultural position. For example, when the A|S|I|A editorial team received Street Theatre Troupe's *Hamlet* script in Korean, it was evident that it was a translation and adaptation of the original text by Shakespeare. To be faithful to the performance text, however, our team's translator decided that it would be more appropriate to translate the Korean performance text into English, rather than return to the original Shakespearean text. Hence, the A|S|I|A website ends up with multiple overlapping layers of translations – from Shakespeare's English to English (by Shakespeare editors and scholars), from English to Korean (by Street Theatre Troupe) and from Korean to English (by our commissioned translator). This gives the viewer new insights and ways of seeing *Hamlet*, but new complications too.

When viewers play the video of Street Theatre Troupe's *Hamlet* and watch the recorded action on stage, they are also able to read the performance text accompanying it, and they are constantly faced with the differences that occur between written text and performance. When they read the English text, it helps them to access the performance as it is an international language. For a bilingual English-Korean user, however, they are constantly aware of the differences, shared lines and cut lines between translations, text and performance.

Yet the English text may also immediately highlight the cultural distance of the viewer from the performance. The haunting ghost of *Hamlet* may then appear foreign to users, who may have limited knowledge of the specific cultural art forms and references used in the Korean performance. Hence, the translation is a double-edged sword. It shows how the performance adapts and redefines the performance of *Hamlet* with its own cultural codes, language and creative choices.

Due to the various navigation points of the site, the way in which one user encounters a video may differ from another. There are thus different possibilities to access the re-stagings of various productions of *Hamlet* – in a different language, from a particular navigational pathway within the website, or even outside the website by doing a Google search on 'Asian Shakespeare' productions. With each re-staging of *Hamlet*, the ghost of Hamlet constantly moves from different mediums, hyperlinks, experiences and modalities that may determine the next entry point, pathway and reception.

The archivist as Horatio

Horatio acts as a friend, an interlocutor and mediator for Hamlet. He is also an audience member, an observer, and an objective eye for Hamlet.

Hamlet
O God, Horatio, what a wounded name,
Things standing thus unknown, shall live behind me!
If thou didst ever hold me in thy heart
Absent thee from felicity awhile,
And in this harsh world draw thy breath in pain,
To tell my story.

Hamlet 5.2.328–33

Horatio prepares the stage and investigates for Hamlet. However, along the way, every manifestation is never fully actualized. Instead, accidents happen and Hamlet reacts accordingly, observing, documenting and commenting with Horatio on the events as they occur.

When a ghost of Hamlet reappears on a video player, a viewer watches the ghost interact with Hamlet. In this example of the Ryutopia Noh-theatre Shakespeare's *Hamlet* (2007) – see Figure 12.2 – Hamlet sits cross-legged on stage throughout the whole performance. In the encounter scene, the ghost appears behind Hamlet (see Figure 12.1). A viewer may be reminded of the performance's theatrical reality, as Hamlet's stationary position emphasizes our passive yet implicated position as a member of the audience or viewer. In spite of his stationary position, the actor who plays Hamlet continues to mediate Shakespeare's *Hamlet* and meets the audience's gaze somewhere in between the performance behind him and in front of the audience. As viewer-users look at the video and most probably replicate the seated Hamlet, the ghosts of Hamlet look back unseeingly at them.

Figure 12.2 A screen capture from A|S|I|A Web of the first ghost scene in Ryutopia Noh-theatre Shakespeare's *Hamlet* (2007)

The video gallery of a recording, which is itself an edited, formatted and highly framed record of a single performance of a production of *Hamlet*, is arrived at from a set of pre-determined pathways. The borders or frames around the ghost (see Figure 12.2) extend to a notepad function, where a user can leave comments or notes which can be read by other users of the archive. From time to time, there are also editor's notes that explain one aspect of the translation or performance. At the same time, there are possibilities of pausing, skipping, losing the internet connection, technological failures or closing the video, moving on to another video, saving a clip and reading a script in another language. These can all be seen as distractions that take the user away from having a continuous experience of the performance but it also places them in a similar position to Hamlet who faces his own distractions and misadventures before we eventually reach the ending.

Despite the distractions, Hamlet is shaped by a certain determinism when he decides to return to Denmark. The script of *Hamlet* and the comments on the notepad function that reappear as web text accompanying the video are supported by an inflexible set of codes and HTML protocols. For every block of text, a user sees a set of time codes attached to the block. For every text-block with its set of time codes, programming codes or mark-up tags are needed to organize the text. Non-speakers of a particular language can copy and add lines from the script to the text blocks because they can learn the common mark-up language (digital codes) such as the '<br/>' HTML tag used for the Japanese translation:

<b>ラジャ・ドゥワ・カヤンガン。</b> おまえたち二人とも座ってくれ。

This process points to a specific form of labour that prepares the scripts for online reading. It is this stage of the archival work that reveals the complexity and labour-intensiveness of intercultural theatre and digital archives and leads to the question: What does it mean to preserve a ghost?

There is always something material about the reproduction of an immaterial presence like ghosts. To produce something on stage that is semi-invisible, immaterial and incorporeal, a theatre-maker has to resort to material means:

<i>(Actor in a white long robe.)</i>
<i>Designer Brief: Western Ghost with Western Armour</i>
<i>A flash of lights OR dim lights; or put a spot on it.</i>
<i> CUE: Smoke / Haze Machine; GO.</i>
p {
font-size: inherit
}
'The ghost has a shadow!'

Aoife Monks (2010) writes, 'Costume is obviously material when clothing the immaterial ghost: its "thereness" interrupts the illusion of the "not-there"' (p. 121). Yet, the costume may also be the material that supports the illusion of the immaterial. For Peter Holland (2006), Hamlet imagines his head as a theatre, a space for a memory-system, while the audience, in response, memorializes his memory in the Globe Theatre in which they sat or stood. The layered pun is of the mind as a theatre and the theatre as a mind; the mind as a theatre of memory and the theatre as a place where the mind investigates how it remembers (221). We remember the costume of the ghost and the ghost together. However, I would like to update Holland's argument a little further by taking Hamlet's response for what it can mean in this age to an almost literal sense: a distracted globe, i.e. the World Wide Web. What happens to Holland's notion of the mind as a theatre, and the theatre as a mind when we add a third memory-system (internet) that memorializes multiple memories – Hamlet's, Hamlet the Ghost's, Japanese and Korean Shakespeares', theirs and yours? In memorializing, does this third memory-system also forget or keep some things out of sight?

The same scene repeated on stage and on the web are each dependent on different sets of logic and language that 'script' the scenes, which on first encounter may be invisible, insignificant or masked behind the surface of things; of objects moving, interacting, appearing and disappearing. Both amount to a different process in support of the main object of the audience's experience; the labour behind the show (whether it is in making the costume, a prop or the make-up to create the ghastly look of the ghost). We regard the page we visit or the theatre we enter, and a whole experience begins to take shape. But we suspend our consciousness of this labour process and we do not ask questions such as (unless you are yourself a technician or a programmer, a technical person): Which script did the programmer use to design the web version of a performance recording? Was it JAVA, Flash, or HTML5? How are the profile lights arranged on the grid? Who is giving the cue to send the next actor on stage?

The entire illusion of the front or the design layout of an online performance is made possible by a language—a tedious and labour-intensive programming language that creates what we watch and experience. In both the theatre and the web, these languages are often concealed. To create a useable, simple, user-friendly website, a great amount of work is needed to script, programme, encode and debug. These things draw attention to themselves without revealing how they are produced.

Where is the virtual scene?

... Remember thee?
Ay, thou poor ghost, whiles memory holds a seat
In this distracted globe. Remember thee?

Hamlet 1.5.95–7

Staging the performance of *Hamlet* on streaming video is another form of mediating the play, from text to performance, and from performance to another performance. It echoes the hallmarks of theatre-making. As Sarah Bay-Cheng argues:

When we re-enact, record and circulate these performances through digital media, we participate in a kind of mediated exchange that takes on all of the hallmarks of theatrical performance, including careful attention to scripts, costumes, and audience response.

Bay-Cheng 2012: 32

The stage is relocated to the virtual. The virtual scene is not an empty display. The virtual is not analogous to the real. It is the real, prolonged and converging somewhere else as an image, from the flat display of the screen (even that is now being redefined with new curved displays) to the user. It is a manifestation of something perhaps intangible and immaterial that is now temporarily simulated or extended by computer software. For that, it has its own reality. The archivist builds this reality by meticulously creating an environment for the viewers to respond to recordings, scripts and the archive's database.

The site-specificity of A|S|I|A foregrounds the reception, where specific performances are archived on the website and where they simultaneously haunt their own reproductions. On the one hand, past productions and productions that are still running are reproduced as a record or document. On the other hand, the website produces the haunting site by which they can make their persistent appearance. Hence, it is only apt to consider where and when this renewed ghosting occurs and not become too caught up in the polarity between liveness and recording. The audiences' viewing of any video is influenced through sensorial prompting, i.e. the relationship between the text and the video in relation to one's present experience. These constitute its staging site (with its specific formal properties) that is accessible from different time zones. However, much still needs to be done to discover disparate user behaviour and reception of this particular virtual experience. For that purpose, this particular archive intends to further develop its notepad function and create an improved environment for user interaction.

Much retelling of the Hamlet tragedy must be told by Horatio, who sees it all and in retrospect is charged with the responsibility of retelling the story to a future audience that perhaps he cannot fully envisage. The ghosts of *Hamlet* continue to haunt the text, not only in terms of the plot but also in each new performance and new translation, and with each new actor who embodies the character Horatio. Digital technology then allows the hauntings to persist in places, time zones and languages in ways we are only beginning to comprehend.

From Copper-plate Inscriptions to Interactive Websites: Documenting Javanese *Wayang* Theatre

Miguel Escobar Varela

In Java, *wayang* refers to a series of theatrical practices. These include, amongst others, *wayang kulit* (shadow puppets), *wayang orang* (a dance drama inspired in the puppet show), *wayang beber* (a narrative performance that uses painted puppets in a scroll) and *wayang golek* (three-dimensional rod puppets). One of the most recent projects that aims to document *wayang* is the Contemporary Wayang Archive (CWA).[1] This archive is the first comprehensive digital video archive of *wayang*. However, the history of documenting *wayang* goes back over 1,000 years. The history of the documentation efforts is as long as the form. An overview of the history of *wayang* documentation offers insight into the complex connections between technology, economic means and epistemological bias. This history will be used here to place the CWA in a historical perspective and to offer a reflection on the ways archiving, theatrical events and technologies of recording are intermingled.

This is not a comprehensive history of the documentation of *wayang kulit*, but a selected overview of how different media constrain and allow certain kinds of documentation. For this overview, the following documents are considered: copper-plate inscriptions from the tenth century, collections of puppet writings and photographs from the nineteenth century, and audio and video records from the twentieth and twenty-first centuries.

Copper-plate inscriptions

The first document indicating the existence of *wayang* is a copper-plate inscription from 907 C.E., which is known as the Balitung or Mantyasih inscription. This inscription was issued by King Balitung, who reigned the kingdom of Mataram (Java and Bali) from 899 to 911. The inscription mentions the word 'mewayang', which means playing *wayang*: 'si Galigi performed wayang for the gods, reciting the Bimmaya Kumara'.

According to Claire Holt, the story *Bimmaya Kumara* is most likely related to Bima, one of the main characters in the Sanskrit *Mahabharata*, which is the main story used for *wayang* performances until the present day.[2] The information on the inscription is sparse. It does not offer much in terms the performance's description, but it does offer two interesting facts: the performance had a religious significance and it was related to the *Mahabharata*. For all its lack of information, the inscription has the advantage that – unlike many records made of other materials – it has been accurately dated. Therefore, this record exhibits what Matthew Kirschenbaum understands as 'forensic materiality', which 'rests upon the principle of individualization . . . the idea that no two things in the physical world are ever exactly alike'.[3] In other words, the specific plate is not identical to any other, and reliable methods can be used to identify the inscription and trace it back to the year 907 C.E. This capacity for easy identification contrasts with what Kirschenbaum terms 'formal materiality' of digital media where there is 'transmission without loss [and] repetition without originality'.[4]

The notion of formal materiality will be important for the last part of this chapter, when we encounter digital archives. But for the time being, let us return to the Balitung inscription. The forensic materiality of the inscription makes it the first record that can be historically placed. This sparse but reliable information has led to many conjectures about the history of *wayang* in Indonesia, which are accepted as the most plausible theories on the origin of *wayang*. For example, according to Holt, this inscription shows that *wayang* was already common enough in the tenth century to be mentioned in the inscription.

This is the first example of a trope presented throughout this chapter: the connection between power and the making of documents. Inscriptions in plates and stones are precious documents for archaeologists and historians attempting to reconstruct the history of Java. However, they are well aware that these documents represent a highly selective, privileged perspective. Commissioning these inscriptions was the prerogative of the royalty. It required access to techniques and expertise of inscription and, as will be the case in many of the examples presented here, these documents are made from the vantage point of people with direct political and economic power or at least with sufficient access to the means for making such documents.

Puppet collections

It is likely that puppets already existed in 907 and Galigi, the person mentioned in the Balitung inscription, was probably a *dalang* (puppeteer). However, no information about the shapes of those puppets subsist. The first dated collection of puppets was acquired by the British colonial officer Stamford Raffles in the early nineteenth century. Raffles was then working for the British East India Company and was the interim governor of Java from 1811 to 1815. As a result of his stay in Java, Raffles published a book on the customs and geography of the island entitled *The History of Java* (1817). There, he mentions *wayang kulit* and related forms but he gives no detailed descriptions of the performances he saw. He briefly outlines the spatial setup of *wayang kulit* referring to the screen as a 'curtain' and briefly describes the function of the *dalang*, attesting that 'without this personage nothing can be done'.[5] Then as now, the *dalang* single-handedly manipulated all the puppets and spoke all character parts in a show that often lasted all night. Raffles specifically mentions a *wayang* performance offered for a ritual exorcism, giving precise details of its duration: 'from seven o'clock in the evening till eight o'clock in the morning'.[6] Raffles also notes that a group of *wayang topeng* (masked *wayang*) dancers received ten rupees ('twenty-five schillings') and a supper as payment for a performance.[7] Of the many illustrations made by Raffles to accompany the book, one shows *wayang* puppets but unfortunately it does not show how they were used in performance.

As well as publishing the book, Raffles was the first foreigner to systematically collect puppets and he spent a substantial amount of his personal fortune in several collections, which included 283 Javanese *wayang* puppets and eighty-three accessories. He did not include any information of where he collected the puppets from but it is probable that they come from both Javanese royal courts: Yogyakarta and Surakarta. Raffles had more interest in the Javanese objects than in the perspective of the Javanese people he encountered. There are no mentions of conversations, but he dedicated substantial efforts to collecting literary texts, animals and plant specimens, as well as ceremonial objects. Modern documentation of *wayang* begins with Raffles; his puppets are some of the oldest, well-preserved puppets in the world, and are currently managed by the British Museum. The collection has allowed scholars to effectively identify trends and differences between the puppets as they were built then and as they are built today, demonstrating that the iconography of the puppets has remained similar.

Raffles remains a controversial figure to this day. He was able to get hold of this collection based on his political power and economic means. He participated in brutal colonial activities that led to deaths and devastation. However, he also had a genuine interest in the cultural artefacts of Java. Regardless of his controversial part in the country's history, his puppets today are of key importance to students of *wayang*. The puppets he collected and words he wrote constitute a different kind of document from the previous example of the copper-plates, but both are instances of deliberate attempts to preserve something for the future. Raffles' puppets also show forensic materiality and they are very important in sustaining the claim that the iconography of the puppets we see today was already common in the early nineteenth century.

Anthropological documents

Raffles' writings on Java were dismissed by later nineteenth century commentators as amateurish. However, according to Nancy Florida, *The History of Java* was the spark that began interest in the scientific study of Java.[8] This interest led to a surge of anthropological writings in the mid to late nineteenth century. These written documents offer insights into the mechanisms of the performance for the first time. This is particularly important for today's scholars since the spatial setup of *wayang kulit* strikes many observers as unusual. *Wayang kulit* has often been described as a form of shadow theatre, since part of the stage apparatus of *wayang* is a screen where the shadows from the two-dimensional leather puppets are cast. It is possible to watch a show from the side of the shadows, but most Javanese people prefer to watch the side of the *dalang*. When people not familiar with the form first encounter *wayang* they often incorrectly assume that watching the side of the *dalang* is a new development. However, from the anthropological writings of the nineteenth century, we know that this spatial setup was already common – and already puzzling – at that time.

The first description of the *wayang* audience comes from Carel Poensen (1872).[9] According to W.H. Rassers, Poensen was surprised that the women saw the shadows while the men watched the puppets. According to Poensen's informants, this situation was already old at the time and explained as an old *adat* (custom). G.R. Rouffer suggested that the distribution of the audience was a 'corruption' of the original situation where all spectators watched the side of the shadows.[10] Rouffer even hypothesized that this meant that the *wayang* was originally a performance offered for the benefit of women. However, Rassers finds Rouffer at fault and argues that this 'original' situation never existed. Rassers suggests that it is possible to conclude, based on the commentary of *wayang* spectators of the late nineteenth century, that some spectators had always watched the puppets rather than the shadows and that, in fact, this was the privileged place from which to watch a performance.[11] According to Rassers, a long tradition of watching the *wayang* from the side of the puppets helps explain some puzzling facts, such as the intricacy of the carving and colouring with which the puppets are decorated.

Postcolonial critiques easily identify a connection between colonial administration and colonial-era scholarship. However, as Bremen and Shimizu note, anthropology is complex and the fact that it thrived in the colonial period does not mean it is inherently colonial.[12] Take, for example, the work of Rassers or of G.A.J. Hazeau, the now practically forgotten *wayang* researchers. Their research was careful, methodical and profoundly respectful of the tradition they were investigating. Dutch *wayang* scholarship has come under much criticism in the past two decades.[13] Part of this criticism is grounded on the accusation that Dutch scholars invented a particular version of *wayang* to suit their needs, and that they did so by overemphasizing the linguistic realm. But a closer look at the work of people like Hazeau and Rassers demonstrates this was not always the case. Despite their training in philology, they prove themselves thoughtful, sensitive observers of non-linguistic aspects of *wayang*.

This is not meant as an apology for colonial-era anthropologists and their documentation work. Like all the makers of records mentioned in this chapter, the Dutch anthropologists were able to carry out their work because of their connections to powerful institutions, which guaranteed access to means and resources. But a nuanced analysis of the relationship between anthropological documentation and the colonial past should dismantle reductionist readings of their documentation efforts as necessarily instrumentalist, simplistic or otherwise contaminated by distinctly colonial endeavours.

The'otherizing' gaze of foreign anthropologists is also problematized by the fact that one of the most famous anthropological photographers of the late nineteenth century was a Javanese man, Kassian Cephas, who became the court photographer of Yogyakarta around 1871.[14] Cephas was a man who moved in between different worlds. As well as working as court photographer he also owned a small commercial photography studio and he was involved in different documentation projects for a scientific society dedicated to the study of archaeology and ethnography. One of the founders of this group was the Dutch physician Isaac Groneman, who collaborated with Cephas on several occasions.

One of the projects on which they collaborated is particularly relevant here: the documentation of *wayang orang* in 1899. As mentioned earlier, *wayang orang* is a type of *wayang* where the characters are played by people rather than puppets. The book was written by Groneman and it included nine process prints by Cephas. It was expensively decorated with jewels and gold; in 1901 it was presented as a wedding gift to Queen Wilhelmina (Knaap 1999: 20). In 1902, Cephas made photographs of *wayang beber,* a version of wayang where the *dalang* uses images in a painted scroll to tell the story. These photographs were meant to accompany the study by the Dutch anthropologist and language teacher G.A.J. Hazeau. However, when the article appeared in print there were no illustrations.[15]

Besides this, Cehpas made several prints of *wayang kulit* in the late
1890s. These photographs confirm the spatial setup mentioned earlier,
where the side of the *dalang* is the most important vantage point for
the spectators.

Like all the makers of documents considered in this overview,
Cephas benefited from the patronage of those in power. He would have
never been able to produce the exquisite photographs he made at the
end of the nineteenth century were it not for his links to the royal court
of Yogyakarta and to the Dutch living in Java at the time. This should
avoid any simplistic reading of Cephas and his work. An attentive artist
can be seen in his work, who captures nuanced expressions of the
wayang performers in ways that were not possible before. A photograph
of particular note is one where Hazeau is seen to be attentively listening
to a *wayang beber* performance in the village of Gelaran (Fig. 13.1).
Hazeau is dressed in batik and sitting amongst the spectators. He is
holding a notebook and looking slightly downwards. But his attitude is
that of contemplative respect. The photograph does not appear to be
staged for the camera. Several people, including children, appear to be
enthralled by the *dalang's* performance. Most people seem unaware of
the photographer, except for two children, sitting on the *dalang's* left,
who look directly into the camera.

As Karel Vanhaesebrouck notes, the connection between
photography and theatre history is complex: 'the photograph is more
than just a *residue* of an event from the past: it allows the historian to
analyse the relationship between spectator and event, between subject
and object'.[16] This connection between spectator and event, and
between the photographer and his subject is masterfully captured by
Cephas. As such, his photographs are not just documents of past
wayang performances. They also document the complex relationships
between artists, foreign and local anthropologists, and technology at
the turn of the twentieth century.

Figure 13.1 *Wayang beber* performance in the village of Gelaran, c. 1902. G.A.J Hazeau is sitting on the right. © University of Leiden, Image Code 3953.

Audiovisual recordings

Although translations and studies of the *wayang* language had been published before, the first comprehensive transcription and analysis of a performance was done by Clara van Groenendael. In 1976, she used tape recorders to record three performances, which were transcribed by six assistants.[17] Groenendael candidly describes her considerations for the selection of which performances to record by explaining that the most important thing was 'the quality of voice and articulation of the *dalang*' that would enable accurate recording and transcription.[18] She also recounts three incidents where the *dalang* objected to the usage of the recording. In one case, a performance was going to take place in a remote village not accustomed to strangers and the *dalang* feared that 'a foreigner loaded with an assortment of mysterious equipment might have a disturbing effect on this closed community'.[19] In another case, the *dalang* was not happy with the performance and was afraid that his creative merit would be judged poorly by the researcher. In the last instance, the *dalang* was afraid of the political ramifications of the recording, since he had got into difficulties with the local authorities.

The candour with which Groenendael recounts the logic for her considerations and the objections presented by the *dalang* demonstrates the complexities of archiving. A performance document is not an objective representation, but the tense confrontation of multiple ways to imagine a performance. Groenendael's documents negotiate what the artists imagine their work to be with the demands that Groenendael anticipates from academic research communities. The transcriptions offered as part of her book are exquisitely detailed. She includes descriptions, transcripts and diagrams showing the places of the puppets, the musicians and even her own position on the stage. This work is of enormous importance today. However, as Groenendal also readily admits, she was able to carry it out based on the fact that, as a Dutch scholar, she had access to the recording technology, time and economic support required for this ambitious project.

Although video recordings of *wayang kulit* have been produced at least since the 1970s, the first academic video documentation was led by Kathryn Emerson, who recorded, translated and carefully annotated six performances by *dalang* Purbo Asmoro. These performances consist of two stories, each presented in three dramatic styles. As such, it constitutes a detailed exploration of the different ways a *wayang* show can be crafted. A project like this could not have been undertaken without the serendipitous combination of talent, vision and sponsorship. Purbo Asmoro has been instrumental to the development of the *garapan* (contemporary-interpretive) style and he is also extremely flexible as a performer. Few if any contemporary *dalang* could present the same stories in three different ways exhibiting the range of artistic interpretations that Purbo Asmoro denotes in his shows. Kathryn Emerson is one of the few people who can translate poetic and archaic Javanese into English. But it is not just the unique combination of talent from *dalang* and translator that made this project possible. As Emerson notes in the introduction, such an ambitious project would be impossible without the funding of several private and public bodies.[20]

This brief historical overview must also refer to the Contemporary Wayang Archive, which consists of twenty-four video recordings, a detailed database of performance information, as well as full translation with notes. Several translation editors remain busy reading and verifying these translations. Unlike many other projects, this archive exists only in digital form. It exhibits what Kirschenbaum referred to as formal materiality, a situation where the records can be easily copied and distributed but they cannot be easily dated. However, the fact that the archive exists solely in digital form opens up the door for other kinds of analysis. At the time that this chapter was written (early 2016) engineers are developing software for the automatic process and analysis of the language, the movement and the stories in the video collection. As Diana Taylor notes, 'different technologies spur different practices (and vice versa) and different things to collect, study, and theorize'.[21] The affordances of new technology for the analysis of performance will continue to change the practice and ideals of documentation, for *wayang* as well as for other performance forms.

In all of the projects analyzed here, documentation takes place at the confluence of epistemological biases, technology and access to economic means. With the benefit of hindsight, many of these projects appear limited, or constrained by the conditions of their own historical moments. Researchers can certainly appreciate the fact that these documenters used their cameras and their chisels, their words and their questions, to document *wayang* for posterity. This is also what the Contemporary Wayang Archive is doing in our time. Hopefully, the digital immateriality of the Contemporary Wayang Archive will endure the test of time, and one day its contents will receive the scrutiny and skeptical admiration now afforded to its predecessors.

Archiving Western Australian New Music Performance

Cat Hope, Adam Trainer and Lelia Green

Art music[1] has become more complex over the course of the last century. The advent of sound recording means the iteration of a work is now more complicated than a score on paper, and the advent of computing means that the work may no longer exist solely on paper, or even on paper at any stage, but rather exists in a number of other forms. How do we navigate the process of remembering and archiving music, and the documents associated with it, particularly when the work may be more closely tied to process and performance than to a score? In addition to existing as a set of rules and expectations, performance as a process is also a means of storing and transmitting knowledge (Taylor 2003). As Reason (2006), Auslander (2008) and Blank (2012) identify, when musical works are transferred into the digital realm, there is a significant need to document them in a way that ensures they remain connected to those elements (cultural, historical and performative) that allow us to make meaning from them.

The Western Australian New Music Archive (WANMA) is a project that aims to distribute experience of new musical activity in Western Australia (WA) from 1970 to the present within the international community (Green et al. 2014).[2] The project has seen the creation of an online digital access point, or portal, to new music composed by Western Australians since 1970. The web portal points to material held by the State Library of Western Australia and the Australian national broadcaster ABC Classic FM.[3] The archive project aims to build the collections of Western Australian new music held by these institutions as a direct result of the access and awareness the portal brings, beyond the materials that are there at any one time. It does this through creating visibility for documents and recordings – making what exists or is known to be missing available to others, but also creating awareness within a specific community around the value of these documents, which focus on music makers and music making in Western Australian during this period.

This archive has prioritized access to the documentation of live performances, including video and audio, but also ephemera relating to specific performances, to reflect the wide range of musical styles featured, including electronic music, sound art, improvisation and more. The collection includes posters, flyers, reviews, programme notes and related photographs. In some cases, these ephemera are the only documents that exist for a work; in other cases, materials provide additional context for more traditional representations of music works, such as scores or published recordings.

The WANMA web portal is housed on external servers that point to works in the State Library of WA collection, where they have been catalogued. Video and audio documents are mirrored on the WANMA servers to enable fast delivery internationally. The portal itself has unique bibliographic content that has been developed especially for it, as well as a system of tagging and linking artists with works, performances and other materials. It includes information about organizations, individuals, groups, venues, concerts and concert series. WANMA began with the gifting to the library of one particular collection, the Tura archive, which was digitized in a pilot project, and formed the basis for the portal. The Tura materials also influenced the way the portal was designed. The collection includes approximately 1,700 digital video and audio recordings, as well as several hundred digital images, including photographs and promotional items such as event posters and flyers.[4] The portal is structured in a way that prioritizes this material and attempts to direct users to it.

An important characteristic of the WANMA web portal is the way in which it creates relationships between different kinds of content in the archive. The archive material itself – the actual documentation of the performance of new music practice in Western Australia – forms the core of the portal content. Holden suggests that 'The work-instance model, in which an abstract intellectual work is instantiated in multiple material "editions, translations, or representations," is the foundation for the past forty-five years of cataloging [sic] theory' (Holden 2015: 873–4). Indeed, the WANMA web portal delivers a range of content, including multiple versions of a work, as well as other supporting information that relates back to a singular work, thus providing a range of contexts for the performance, presentation and genesis of these works. When music is considered in terms of these different points of experience, it contains a range of pointers to other materials – people, places, ensembles, organizations, events, programmes, posters, flyers and critical reviews. Linking this data together builds a holistic impression of the existence and evolution of the music scene in Western Australia over that time. As Alexander points out:

> the active process of archiving performance, meaning the denotation and connotations of cultural experience and the realization [of] that performance; the artistic expression of thought, feeling, and experience – can be archived; not just for its tropes and figures or captured in cellulose or on papyrus, but the ways in which performance is culture, expression, and artefact and how performance has a historicity of experience – that can be mined and cataloged [sic] for knowledge.
>
> Alexander 2012: 271

So where new music-things happened, with whom, how and to what ends, are all important facets of WANMA, documenting the supply and connection of different individual components that together create a narrative linked to a place and time.

The WANMA web portal provides a framework by which visitors can explore the relationships between the collection materials and the descriptive information to which they relate, informing and complementing the documents that exist in the collection itself. The use of various data sets (performers, ensembles, organizations, locations and events) as organizing components of portal content to link between the various collection materials, illuminates complex relationships and provides additional context for particular performances. These connections help communicate the various nuances and details of the Western Australian new music scene as a community of practice (Lave and Wenger 1991) composed of individuals whose relationships to particular performances may be multi-faceted.

The documents used as a starting point for the archive were a combination of different versions of works and associated ephemera. For example, an audio recording of a work could take the form of one, or a combination of: studio recordings, live recordings, video recording (sometimes multiple renditions) of a performance, homemade recordings, published recordings or radio broadcasts. In some cases, there was no audio recording but a score. An archived work would then be augmented by photographs of the performance, promotional photographs of performers, posters, flyers, programmes, reviews and even introductory speeches. All these elements are linked in the portal using tagging and complex linking infrastructures. For example, Lindsay Vickery's *Rendez-vous: An Opera Noir* (2001) is documented within the original Tura archive materials in the form of a digitized VHS recording of the full performance and photographs of the rehearsals featuring Vickery alongside members of the ensemble and actors from the performance. In addition, physical copies of the event poster were acquired by the library from a private collector to be digitized and added to the archive, with the original studio recording of the work already physically housed in the library's music collection. In this instance, the linking architecture makes explicit the relationships between the digital documents of the work in the archive,and the library catalogue entry for the physical sound recording. All the individuals involved in the work are linked to one another on their own individual profile pages on the portal, so that visitors are able to move across profiles and access relevant information about them.

Commissioned and recorded performances by international and interstate artists were included in the archival materials gifted to the library at the start of the project, as they were often programmed alongside relevant Western Australian work. The curatorial team were able to quickly ascertain which material was Western Australian through their familiarity with the scene and the participants engaged in it. Promotional materials from visiting artists were removed. Local artists involved in visiting artists' performances and concert programmes complicated the decision-making process, and it was decided that visiting artists featuring local collaborators would be included in the archive. For example, in 2004 UK-based composer Gavin Bryars visited Western Australia as composer in residence at the Perth International Arts Festival. Performances of Bryars' works included Western Australian new music composer and performer Roger Smalley as conductor, and were performed by the Western Australian Symphony Orchestra, so these were included in the archive. A slightly different example of a curatorial decision concerns the works created by Sydney-based violinist Jon Rose, who has composed a number of pieces in Western Australia, using the Western Australian landscape as a key element in the composition and performance process. These are also included.

This inclusive definition of participation, and of Western Australian, has made the permissions process somewhat complex and detailed. A broad range of recording quality has been included – from professionally-produced recordings and documentary footage, to rough lo-fi recordings or demos and blurry hand-held video footage. As mentioned previously, different performances of the same work have been included where possible, for example Melanie Robinson's composition *Hey Mister* (2006) is featured in four different versions, performed in different locations as part of new music ensemble Wood's tour of the remote Western Australian Kimberley region. This allows an understanding of the social and cultural 'biography' (Kopytoff 1986: 67) of a piece. As Morgan suggests, 'reviving a performance that was essentially within a microcosm of historical time at its first performance will have difficulty in surviving unless adjustments are made within the ongoing present' (2010: 2). WANMA attempts to chart this ongoing present, suggesting it as an integral aspect of the performance material collected in the archive, and demonstrating that differentiations that characterize alternative performances are worthy of investigation and recognition. In other cases, different 'iterations' of the same work are featured, with both live and studio versions of that work included. The richness of material collected enables the archive to be a hyperreal extension of performance (Kuhn 2011).

Engagement and participation are key elements in building the archive as an active resource. As noted by Holden, 'There should be increased interdisciplinary interaction between librarians and members of musical communities in order to further understand how the work is defined outside the world of information science' (Holden 2015: 891). This 'community view' must be communicated to the library in some way. A soft launch of WANMA's beta portal within a State Library of Western Australia context invited comment from the new music community featured, or wanting to be featured, in the archive. It also served to identify important collections that could be included, enriching the project's development and engaging musicians and associated participants. The portal is designed so that artists may edit and update their bibliographic information and add work titles, encouraging the community to interact with the collection. Performers may also include descriptive information about new works, or submit material for consideration in terms of a contribution to the archive itself. Numerous contributions were forthcoming when the community saw that such a wide range of documents were appropriate for inclusion in the archive.

Not all documents in WANMA are deposited via the website by copyright holders, however, and many of the documents in the original pilot collection were commissioned and paid for by Tura. At the time of creation, they were made merely with a view towards documenting events, with no view towards including them in a library collection. With some large ensemble performances, for example, permission to document the work had only been sought from the composer. Negotiating with rights holders is complex, and whilst the library has procedures in place, approaching individuals to include their creative works in a freely available digital archive was unprecedented. The team devised a unique permissions agreement that was forwarded to all rights holders in the collection, including composers and performers as well as curators and even recording engineers in works recorded after 2005 (ArtsLaw n.d). Most of these rights holders were easy to contact, via Tura, and were generally prepared to grant permission for the incorporation of their work into the archive. Sometimes it was not possible to communicate with the relevant parties. At first, these permissions and licensing processes were seen as a necessary part of the curation process. However, after reasonable attempts to gain permission had been made, the curators decided to include the materials pending further information.

Perth, the main city in Western Australia, has a population of approximately two million (ABS, 2015) and the new music scene is relatively small. By the end of 2015, all of the original 1,700 audio and video items were included in the archive, with permissions being sought from more than two hundred and fifty individuals. Licensing agreements were generated for each individual to include both their contributions to the Tura material, and material already in the library collections, gleaned from an audit of the catalogue. Although the digitization of the physical materials already contained in the library collection was beyond the scope of the project at the time, this material was included so that rights holders would be made aware of what materials of theirs were already held within the library catalogue so that they might contribute missing materials to WANMA. It is planned that existing hard copy library catalogue items will eventually be digitized to maximize the benefit of the connections provided in WANMA, however, and this permissions process ensures that no further rights permissions will need to be sought when digitization occurs.

Another challenge of a resource such as WANMA that includes ephemeral material was the lack of available metadata for items that had not previously been catalogued or identified, and which existed – in contrast to published items – as undocumented artefacts. The library's Liaison, Acquisition and Description team were required to identify individuals who featured as performers in video recordings, as well as identifying the title of particular compositions that were being performed in these recordings. In the process of cataloguing (and sometimes digitizing) these recordings, screen shots were taken of unidentified individuals in the videos, that were then forwarded to the curators (and sometimes further afield) for identification. This way, ancillary performers could be identified in catalogue works where initially only the composer or soloist had been named.

Some items were prefaced by introductions, naming the participants. However, access to these introductions was complicated by the fact that many had been edited out in the digitization process as separate, stand-alone video recordings and unique performance documents in their own right. By separating out introduction from performance, the introductions, many of which were made by Tos Mahoney, were contextualized in the portal as separate entities that provided information that framed and informed the performance footage itself, such as the tone of the event. This lent a particular archival aesthetic to the collection, with cross-links such as keywords and tags required to reconnect performances to their introductions, framing both works in their own right.

An early issue with the library catalogue was the awkward nature of the delivery of online materials, which highlighted the difference between the required functionality of the WANMA web portal and the systems in place within the library's digital catalogue. Any multipage document was presented as an interactive on-screen document, complete with audible turning pages. This was hardly suitable for music scores. Audio files could only be downloaded, not streamed for listening in real time, and were represented by an outdated image of a CD or television, due to the nature of the particular Application Programming Interface (API) used by the library. To overcome these limitations, the WANMA portal maintains its own server to provide a mirror to the items in the library catalogue which are also included in the archive. This commercially-supplied data server system includes international nodes meaning that downloads can occur quickly and easily, no matter from which part of the world the materials are being accessed. Without this, a user in Norway would have to connect to the server in Australia to download materials, causing delays. The commercially-supplied server system was also preferred over popular services such as video providers YouTube and Vimeo, or audio services such as SoundCloud and Bandcamp. Each of these extant services has limitations – from the inclusion of advertising, to restrictive copyright agreements, stability issues, logo inclusion, creeping costs and designed and branded delivery windows. Maintaining a commercial, non-branded server system keeps the delivery of materials simple and controllable. The potential compromise is sustainable longevity, and whilst this has been acknowledged, no formal commitment has been made.

Holden discusses the fact that despite academic enquiry having a traditional bias towards the Western classical music tradition, the field has broadened of late 'to recognize folk, rock, jazz, hip-hop, and electronica as valid genres of academic study' (2015: 874). He goes on to suggest that these styles all have their own functional requirements that 'represent bibliographic relationships that should be taken into account in the modern information environment' (Holden 2015: 874). Music, and new music specifically, is no exception, and WANMA does and will include items that do not as yet have a means of traditional archival identification, such as Library of Congress MARC standards, which provide metadata for catalogued library items. This issue also reflects the International Federation of Library Associations and Institutions' recommendations for restructuring catalogue databases to reflect more accurately the conceptual structure of specific information resources as opposed to more traditional cataloguing practices, known as Functional Requirements of Bibliographic Records (IFLA 1998). As pointed out by Miller and Le Boeuf (2005), these requirements are where the differences between a work and a recording of that work come into play.

New music practice often incorporates new technologies, including compositional tools that are based around proprietary and sometimes interactive software, as well as specific hardware for physical playback. Whilst the Tura collection contains relatively few examples of this media, accurately representing compositions that rely on file formats that may no longer be supported by contemporary digital tools throws up a significant problem in terms of documenting new music. The aim of the archive is to present scores in a format that means they can be performed into the future which, as Sterne (2009: 56) points out, presents an inherent paradox for traditional archival and preservation practices. Currently, the library is unable to hold software in its collection, and many paper scores that include electronics feature instructions on contacting the composer for access to software materials, with some composers having already died. From a different perspective, the inclusion of multiple live performances may assist in the re-creation of electronic parts if the software is not accessible or available. Performance documents such as video provide more information about a music scene; they can teach us about how scores are iterated; how they actually sound and what performers do that turns scores into live pieces of music. Auslander argues that 'It is assumed that the documentation of the performance event provides both a record of it through which it can be reconstructed [...] and evidence that it actually occurred' (Auslander 2006: 1). This is emphasized in the case of music with interactive electronics, where the role of documentation is vital, and is an important area for future research.

Performance documents are as yet to be truly understood for what they are capable of offering our archives and collections. 'It is perhaps easier to imagine that we can observe and critique an explicitly "staged" authenticity in moments of performance; that they might hold themselves up rather more openly for scrutiny than other frames for the consumption of "heritage"' (Kidd 2011: 24). Performance documents may assist us in recreating works that currently cannot be preserved fully. They do this by providing a rich combination of elements – pointing to a community of practitioners, audience, documenters, presenters, publications and environments. Such repositories of performance documentation, including WANMA, assist us to identify people in these communities, and while they point us to more than the original work itself, the connections between these elements need to be established in some way, and archived in a way that is stable and lasting. Communities can contribute to their own archives easily and readily with the appropriate digital technologies and preservation policies. Digital archives struggle with intellectual property rights. WANMA, however, as an archive that is accessible through a web portal, tackles these challenges head on in an effort to provide a means for documenting performance in a way that truly reflects the breadth of performative possibility, connecting an interested community to that documenting process.

15

Participation and Presence: Propositional Frameworks for Engaging Users in the Design of the Circus Oz Living Archive

Laurene Vaughan

Situated at the nexus of digital humanities, interaction design and computer science disciplines, the design of living digital archives for cultural institutions is one of the key areas of development in the digital humanities. There are many ways to approach their design, and a successful design will embrace the expertise of this range of disciplines in its realization. This chapter focuses on the strategies used in the design of the Circus Oz Living Archive and in particular strategies that were used by the team around user engagement – in both the design and development of the archive and for its ongoing use from an interaction design perspective.

User participation is a fundamental in the design of a digital living archive. Designing infrastructure and strategies that will enable participation is essential to the success of a project. This has been the basis of significant amounts of design research in the fields of Interaction Design and Human Computer Interaction (HCI) over the past fifteen years (Dourish and Bell 2011; Suchman 2007; Moggridge 2007; Lowgren and Stolterman 2007; Dourish 2001). Some might even say that it is the Holy Grail of online collaboration, and is a vital aspect of the design of living archives (Whitelaw 2009).

228 Documenting Performance

The Circus Oz Living Archive

The Circus Oz Living Archive was developed between 2011 and 2014 with a beta version being released in 2012.[1] Circus Oz is Australia's premier circus company and since 1978 the company has made recordings of their performances, rehearsals and media activities. These have been recorded in every commonly-used format that has been created during this time. In 2009, a collaboration between Circus Oz and a team of academic researchers led to the project known as the Circus Oz Living Archive (COLA). It became a collaborative investigation, bringing together academics from across the humanities and sciences as well as archivists, cultural organizations and members of the Circus Oz Company.

The archive as it existed at the beginning of the project was essentially a storeroom that held the documentation of their performances in an ordered but not formal system. The ambition of the project was to open the door to the cupboard, consolidate this collection, transform it into a consistent digital format and then build a system that would make it accessible on the internet. It was envisioned that this newly accessible archive would open the way to new forms of audience engagement and conceptualizations of performance. Numerous publications about the origins, design and role of COLA from a range of perspectives have been published by the project team and are listed on the project website.[2]

Designing for/with liveness

The fundamental conceptual model that underpins the COLA is the augmentation of the static records of the live performances of a circus company for future application. As an historic record of the company this archive is empowered with authority as the collected voice of history. Yet in this case the facts of the recordings are a little hazy, held in the minds and memories of the circus members rather than as listed facts in a log that is filed. As such, the truth of what is held in this archive is often uncertain and it may be contested.

There are two key ways that we can conceive of 'living' in relation to the design of living archives. Typically, the term living archive refers to the animation of static or inaccessible collections in a manner that enables people to visit or make use of the collections (Burdick et al. 2012). Although much of the discourse on living archives focuses on digitization, if we frame living in terms of ease of access, then this discourse is as relevant to an analogue, digital or digitized collection. Living can refer to modes of opening up access to archives and stripping away barriers to use – physical, social or procedural. In this way, the classification of being a 'living archive' actually refers to something more than digitization or ease of access, and extends to ambitions for participation and new contexts of access.

The development of new types of archives that may attract new audiences can be a viable response by cultural heritage institutions to the concern that the public's interest and engagement is dwindling (Burdick et al. 2012). In this way, the living archive becomes a means to seek out innovative ways to engage or reignite people's interests and passions in a manner that is aligned to contemporary socio-cultural-technical practices.

For Circus Oz, diminishing audiences and fragile collections were not the driving force behind their desire to develop a living archive. As a performing arts and cultural institution, their aim was not to save their archive as a static historic record, but rather to make use of their archive as a means to expand their capacity to perform.

Undertaking the challenge of transitioning the archive from being a physical holding in a storeroom to an interactive digital platform involved far more conceptually than merely digitizing videos, building a database and designing an interface. In this particular case, historical records were given a new lease of life and transformed. This also enabled a re-conception of the ways that people engage with the archive. This included the public, those that manage and maintain the archive, and those whose work is the life substance of the archive itself.

Designing for presence

Structurally, a digital living archive is a digital, often online, interactive platform that performs the functions of presenting data (image, text and/or audio), that is housed in a database, accessed via a search engine which ensures that it is able to be interacted with via searches, comments, views or links to other sites. In this way, there are many similarities between a living archive and any other online communication platform; it is a socio-cultural communication platform. The challenges that are faced in its design by interaction designers and computer programmers are consistent with other participatory communication platforms. A variety of sources of literature and professional practices have informed the design decisions throughout the making of the COLA. Devising ways to engage with the circus community in the design of the archive, as well as developing an experience of design approach that would guide the way that people used or engaged with the COLA into the future, were of particular interest from a design perspective. Participation and presence were the two conceptual frameworks used to guide this activity.

Presence within the framework of a living digital archive can have many incarnations. There is the presence of the works in the collection held in the archive; of the performers that make up each of the works; of the audience at each of the performances; of the visitors to the archive; and of the archive in the life world of the audience, the performers and

Circus Oz. This diversity of contexts for the archive, and the socio-cultural contexts of its use and making, both provides and calls for designers to create in a comprehensive manner, accepting and even embracing the unknown in their design outcome. It also raises the possibility for a fresh approach to the design of participation.

Designing with/for people

The methodology for the design of COLA was a typical iterative, interaction design process. It involved exploring the material of the archive, exploring options with the circus partner, exploring the literature and other pre-existing platforms. There were seven different academic domains involved in the project, and each considered the possibilities and impacts from their respective domains. Engaging with the Circus was essential to the project methodology. To achieve this a reference group from the circus community was established. This group provided vital contextual input and were the trial users for technical developments. Events to collect content, trial developments and receive critical feedback were a key method in the research process. This process was documented in the project blog and wiki. These were publicly available and were an ongoing means for disseminating the research and engaging with a broader community of participants. It was through this mix of participation and dissemination methods that the project design melded a focus on people as agents in the design process, in conjunction with the computational and technical demands of a large digital video archive.

Pelle Ehn proposes that there are two complementary approaches that can be used in the design of things that are to have meaning for people. These are participatory design and meta-design. 'Participatory design is characterised as an approach to involve users in the design and, as suggested by Redstrom (2008) in the design process encounter "use-before-use" [. . .] meta-design suggests to defer some design and participation until after the design project and open up for use as design, design as use time or "design-after-design" (Redstrom 2008)' (Ehn 2008: 92). This proposition for engaging in design through use or design-after-design does require changes in process and approach to a project for a design team. They must accept that their design work will not necessarily result in the planned solution, and they must design a system or thing in such a manner that allows for this to happen. In the design of COLA a participatory methodology was used, and the possibility of meta-design as a means for enabling the possibility of the archive having a life emerges in the process.

Discovering the possibility of narrative

It was in the very early stages of the COLA project when the research team exposed some of the archive footage to the Circus Oz community, that the power of this archive became apparent to both the researchers and the broader stakeholders. As the members of the Circus Oz Community viewed themselves in a selection of video footage, it was observed that there was an affective connection between the company members, their friends and family, and the content of the archive. They were transfixed on the images, at times they were delighted and for the older members, wistful. As they sat and watched the videos, the company members adopted multiple positions in relation to the videos; they were both viewers of the content of the archive, and the substance of the archive narrative at the same time. It could be said that they were present on both sides of the screens that were being viewed. As the company members watched the videos they would exchange stories about the performance. They would clarify names and locations of performances. They were adding details to the collection in the archive.

The design of participation in any digital platform is one of the key challenges for a design team. The shift from use to repeated use and then active participation is essential if a digital archive is to be classified as living. From discussion boards, to customizable interfaces or voting or ranking systems, researchers have been designing ways for people to actively participate in digital platforms or archives. Based on the initial observations of users, the COLA team proposed that stories from archive visitors would be the means for breathing life into the archive. This is what was observed in the initial workshop – it was through narrative, realized through the sharing of stories between people, that the content of the archive was given meaning. As such, it was resolved that story prompts would be the key means for engaging users to participate in COLA and by default with the circus. It was proposed that a mix of story and personal reflections, combined with personal or customizable collections of favourite videos, would be the participation model for this living archive. These two key features would be the means for archive visitors to contribute to the archive, and to create a public record of their engagement with the archive and with Circus Oz.

Enabling a comments feature to a webpage is not an innovative solution to participation – in fact it is the norm. This digital practice of writing into communal spaces on the web has a long history in internet terms. In COLA, the aim was to expand on known practices for digital participation and create a strong link to conventional methods for an audience member or fan of the Circus to communicate with them. From a digital communication perspective, the experience of posting a comment would be consistent with what people might do on any other social media site. As a fan of the Circus, writing a letter to the organization is quite a traditional method for connecting to the performers. It was proposed that this familiarity in media and practices could overcome some of the barriers to participation that might exist. Underpinning the COLA project was a desire by the Circus to explore how they might be able to challenge and explore new conceptions of circus performance and performance attendance through their archive. Working with and around resource, space and time limitations, is an ongoing issue for the company. As such, based on this combination of communication norms, and the bigger ambition to break outside of norms of performance, the project team proposed to allow anyone to contribute text to the archive. It wasn't essential that people's stories be true, especially when recounting the experience of having been at a performance. What one person experiences and remembers may be different from another person, and these different recollections co-exist in the analogue world and would do so in this digital one as well. This would be a means to challenge these boundaries of time and space, and also authority in relation to circus performance and history. Two particular prompts were designed to enable people to contribute individual narratives in the archive: 'I was there and ...' or, 'I wasn't there but ...'. These two simple prompts would allow the archive visitors to do more than just search, read and watch the videos. By contributing to either of the text options people were able to write their way into the archive, into the performance, and into the history of Circus Oz.

By entering text in response to the prompt 'I was there and ...', whether the contributor was a performer or audience member, that person was recorded in the archive as having been there in the tent for the performance. The COLA contributors have a voice in the record of what *did* take place, what they *remember* to have taken place, or perhaps with less certainty what each individual contributor *thinks* took place. This ambiguity established a certain level of indifference to the 'truth' of what really took place and allowed for serendipity and collective wisdom to emerge through exchanges in the archive. The one thing that was certain is that the contributor was there, and this is what they remember.

In contrast, by writing into the space of absence ('I wasn't there but ...') an archive visitor was able to subvert the necessity of a recollection being based on their attendance at the performance then, and allow them to be present at the performance now, through the archive. As a visitor to the digital archive, anyone can imagine or make connections regardless of their lack of presence at the time of the live performance, for they are present now in the collection. The COLA contributor's performance now as a writer and/or collector in the archive in the present, is essential to the livingness of the archive.

These simple narrative prompts provided a way for users of the archive to record their presence and contribute to the archive's ambition to live. Despite the best plans and trials of such design solutions, it is impossible to ensure that people will make use of such devices in practice. Numerous 'solutions' have been developed to measure the success of discussion tools in online platforms – the measure of clicks, downloads, word counts and frequency of return visits. Conventional wisdom is to believe that the more internet traffic, the greater the success of a tool. In reality, when we measure traffic, we measure actions far more than engagement or presence: we measure popularity. Hallnas and Redstrom (2002) argue that there is a need for interaction designers to shift their focus away from *use* to a focus on *presence* if we are to truly design ubiquitous technologies. In their argument, presence is discussed in relation to the way in which a thing (object or system) makes its way into the life world of its user or owner. Ultimately, when a thing is assimilated into the life world in a manner that it is no longer recognized as being other or strange, then, they argue, we can conceive of the thing as having presence in a person's reality, rather than functional use. 'When we let things into our life world and they receive a place in our life they become meaningful to us' (p. 113). Hallnas and Redstrom's argument for the significance of designing for presence provides two important prompts for what I see as being integral to the design of living archives.

The story prompts that were designed as a means to engage people with the living history of the archive were designed with the intention of creating meaning. By positing a story, a visitor to the archive can make a direct public connection to the archive and to Circus Oz. In this way the system holds the potential to enable meaning of the order that Hallnas and Redstrom propose. The extensive workshops that were undertaken with the members of the Circus Oz Company were another means for supporting this level of meaning making through repeated and phased engagement with the project as it evolved. It was hoped that this would create deep connections to the archive. And yet despite concerted efforts engagement with the archive has been slow. Does this mean that the COLA is a failure? That this archive has meaning, and yet it has no presence in the life of its potential visitors or Circus Oz? Perhaps, is a possible answer to these questions, but what if the notion of meaning making and presence that Hallnas and Redstrom propose is expanded? What if, in the design of digital systems designers focus their efforts on designing for user presence rather than use? What if the integrity of the long suffering lurkers who have been derided for as long as these systems have been being built for their action-less presence in the system is embraced? What if issues of temporality in relation to place in the life world were to be embraced, and measures for the success of systems were reframed? Scale, time, speed and quantity are the conventional measures, but designing for meaning making may be slower or require very different measures to those that most analytics present.

If the aim of the digital age is to design 'computational things' that will have meaning whilst also adopting a presence in our lives beyond functional use, then there is a need to design new ways for thinking about how people are engaged with such things.

Conclusion

The design of a digital living archive for a performing arts company such as Circus Oz brought with it many exciting opportunities and challenges. What became apparent through this research is that despite the fact that COLA is the digital manifestation of the material of code and the social and professional practices of the circus, this archive is a digital system and a living entity. The archive was designed to live, but what that life will be, is yet to be known.

Designers are accustomed to working into the space of the unknown and the propositional but with a mandate to manifest the tangible and useful; however, this can never be ensured. This was the case with COLA. The variables that sat around the archive in its form and use were many. How, or if, the practices of its users will realize its potential is the exciting aspect of this project.

As has been discussed through this account of one digital archive, designing for user presence embraces and enables affect and is not limited to frameworks of truth or use. Designing for presence challenges expectations of user behaviour and use analytics; it challenges expectations of interaction and participation. Can a living archive be still rather than dormant? Can it be quiet and still live, without being classified as dead?

Part Four

Documenting Bodies in Motion

The final section of this book is concerned mainly with ways of documenting the human body in motion. Outside cultural forms of performance, the necessary technology to document moving bodies has arguably been satisfactorily achieved through the various forms of motion capture technology that sample the movements of one or more performers many times per second through specific sensors. However, this type of technology only captures the moving parts of a performer so that they are later mapped on to a 3D model, leaving out the nuances that photography and video are better suited to document.

Ben Spatz makes a case for better use of video in documenting performance. He advocates for a process described as dense video. This is described and proposed as a better way to analyze psychophysical acting. Spatz's 'What do we Document? Dense Video and the Epistemology of Practice' (chapter 16) is ultimately an invitation for psychophysical theatre practitioners and performance scholars to consider how useful performance documents in video and other multimedia forms can be, in conjunction with more body-based transmission of knowledge about such practices.

Alissa Clarke takes a similar but rather diverging point of view and proposes writing as a way to document psychophysical acting. Chapter 17, 'Pleasures of Writing about the Pleasures of the Practice', deals more with documenting psychophysical performance training rather than performances intended for public audiences. In itself, this is a rather interesting perspective that highlights the possible depths for documenting performance, by focusing on performer training. Such activities are normally only documented for didactic or pedagogical purposes.

Bringing the central focus of this section to the fore, Laura Griffiths' 'Dance Archival Futures: Embodied Knowledge and the Digital Archive of Dance' (chapter 18) discusses recent innovation in documenting and preserving dance works. Drawing on various digital archives of dance, with specific attention to the work of the contemporary dance company Phoenix Dance Theatre, this chapter provides some useful contemplation of the possible future uses of documented dance. This is particularly useful when considered as a prelude to the final chapter in the book, Sarah Whatley's 'Documenting Dance: Tools, Frameworks and Digital Transformations'.

Whatley's contribution provides an overview that tackles historical developments in documenting dance alongside the shift from analogue to digital methods of document creation. Highlighting aspects of the academic journey that has led to the publication of this book, the final chapter also deals with contemporary strategies and methods for documenting dance, which are also of interest to the broader spectrum of performance and the ways it is documented. What is very evident from this and many of the other contributions in this book, is how the more successful examples of documenting performance involve collaborative efforts between performance makers, documentation professionals and, increasingly, members of the audience.

16

What do we Document? Dense Video and the Epistemology of Practice

Ben Spatz

Document, event, technique

Much recent thinking about performance documentation has coalesced around an apparent opposition between the relative stability of the document and the ontological ephemerality of the live event. Indeed, if we begin from the problem of translating a singular and ephemeral event into a stable document, then failure is guaranteed. But the problem of documentation is illusory insofar as the performing arts have no special claim to ephemerality. As I have argued elsewhere, it is not performance but life in general – the world, the real, *being* itself – that escapes documentary capture (Spatz 2015a: 234). In fact, the questions faced by a documenter are not entirely different to those faced by a theatre director or choreographer who works through the craft of composition to condense various embodied and dramaturgical materials into a repeatable performance score. Nor do the spectators who attend a live performance necessarily have better or more direct access to the underlying processes that gave rise to it than do those who encounter the work through written or recorded documents. Understood in this way, documenting performance presents not the insoluble problem of grasping the ungraspable but rather the concrete challenge of isolating and articulating those aspects of a practice that can be shared and transmitted through the available tools. As the tools change, the potential for sharing and transmission also changes.

Both transmissible documents and live performance events owe their existence to underlying phenomena that structure practice over time. Rather than opposing these two kinds of phenomenon as ontological opposites, I would like to consider some of the ways in which specific kinds of events and documents relate to the practices from which they emerge. If the totality of a live event cannot be captured by any document, what can be documented is the practice out of which the event arises – as well perhaps as the structure of that practice, including transmissible knowledge or technique. As soon as we refocus our discussion on practice and technique rather than performance, much of the conceptual twisting around issues of liveness and ephemerality evaporates. We are then left with two different and complementary strategies for encountering practice: documents and performances. Just as performances may be shared with many different types and sizes of audience, there are many different kinds of document with different possible relationships to practice. Some documents, like some performances, aim to reach a broad and general audience. Other documents are designed for a specific community, perhaps one grounded in shared knowledge and practice. It is the latter that I want to consider here.

In praise of video

The past decade has witnessed an explosion of ways to document performance. With the advent of inexpensive digital photo and video technologies, and further amplified by the internet, the possibilities for documenting performance have proliferated radically. First there are the various configurations of book or booklet and DVD, such as those produced by Paxton (2008), Zarrilli (2009), Allegue et al. (2009),

Hodge (2013), and Hulton and Kapsali (2016).[1] These are important landmarks in the development of performance documentation, yet the format of the DVD already feels outdated in comparison with what can be realized online. DVD menus are notoriously clumsy to navigate and video distributed in this format is limited to Standard Definition resolution (720 x 480). In addition, while it is difficult to estimate the precise longevity of optical media, the possibility of data loss through physical deterioration is especially significant with physical objects like DVDs, which may remain untouched in an archive for many years. With even the commercial film industry increasingly moving towards streaming media, it seems unlikely that the DVD format can tell us much about the future of the audiovisual.

Shifting to online digital spaces, we must first take note of the high-end, custom-designed online databases that have been produced for well-known choreographers like Siobhan Davies and William Forsythe (Siobhan Davies Replay 2007; Motion Bank 2013; see also Whatley and Varney 2009). These are extraordinary in their breadth and undeniably important in theorizing the future of performance documentation. However, the scale of such ventures means that a plethora of material may be available without any clear routes for navigating through it. In addition, the production and maintenance of such bespoke databases – to say nothing of their continual updating – is an expensive project requiring the skills of digital archivists and programmers as well as scholars of performance. Notwithstanding their value for the field at large, the cost and complexity of these projects rules them out as models for individual scholars and practitioners developing documentation strategies on a smaller scale. Instead, such individuals and small groups may share audiovisual and other multimedia documents through online platforms like WordPress, which supports University of Winchester's Experiments & Intensities series (E&I 2015) and the new website of the journal *Theatre, Dance and Performance Training* (TDPT 2015);

the research catalogue, developed to support the *Journal for Artistic Research* (JAR 2015); and Scalar, a creation of the Alliance for Networking Visual Culture in California, which has been selected by *TDR* as the basis for its online space (Mee 2013: 150). The aim of these platforms is to make multimedia publication available to those without the skills or resources to design and code their own digital archival spaces.

Excitement about the possibilities afforded by such platforms is at a high point. Yet in the slew of recent publications addressing digital performance documentation and archives, one apparently simple approach to documentation has gone curiously unremarked: that of video itself as a linear framework with potentially nonlinear content.[2] Before considering its specific application to performance and embodied practice, it may be instructive to note how the potential of video is being explored in other fields. As one might expect, the video essay has become an important genre of critical work in film and media studies. The online journal *[in]Transition* bills itself as 'the first peer-reviewed academic journal of videographic film and moving image studies' (Media Commons 2015). The advantage for film and media scholars is that the object of their analysis is already available to them through the vast reserves of digital video stored in existing archives, libraries and online. Their task is to continue and expand the critical work already taking place in forums like *Cinema Journal* by developing new modes of composition in which analysis and its object are contained within the same frame. *[in]Transition*'s website contains a wealth of online and print resources dealing with the video essay, ranging from the aesthetics of composition to the legalities of fair use, which have much to offer those concerned with documenting performance. Further afield, a much simpler version of the video essay has become an important way to share clinical medical knowledge through channels like the *Journal of Visualized Experiments* — 'the world's first peer reviewed scientific video journal'

(JoVE 2015) – and *The New England Journal of Medicine*'s multimedia section (NEJM 2015).

It is surprising that the video essay has not already come to greater prominence in performance studies and related fields. While sites like the Research Catalogue, Scalar, and Experiments & Intensities offer exciting design potentials, publications developed for those digital environments are not guaranteed to last beyond the lifespan of the platform. Video files, in contrast – as one of the basic building blocks of digital space – are more technologically robust. They can be easily transferred from one platform to another, hosted on multiple platforms at once, and scaled down to smaller resolutions as needed. Massive video hosting websites like YouTube and Vimeo can serve as backups or even primary servers for peer-reviewed journals. While all digital media must be continually ported from one technological generation to the next to remain accessible – and this is a serious issue for digital archivists – an MP4 file produced in 2015 is more likely to be readable in 2020 than a custom-built web interface. To produce edited video documents of course requires a bit of skill, as well as access to a computer and a working copy of a video editing application like Adobe Premiere, FinalCut Pro, or even iMovie. But such resources are well on their way to becoming as commonplace as the word processing and desktop publishing tools now used to produce books and articles.

What platforms like Scalar and the Research Catalogue offer in formal innovation is exchanged for the well-tested rhetoric of the linear motion picture, which has more than one hundred years of history. The standalone video may not be the most exciting form of 'new media', but it is tried and true as a medium of both expression and communication. Why then is the scholarly video essay not already accepted as a basic form of contribution to the major peer-reviewed journals in our field? Why is there no journal of performance studies that accepts contributions only or primarily in this form?[3] It would appear that, in our zeal to explore the ever-expanding nonlinear spatiality of the web, we have skipped over the apparently simpler genre of the audiovisual.

Dense video and digital epistemology

The WordPress blog associated with the journal *Theatre, Dance and Performance Training* includes a 'Studio' section 'dedicated to the audio-visual documentation of training practices'. Among the first round of posts was a four-minute video I produced called 'Sequence of Four Exercise-Actions', which documents a training session I led at the Centre for Psychophysical Performance Research in Huddersfield, northern England (Spatz 2015b). In this video, I explored for the first time some of the more complex editing and montage techniques that can be used to increase what I call the density of a video document. Through carefully placed embedded video citations and textual annotations, I attempted to guide the viewer towards a richer understanding of the documented practice by enfolding multilayered, nonlinear content within the overall linear structure of a four-minute video. Within its limited scope, I considered this video successful and soon undertook another project with more ambitious aims. This second video, 'Judaica: Designing a Laboratory for Song-Action', is still in draft stage and remains unpublished as of this writing. It differs from the first in several respects and raises a number of additional challenges, which I will address later. First, however, I will elaborate on what I mean by density in this context.

I take the density of a document to be the richness of information found in any given frame or excerpt. The density of prose can be increased by the use of footnotes, parenthetical annotations, citations and references, specialized language, longer or more elaborate sentence structures, and other textual complexities that tend to distinguish academic writing from popular non-fiction. A similar range can be elaborated for video: what we might call a simple linear video is one consisting of a single take, an uninterrupted recording that documents a moment of practice. To stand as a citable document in the growing archive of our field, I propose that such a video ought to at least have two basic elements of metadata: a title frame – identifying the author, practitioners, location, and date – and continuous time code (essential for stable referencing). Beyond those basic elements there are myriad ways in which the density of a video document might be increased. The training video 'Sequence of Four Exercise-Actions' contains several different types of textual annotation running across the bottom of the frame, including the names and roles of practitioners; names and descriptions of the exercises shown; references to books and articles that analyze related practices; and pedagogically-oriented commentary. It also includes excerpts of secondary video and one still image, which are embedded within the frame and run parallel to the main video. The embedded video comes from two sources: from the same training session – to show what happened before or after the four minutes documented in the main video – and from an earlier set of videos in which the same exercises are practised by the person who invented them (Balduzzi 2013; see Spatz 2014). At one point, three videos are juxtaposed within the same frame to demonstrate how a given exercise may be 'transmitted from person to person, traveling across space and time' (Spatz 2015b: 03:02–03:12).

The second video, 'Judaica: Designing a Laboratory for Song-Action', is considerably longer than the first, its current version running twenty minutes rather than four. As in the difference between a four-page article and a twenty-page article, the larger duration poses additional problems in terms of structure and organization. More significantly, because it documents a practice in which song and speech have central importance, this video grapples with differences in how visual and aural materials are received. In the first video, I was able to present four continuous minutes of recorded footage with additional videos layered on top. This worked because the soundtracks of the embedded videos could be muted without too much loss of information. But while two videos can be placed within the same frame without interfering with each another, two audio tracks playing simultaneously quickly become confused and confusing. Thus, if I want to compare two performances of the same song, their juxtaposition must involve sequential rather than simultaneous montage. This makes continuity a problem: if I choose to include five or ten minutes of continuous audio recording, I am limited in the extent to which I can embed or layer additional audio tracks on top. This may seem a merely logistical issue, but I think it suggests the extent to which audiovisual recording remains underexplored as a mode for documenting performance, particularly in academic contexts where density is desirable. Those who find academic reading pleasurable enjoy the density that skilled writers are able to achieve through the careful shaping of sentences and paragraphs as well as parenthetical statements, footnotes, and the other nonlinear techniques mentioned earlier. At this point we know relatively little about how such epistemic density can be layered within a video essay.

The challenges facing those who might want to produce *dense video documents*, for example as research outcomes of an embodied research practice, are numerous. They range from logistical concerns – such as finding a workspace with a visually clean backdrop (compare Spatz 2015b with Balduzzi 2013) and compensating one or more skilled videographers – to those that are critical, aesthetic and editorial. The spatial and temporal relationships among video channels, audio channels, textual annotation and other media all must be considered in the context of a project's scope and duration and what it aims to document. In a sense, none of these challenges is merely logistical. Taken together, they suggest a new 'digital epistemology' (e.g., CRASSH 2015) that arguably has already changed the way we understand what we are doing when we move, dance, sing, speak, interact, improvise, tell stories, walk through a city or whatever else may be captured on video. In the two experimental prototypes discussed here, I aimed to create documents that would be dense enough to warrant multiple viewings and which might, like a good article, cause the viewer to stop and rewind while watching in order to more fully appreciate their layers of juxtaposed, intermedial content. In erring towards density, I may have risked allowing the pace to become too fast and the screen too busy. But that is a matter of style. My point here is that we have yet to begin a serious, field-wide investigation of video as a medium through which to document and articulate the performance-oriented practices that concern us.

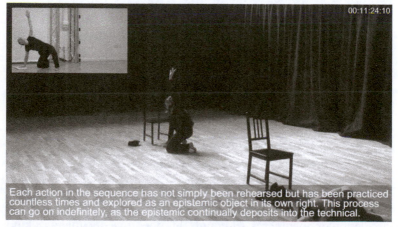

Figure 16.1 'Judaica: Designing a Laboratory for Song-Action'. Still frame from a dense video documenting the *Judaica Project* 2012–15. Urban Research Theater and the Centre for Psychophysical Performance Research, November 2015 (draft version). Practitioners: Ben Spatz, Sióbhán Harrison, Jennifer Parkin

What do we document?

To return to the epistemological considerations from which I began, neither of the cited video documents refers specifically to performance in the sense of documenting an ephemeral public event. The first, shorter video focuses on a training session in which I worked with university students in the context of an undergraduate drama course. The second video is more complex, not only because of its duration and the fact that it documents vocal as well as physical practice but also because it is intended as a document of research rather than training.[4] Rather than documenting performance, these documents should be understood as functioning in parallel to live performances in that they too offer composed surfaces through which to glimpse the depth and complexity of ongoing practices.

Performing arts discourse tends to accord primary significance to public performances and to treat the practices that give rise to them as preparatory in nature (either 'training' or 'rehearsal'). Yet for many performing artists this hierarchy is reversed, with the public event of performance serving to make possible – both socially and financially – a deeper and more intimate studio practice. While both of these approaches are legitimate, here I am invoking a third possibility in which the circulating document has primary status. Such an explicit de-emphasis of both long-term practice and public performance may strike those in both camps as anathema. How cold to put the document first! But a closer examination of academic knowledge transmission – whether in the humanities or sciences – reveals that there is nothing inherently cold about document-oriented practices. Scholarly research, whether individual or collaborative, is reliant upon the circulation of documents. Although this does give documents a kind of ontological priority, it is clear at least in academic fields that documents have historically served to found and support communities of knowledge rather than to displace them. It is arguably only because of transmissible documents that fields such as mathematics, philosophy, sociology, literature and history exist. What fields of practice might come into being through the development of substantial, well-organized and diverse dense video archives? What communities of knowledge might become possible when video can be shared, annotated and excerpted as easily as text? What territories of research will become accessible when practice and performance begin to organize themselves around the production of documents rather than treating them as secondary byproducts?

I have no wish to devalue those practices that are oriented towards performance or which take sustained embodied practice itself to be inherently valuable. I only wish to observe that, alongside those long-standing traditions, a third domain is emerging in which the circulation of multimedia documents takes on primary importance. We do not yet know how this domain will relate to those of performance and performance studies. Neither, at this time, can we say what forms those documents will eventually take or how they will achieve their particular epistemic densities. Let us not then be too quick to dismiss video, which after all is the most recent substantive documentary medium to have emerged from the technological explosion that defines our era.

Pleasures of Writing about the Pleasures of the Practice: Documenting Psychophysical Performer Trainings

Alissa Clarke

Whilst emphasizing the perpetually innovative evolution of documentation, Suzanne Briet's seminal 1951 text – *What is Documentation?* – places emphasis on standardization, organization, classification, hierarchy, selection and exclusion, and the continuing centrality of the text. It can, thus, be aligned with Diana Taylor's depiction of the 'archive', as distinguished from 'the embodied memory' of the 'repertoire' (2003). Indeed, just as Taylor highlights how 'Western epistemology so privileges writing and archival systems of transmission that it often fails to account for embodied practices as an "act of transfer"' (2007), so Briet rigidly underscores that 'a star', 'a pebble rolled by a torrent' and 'a living animal', all of which might be viewed as involved in active enlivened matter-based processes and actions, cannot be seen as documents (1951: 10). Thus, this logocentric dominance and the apparently 'indescribable' state of sensorial processes (Zarrilli 1988: 101) results in a perceived 'aporia between logos and the body' (Kobialka quoted in Dolan 2005: 168).[1] It is, therefore, unsurprising that previous studies investigating the textual documenting of embodied performance and performer trainings have predominantly focused upon the difficulties of making such documents. These difficulties normatively appear as a war with words or as a limitation of register (Melrose 2006: 120–35), where words may 'betray' (Artaud 1958: 71) or 'asphyxiate what we would like them to give birth to' (Barba 1995: 50).

Whilst not ignoring or underestimating the challenges raised by articulating the processes of the body in training, this chapter refuses the negative positioning of written documents, and challenges the over romanticized perception of performative and pre-performative embodied processes as magically beyond documentation (Foster 1995: 9). Following this, psychophysical performer trainings, trainings that pursue an interrelationship between body and mind, can generate multiple creative embodied pleasures that the participant or practitioner wishes to express, and so critically and reflexively examine. I argue that the potential to articulate the embodied sensations of pleasure provoked by psychophysical performer trainings lies in possible modes of activating and conveying the pleasures of writing about one's practice. This argument builds upon the abundance of contemporary performance studies theorists (such as W.B. Worthen 1995, 2008; Della Pollock 1998; Ann Daly 2002; Claire MacDonald 1999, 2004; Peggy Phelan 1998), who have addressed and deployed the concept of 'performative writing', and those key practitioners who have explored the creation of embodied written reflection within or directly stemming from the training and practice space. The latter include Grotowski and Barba's lyrical forms of expression, which offer the 'performer-as-reader ... an intuitive grasp of the subject' (Zarrilli 1988: 101), despite their denigration of attempts to lexically articulate the performing body and their ban on such attempts at verbal or written articulation and explanation in the training space; Miranda Tufnell and Chris Crickmay's sensorial evocations of and incitements to practice in *Body Space Image* (1990) and *A Widening Field: Journeys in Body and Imagination* (2004); the personal, collaborative and sometimes visionary forms of female performers' writing produced by The Magdalena Project's *The Open Page* (1996–2008); Susan Leigh Foster's game changing work 'Choreographing

History', which called for 'figures of speech and forms of phrase and sentence construction that evoke the texture and timing of bodies in motion' (1995: 9).

And yet, whilst most of these sources engage with often playful and joyous forms of writing, a highly fruitful pursuit of pleasure is absent. In 'Another Kind of Writing: Reflective Practice and Creative Journals in the Performing Arts' Mark Evans describes the changes wrought in his students' reflective writing on their embodied performance practice through dancer, craniosacral therapist and Alexander technique teacher, Miranda Tufnell's, work with the deployment of writing within a space of movement.[2] Evans explains how Tufnell facilitated his students to create more sensorial, evocative, provisional and multiplicit forms of reflective writing (2007: 72–3), and highlights the importance of the enjoyment that stemmed from the pedagogical process, but emphasizes that 'Enjoyment was not in itself an aim of this project – that would have been indeed a primrose path to dalliance' (2007: 74). Whilst accepting that such sentiments in this case may necessarily be shaped by the pedagogical context at work, this chapter develops upon the missed opportunity to dally displayed by these previous explorations of written documents. In pursuing this primrose path, it demonstrates how the encounters and intersections between embodied and lexical pleasures can feed and mutually support one another, whilst producing further such fruitful pleasures. This argument is grounded within consideration of the working and writing practices of an international range of practitioners, focusing particularly on my own pleasurable experiences as a participant and participant-writer within Odin Teatret, Phillip Zarrilli, Sandra Reeve and Eva Schmale's practices.

All of this material is explored in apposite dialogue with Hélène Cixous' depiction of the sensorial processes of the urgent and energized 'drive to write' (Cixous 1991b: 1). Despite her explorations of embodiment, Cixous' theories are near absent in writings upon body-based performer trainings, and where her work appears in explorations of documenting performance (Furse 1997; Cutler 1998; Jools Gilson-Ellis 2003; Prendergast 2003), these explorations have, understandably, focused solely upon the feminist potential of Cixous' early concept of *écriture féminine* and a very limited use of Cixous' early most well-known text, 'The Laugh of the Medusa' (1981). Thus, the very practical possibilities of Cixous' theorizations across her oeuvre of, what I propose are, intensively and detailed psychophysical processes of writing, appear to have been missed. Hence, I propose that Cixous' portrayals of exhilarating psychophysical processes of writing can significantly enhance and elucidate the fruitful encounters between the embodied and lexical documentary pleasures within and surrounding the psychophysical performer training space. Indeed, whilst these portrayals of psychophysical processes of writing are especially evident in Cixous' later texts, they do span her entire oeuvre and can be viewed as stemming from her earlier and far better known theorizations of *écriture féminine* and embodied feminine pleasure. Examination of these earlier theorizations becomes important in the next section of this chapter, as I consider the desire, and the lexical frustration of that desire, to articulate the sensorial pleasures of the practice within Sandra Reeve's workshops.

Articulating pleasure

Focusing upon enhancing participants' awareness of their own evolving daily movement patterns within and interrelated with changing groups of people and environments, Reeve's workshops are predominantly conducted in rural outdoor locations. These workshops, entitled 'Move into Life', display the influences of Grotowski, Theravada Buddhist mindfulness practice, and Reeve's background as a Shiatsu practitioner and as a Dance Movement Psychotherapist. 'Move into

Life', though, is particularly centred around Reeve's twenty-seven years of studying with Javanese movement artist, Suprapto Suryodarmo, and his methods of 'guiding' non-stylized movement through movement (Reeve 2005). Using action, gesture, music, noise, verbal suggestions and simple movement tasks, Reeve guides participants through movement that stems from their mind, body or feelings, in order to 'bring out the potential of how they [a]re already moving' (Reeve 2005). When guiding people, Reeve will often encourage participants to 'Follow your bliss', and to then 'note down movements that [you] liked' (2012b), considering 'why' a movement or moving in a certain area 'brings you delight' (2012a). This encouragement of reflexivity about movement preferences in that time and space, highlights the way in which Reeve's guidance and her use of simple movement tasks work 'as a way of stimulating awareness and expression of [participants'] internal landscapes [...] without losing contact with the external environment' (Reeve 2008: 109).

Such self-awareness and pursuit of delight is evident in one participant's articulation of her experience of the first exercise outdoors during Reeve's workshop, 'Journey: Valley to Rock to Sea'. This participant exclaimed that she had felt such joy and gladness at moving alongside everyone within the beautiful environment that the only way in which she could describe this wonderful sensation was as 'bursting'. When later I asked whether she had increased this highly pleasurable sensation of bursting through articulating it, Reeve's participant responded that she felt that the bursting had been dissolved through talking about it, even though the feedback had been very supportively and encouragingly received. This dissolution echoes the psychoanalyst Leclaire, who declared that 'Whoever speaks, by speaking denies bliss' (quoted in Barthes 1975: 21).

This lexical destruction of embodied bliss could be perceived through Cixous' emphasis upon the problems of articulating feminine *jouissance*, sexual bliss, through dominant phallocentric discourse.

This dominant phallocentric discourse is rooted in what Lacan terms the 'symbolic' order of patriarchal culture, which upholds patriarchal power and law. The symbolic order and its discourse are 'associated with authority, order, fathers, repression and control', which is manifested through definite, controlled and prescribed patterns of words and grammar (Barry 2002 [1995]: 128). In 'Castration or Decapitation?' Cixous describes how the woman, or, within the context of this chapter, any person positioned by 'Freud/Lacan [...]' "outside the symbolic"', 'cannot speak of [their] pleasure', with the consequence that 'unable to speak of pleasure = no pleasure, no desire' (1981a: 45). This dominant and prohibitionary positioning of the word suggests that bodily desire and pleasure can only be enjoyed as a result of, and through, being able to express this pleasure.

Cixous calls for the subversion of this logocentric, phallocentric discourse through the deployment of *écriture féminine*. This playful, processual and pleasurably uncontrolled feminine pattern of writing is rooted within sexually specific means of bodily pleasure. It is rooted within multiplicity and excess, where 'woman's capacity for multiple orgasms indicates that she has the potential to attain something more than Total, something extra – abundance and waste' (Wing 1996: 165). Cixous is clear, however, that this embodied feminine form of writing and its associated pleasures are 'not the endowment solely of women' (1991a: 149). She emphasizes how such abundant, playful *jouissance* has been denied to both men and women through the cultural dominance of rigid pompous phallocentricity (1981a: 51). Indeed, I would argue that the psychophysical extra-daily pleasures experienced by male and female training participants create one means of accessing such *jouissance*. Therefore, Cixous' portrayal of an expression of feminine bodily pleasure that forms part of, as well as enabling, the experience of that pleasure, offers an extremely useful fresh framework to male and female participant-writers, through which they could attempt to lexically articulate an experience of embodied bliss without negative consequences for that experience. Thus, this chapter follows Cixous' emphasis, proposing a dialogic, interwoven relationship between the pleasures of the body and the word.

The drive to write

This interwoven relationship between the pleasures of the body and the word can be traced within the construction of the notes that I made during the 2004 'Odin Teatret South-West Residency' in Exeter, in southern England. The intensive and interwoven combination of work demonstration, solo performance, workshops, talks and film showings of training during the residency with the director, Eugenio Barba, and one of the performers, Julia Varley, of this longstanding psychophysical performance company, and the reflections that they generated, provoked a state of full psychophysical engagement. In 'The Echo of Silence', a work demonstration with Julia Varley, rooted in the possibilities and strengths of her vocal vulnerabilities, the catch and breaks, ambiguous accent and rich laughter notes within her voice reverberated through the attentive bodies of those listening. The impact of this was enhanced through the body memory of a vocal training workshop with Varley earlier in the day, which had provoked a state of highly concentrated shared collaborative focus and full embodied awareness, as Varley facilitated the group to create a collective international song formed through snatches of tune supplied by different participants. At the same time, Varley encouraged the group to support individuals through vocal resistances and embarrassments by echoing and so firming up their sound or by creating a soundscape over which the individual could more easily deliver their text. These states and experiences of highly focused individual and collective psychophysical concentration led me to an intensely engaged process of documenting throughout each of the events, conducted through a state of embodied excitation. That excitation provoked further engagement with, reflection upon, and so even greater excitation in writing about, the stimulating pleasures of the psychophysical practice. Reviewing and analyzing this embodied excitation and the processes surrounding it, can provide a means of understanding how a pleasurable form of articulation might be experienced and shaped.

This embodied excitation was manifest through, and provoked heightened awareness of, flushed cheeks, heat, quickened breath and heartbeat. Echoing Foster's emphasis on the specific physical conditions involved in being a 'body writing' and 'a bodily writing' (1995: 3), these sensations were bound up with a strong clasp and vigorous propulsion of the pen, movements that emanated from a forceful centring within the lower abdomen. This invigorated, activated physicality was reminiscent of the exhilarating sensations experienced whilst completing the percussive highly charged South Indian, *kalarippayattu*, martial art sequences within Phillip Zarrilli's Asian martial and meditational arts-based pre-performative training. Such invigorated physicality and excitation mirrors Cixous' portrayal of the results of the 'drive' (1991b: 1) or 'desire to write' (1998b: 144). This 'drive' stems somatically from the force of breath (Cixous 1991a: 9) and a strong connection with the lower abdomen (Cixous 1997: 90). This echoes the way in which in Zarrilli's form-based training, energizing 'breath and impetus for movement into and out of the forms originate' from the support of the lower abdominal centre (Zarrilli 1990: 136). Indeed, as can be seen through my response to the Odin Teatret residency, this drive to write can be incited and actualized by psychophysical pre-performance practice.

When experiencing this drive to write, Cixous variously describes how: 'The scene is in the entrails with turmoil, élans. Knees knock, the heart catches fire' (1998b: 141), 'Everything beats faster' (1998b: 144), 'it precipitates itself in spasms, in waves, the length of the arm, passing the hand, passing the pen' (1993: 2). This heat and fire, 'turmoil', 'spasms', 'waves', and subsequent vigorous activity engendered by the drive to write, recall Julia Kristeva's positioning of unconscious 'drives' as '"energy" charges as well as "psychical" marks' (1984: 25). These energetic writing drives can be viewed through Barba's depiction of, and engendered by, the extra-daily energy activated by the psychophysical performer. Barba describes how 'The performer's dilated body' (1995: 98), like the writer's body aflame to write, 'is a red hot body, in the scientific sense of the word. The particles which make up daily behaviour have been excited and produce more energy. They have undergone an increment of motion, they move apart, they attract each other, they oppose each other with more force, more speed, within a larger space' (1995: 98). The particles in the performer or writer's red hot body display an energy energized through the production of more and more energy.[3] This reflects the way in which, as Cixous explains, the result of writing of and through one's desires through the desire to write is that 'my desires have invented new desires' (1981b: 246), so leading to accumulative waves of desire to write. Thus, in the manner of feminine abundance, the performer/desiring writer 'wast[es]' (Barba 1995: 16) 'excessive energy' (Barba 1995: 19) or excitations.

At maximum intensity these excessive, heated excitations and accumulative waves of desire can provide an experience for the performer/writer akin to the bliss of 'bursting'. Indeed, one can view Reeve's workshop participant's intense desire to lexically represent her experience of bursting through Cixous' portrayal of the accumulative waves of desire to write. In 'The Laugh of the Medusa' Cixous proclaims: 'I, too, have felt so full of luminous torrents that I could burst – burst with forms' (1981b: 246). The participant-writer can work to burst with forms upon the page in order to evoke these connected practical and written experiences of bursting.

The beginnings of such textual bursting were evident within my handwritten account of the Odin Teatret residency, which echoed the multiplicity, excess and processual state of *écriture féminine*. In this document, the non-sequential placement of asterisked afterthoughts, simultaneous and multiplying ideas, all expressed though fragmented notes and sentences, were suggestive of 'a volcano spitting lava' across the page (Cixous 2004: 118). Such textual bursting is 'writ[ten] *before,* at the time still in fusion before the cooled off time of the narrative' (1998b: 141; emphasis in original). It is 'written close to the very drive to write' (1991b: 1).

Urgency

Evans recommends using play to embrace experimentation and incompleteness in written reflection, which 'enables it to play with meanings, to reveal meaning-making, and to dispel the kinds of student anxieties over style, correctness and erudition', which linger long beyond student days, and 'distance [the individual] from a mature sense of self-as-learner' (2007: 75). Another mode of tackling such distancing can be found by activating and writing through this bursting desire, where the participant-writer must of necessity shed any remaining inclination for the correctness, order and control of the symbolic order, as the speed of the excessive energy particles and of the torrential waves of desire leaves no time to polish and edit. Cixous and Calle-Gruber describe how when 'writ[ing] (from) the overflowing of writing', the writing '"gallops, it gallops me"' (1997: 40). This leads to an urgent need to communicate, to 'burst with forms', with all possible haste. Indeed, Cixous' depiction of the 'feverish notation' (2002a: 417) resulting from this urgency can be traced through the actions that I observed deriving from my body whilst documenting the Odin Teatret residency: the hand vigorously pressing downwards upon the frenziedly writing pen barely raised from the page and refusing to stop for fear of breaking the pleasurable flow of mutating excitations and ideas.

This deployment and inhabitation of urgency and speed is made absolutely necessary during, and is further fuelled by, the documenting of the pleasures found in psychophysical training processes. After participating in Reeve's 'Guiding through Movement' workshop, one student declared that, due to the pleasures of the workshop, he had never felt a two-hour session go more quickly. This example underlines the way in which the psychophysical training pleasures that the participant-writer experiences and documents make the time and, therefore, also the pleasure itself, pass at a tremendous pace. This is the case even where that pleasure is of the languid, tranquil kind.

However, even when feverishly noting these pleasures, as Cixous points out, 'writing moves at the pace of the hand', 'far behind' (1998a: 39) these sensorial experiences and associated thoughts and ideas. In an attempt to revoke this disparity of pace, when documenting the Odin Teatret residency I scrawled hard and fast across the pages that I crumpled as I grabbed at them. I tried to turn the pages fast enough to match the speed of the writing that pursued the thoughts and sensations immersed within, and provoking self-reflexive consideration of that, pleasure. This attempt embodies Cixous' portrayal of the tough, but exhilaratingly exciting 'race' or 'chase' (1998b: 141 and 144), that may be experienced by the writer, where one's blood is up in the thrilling 'pursuit of a thought which bolts off before [one] like some marvellous game' (1998b: 139–40). Here 'game' refers to both the placement of the pursued moment / thought as prey, and to the way in which the 'book writes itself ... With jubilation and play' (1998b: 141).

When analyzing Cixous' handwritten notebooks Susan Sellers underlines Cixous' creation of a personal 'shorthand' (Cixous 2004: 121) of abbreviated words, and the moments where 'her letters trail into almost undecipherable marks' (Sellers 2004: x). These writing tactics enable Cixous to go faster and so 'to catch more' (Cixous 2004:121) of that which is pursued. These tactics of the hunt could similarly be traced in the fragmented notes and patches of scrawled illegibility bouncing above and below the lines of the page in my documents of the Odin Teatret residency. The participant-writer can consider the advantages to the chase provided by such tactics, and the way in which these presentational techniques can also work to represent the jubilant speed of the chase and that which is chased. Indeed, my documenting of the residency serves to produce the impression of rapid movement between notes and thoughts without pause. Such rapidity is conveyed by the presence of excessive enjambment, and frequent points where, as a consequence of that pen 'barely raised from the page', one word appears to be fused to the next. This intensifies the rate of the fast flowing rhythm created by these textual forms to the pace of the 'luminous torrents' depicted by Cixous. This fast flowing rhythm increases the lightening-paced pleasures experienced by the writer, and speeds the reader's gaze around the page into a headlong race with the running text and that which the text is pursuing. Where the reader, whilst on the run, rewrites that running text and, therefore, the race, they construct further jubilant ideas and experiences to be followed in articulatory pursuit. This creates additional layers and possibilities of pleasurable pursuit to be played with amidst this 'marvellous game' of document creation.

Tension and constriction

However, in contrast to this emphasis upon playfulness and the positioning of this race as a game, Cixous, also describes how 'I chase after what goes beyond me. On occasion I try to go after four hares at once' (1998b: 144). Such an attempt is necessary where sensorial experience and ideas, as demonstrated in the textual lava documenting the Odin residency, thwart *symbolic* emphasis on the linear and singular. Yet, this demanding chase, Cixous explains, 'makes me all out of breath and contorted. So I stop and get back my breath' (1998b: 144). This pained physicality, far removed from the release suggested by the speed earlier, displays what the psychophysical practitioner, Elsa Gindler, underlines as the 'constricted breathing' that 'is closely related to unhealthy physical tension' (1995: 10). Indeed, my own experience of this pained physicality in the urgency of the written chase can be reviewed through the somatic knowledge, which I gained during Eva Schmale's *Gindler Work: Sensory Awareness* workshop.

Rebecca Loukes outlines how Gindler was 'a pioneer of a psychophysical awareness practice', and 'though her work has influenced twentieth-century theatre and dance in a variety of ways, she herself was not a performer or performance maker' (2006: 387). Gindler's, and, thus Schmale's, work echoes the emphasis within Reeve's training upon 'the basic movements of daily life: walking, sitting, standing, crawling and lying down and the transitions between them' (Reeve 2006b: 19–20, n. 1). Work upon these daily movements serves to bring participants to a consciousness of, and an ability to move beyond, their movement habits. Within this context, halfway through her six-day workshop, Schmale drew upon an exercise used by Gindler and asked participants to allow ten minutes extra when walking to the workshop and to closely observe their process of walking. These extra ten minutes were to be taken to allow participants to 'thoughtfully' enjoy the process, rather than working towards the result (Gindler 1995: 6) of the final destination.

However, I initially, very uncomfortably, experienced this use of extra time as conflicting with my habitual tendency towards tension and rushing, and associated hurried, shallow breathing. These tendencies derived from an anxious 'endgaining' attempt to compete with time, and a fear of being late and, hence, out of control. I can trace these same habits in the urgency of my written pursuits. As I experienced whilst documenting the Odin Teatret residency, where this anxious endgaining dominates, the quickened pattern of breathing

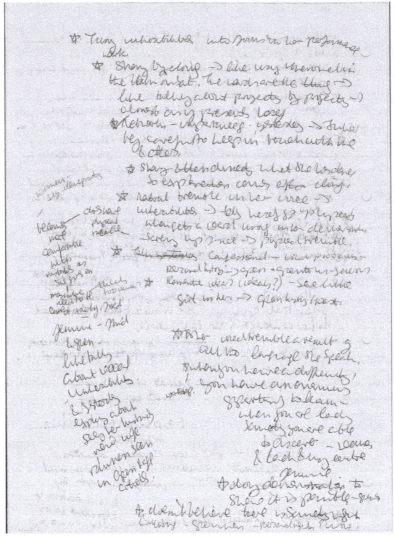

Figure 17.1 Tense rushed writing. Image courtesy of Alissa Clarke

and firm grip of and vigorous pressure down upon the pen can easily evolve into that hurried, shallow breathing, or, at worst, breath held without release, and a tensed hand and wrist. This tension almost pushes the pen into the paper as the writing hand rushes across the page, ineffectively endeavouring to express the ideas coming from 'all directions' in time. The textual consequence and representation of this anxiety, constriction and rushing can be viewed in my documents through: darker, thicker, tighter marks and heavy indentations upon the page (see Figure 17.1). This anxiety is also evident through an unwieldy attempt, in the manner of the *symbolic,* to organize and tidy these overwhelmingly numerous ideas into abrupt lists of bullet points. Gindler attributes such constricted rushing to the habitualized perception 'that the demands made upon us by life are [...] overwhelmingly difficult' and should 'be carried out with' 'maximum effort and turmoil' (1995: 10). Indeed, the physical difficulties and mentally-enforced endgaining that may result from the writing chase can be viewed as the consequence of trying too hard, and thereby prohibiting the possibility of being able to match the pace and direction of that pursued.

'Knowing through pleasure'

Such effortful over-exertion can be further fruitfully re/viewed through Cixous' depiction of a controlling masculine 'knowledge of knowing, which has to do with mastering' (1987: 2). Using 'the story of *Eve and the Apple*' as a key example, Cixous associates the 'knowledge of knowing' with 'the word of the Law (or the discourse of God)' (1991a: 149 and 150), which as negative prohibition and 'pure antipleasure' bans eating from the tree of knowledge (1991a: 154 and 151). This form of knowledge characterizes my normative mode of operating within these trainings. Echoing Evans' emphasis on the problematic strong scholastic influence of desire to work effortfully to achieve a state of correctness and praise in a distancing of one's own learning needs and desires, a recurring habit during training experiences is to do what I feel that I should do, to place maximum effort and turmoil into following what I think would be considered the 'correct', law abiding thing to do. Similarly, one of Zarrilli's male participants acknowledged an initial discombobulating tendency to 'try and please the teacher' (Participant F 2005). This tendency was combined with a normative initial propensity for mystifying and romanticizing this intercultural form of bodymind practice so concentrated upon the development of the participant's internal focus and awareness. These initial tendencies moulded Participant F's written reflections into an attempt to demonstrate the mastery bound up with the knowledge of knowing. Following the phallic grandiosity, over-seriousness and pride of this pattern of knowledge, these first reflections tried far too hard to impress the external reader with great discoveries and knowledge. Participant F describes how his reflections were written with an eye towards posterity, to what, he explained, 'would be really meaningful . . . in a few months or something' (2005). This mirrors Zarrilli's own troubled description of how, when writing about his developing bodymind and observations of an optimal state of practice when training in India, how 'difficult [he] found it to describe [his] experience in language that neither objectified nor . . . romantically subjectified and/or reified [his] own experience, applying to it a thin gloss of self-congratulation' (2002 [1995]: 185).

Yet, just as Reeve makes the individual overtly aware, and able to plot the process, of doing what they want and need to do, so Zarrilli's participant describes a change, a movement away from this self-congratulatory self-consciousness and knowing through knowledge as, he explains, 'eventually, you realise the training's just for yourself, and not for [impressing] other people' (2005). The participant's pursuit of their own needs, pleasures and desires in Zarrilli or Reeve's work embodies Cixous' portrayal and advocation of the feminine mode of 'knowing through pleasure' (1987: 2). Knowing through pleasure is epitomized by Eve's adherence to her desires and the subsequent sensorial joys of eating the apple (1991a: 151–2). Cixous, connecting Eve's position with that of Percival in the *Quest for the Holy Grail*, is definite that knowing through pleasure is a feminine, not female, state (1991a: 149). Indeed, just as Eve 'struggling to choose between the abstract, absent Law and the present concrete apple' opts for that immediate 'oral pleasure' (Rubin Suleiman 1991: xv), so Zarrilli's student now writes about the concrete 'small things that have actually helped me, rather than big, kind of philosophies' (2005). Demolishing the earlier romanticizing tendencies and attempts to win the favour of the audience or reader, this concrete writing is 'more personal and more casual ... and more sort of anecdotal, as well' (2005). Mirroring the daily application of the Gindler practice, the careful simplicity encouraged during feedback in Reeve, Schmale and Zarrilli's work, and, particularly, the precise observation and awareness that Gindler pushed students to achieve in their journal entries reflecting on their workshop physical tasks and exercises (Loukes 2006), the student now documents moments 'Like, I was whisking eggs the other day and I realised that if you're loose when you whisk eggs, [with] your hand, you do it better than (*he makes whisking motions with one hand in a furious and tense way*) if you're trying really hard, like that' (2005). This unglamorous, detail-focused documenting serves to thwart the potential selfish narcissicism that could result from doing what one wants and single-mindedly pursuing one's desires, whilst also demolishing any sense of grand mystifying narrative. At the same time, in the content and attitude of the writing, it adheres to Gindler and Schmale's emphasis on release of negative tension and constricted breathing through the deployment of 'greater economy of strength' and the pursuit of 'ease' within one's actions, leading over time to a 'strong feeling of inner strength, of effortlessness in accomplishment – in short, a heightened *joie de vivre*' (Gindler 1995: 10 and 14).

Achievement of such full blissful ease and effortlessness through knowing through pleasure provides a way for the participant-writer to be able to openly receive, release into, and thus follow, inhabit and express, the action and flow of the speed of the pleasurable experiences without constriction or fatigue, so 'Let [them]self go, let the writing flow, let [them]self steep; bathe, relax, become the river, let everything go, open up, unwind' (Cixous 1991a: 56–7). Thus, where such enjoyment is experienced across both the workshop and the page, the participant intensifies their ability to access and incite those tranquil pleasures, which, Gindler declares, 'fill us with well-being and vigor' (1995: 5).

Dance Archival Futures: Embodied Knowledge and the Digital Archive of Dance

Laura Griffiths

This chapter responds to recent innovation into the documenting and preservation of dance. Numerous digital platforms now exist which facilitate new insights into dance-making processes by the virtue of new technologies. Such innovation affords new insights into dance making and practice through digital tools that can reveal the multiple layers of information available. The aim here is to discuss how such new initiatives remain heavily dependent upon the physical body as a means for grounding the technology. The reliance upon video-based components still prevents digital manifestations from capturing the traditional context of space and collectivity associated with dance making and performance, they remain incomparable to the lived, experiential processes of the body.

For both the spectator and the performer, the multiple modes of dance experience are besieged with un-saveable, non-verbal, intangible elements that are prevented from becoming 'fixed' in space and time, and therefore resist the permanence of the archive. The body is frequently regarded as an archive (Pavis 2003; Lepecki 2013), a source of knowledge gathered, preserved and revisited concomitantly with its lived existence. This has given currency to the dancing body as an additional source of archival information and prompted a re-consideration of what dance preservation is. This chapter assesses the interplay between the digital archive and the knowledge manifest in conventional dance-making processes where knowledge is preserved in the body through lived experience. It draws upon examples from multiple digital dance archives and observation of the dance reconstruction processes of contemporary dance repertory company Phoenix Dance Theatre.

Ephemerality and the archive

The relationship between the archive and performance is negotiated widely and extensively across performance studies. Performance as a disappearing act is problematized in relation to the value that can be articulated post-performance based upon the 'remains' or 'detritus' of its fleeting existence (Phelan 1993; Reason 2006). Archival processes bind together methods of appraisal and organization to preserve the provenance of an archival material. As a grounding principle of the archival profession, provenance further illuminates the impact of performance's ephemerality upon its archives and also offers a context for re-considering digital archival practices in dance. Provenance recognizes that 'the significance of archival materials is heavily dependent on the context of their creation' (Hensen 1993: 67). The concept ensures that the origins (inclusive of original purpose and function) of archival materials are reflected in or 'should be directly related' to their arrangement and description with the archival repository (ibid.). In dance-making contexts, documenting has traditionally followed the performance event, insofar as it has highlighted 'product rather than process' (Melrose 2007: 75). Moreover, the archive typically 'intervenes not only after the production of the work, but after its evaluation (and selection) by others' (2007: 75). Melrose's argument that the documentation of performance-based practices traditionally augments the selective and hierarchical nature of the archive is placed with a view to realigning processes of documenting dance 'away from product and into decision-making processes' (2007: 6). Applications of this shift away from the dance 'product' (i.e. the final work) towards the knowledge constructed through and available within the process are increasingly evident in the digital archives of dance. These new modes respond to more recent recommendations that dance should be 'approached as a transformation process rather than as a fleeting act – contrary to the prevalent thesis about dance's disappearance' (Cvejic 2015).

In response to ephemerality, Diana Taylor recognizes that the logocentrism of the archive has led to a separation between the knowledge manifest in 'the knower' in time and/or space and how the repertoire is shaped by how people participate in its 'production and reproduction … by being part of the transmission' (2003:20). This perspective is key in recognizing that archival memory and its relationship with archival knowledge is especially problematic in relation to performance-making practices that are embodied. The slippages between Taylor's notion of the 'archive and the repertoire' can be aligned with notions of archival evidence as discussed by the historian R.G. Collingwood (1946). Collingwood observed that historical evidence exists as both 'potential' and 'actual' (1946: 280). 'Actual evidence' about a subject is all the extant statements about it and 'potential evidence' is that part of these statements which we decide to accept (ibid.). Whilst the archival discipline continues to evolve, such notions of 'evidence' highlight the traditional position of the archive as selective and hierarchical inasmuch as the archivist is no longer understood as a 'passive' keeper of 'documentary residue' but rather active shapers of … archival heritage (ibid.: 46). Collingwood's notion of 'potential evidence' can assist in revealing the knowledge manifest in the embodied, ineffable components of dance 'repertoire' as emerging sources of 'actual evidence'.

The digital and the spatio-temporal

Online dance archives have not only extended the accessibility of historic dance material but also impacted upon the way in which dance is made available in archival repositories. The Siobhan Davies *RePlay*[1] archive was the first notable online host for dance-based material and exemplifies how the 'raw materials' of dance making can be made visible in digital contexts (Whatley 2009). Such 'raw materials' take shape in the digital archive as material that stems from making processes, insofar as they have been produced simultaneously with aspects of the choreographic process, or that have been constructed to exemplify aspects of dance-making activities ordinarily absent from the archive. The *RePlay* archive contains 'scratch tapes' which 'document the thinking, experimenting, sketching stage of the dance-making process'. Whatley explains that this material 'became a rich resource for accessing the cognitive and corporeal stages through which the dancer develops a response to a choreographic task' (2014: 123). Such documents offer insight into how dancers 'learn to perform dances, and to understand them in a dancerly way' (McFee 2012: 8) in the sense that the conditions that surround choreographic creation, facilitate choreographic cognition and the formation of experiential, tacit knowledge. Central to such processes are the elements of 'time, space and motion', which provide the 'media for choreographic cognition' (McKechnie and Stevens 2009: 39). Studies into the neurocognition of dance practice also reveal the importance of bodily-space relations as 'Dancers often use spatial directions in an egocentric frame of reference, relative to their own body, as mental cues for supporting movement performance and for shaping movement quality' (Bläsing 2010: 93). Developments in digital archiving are extending the possibilities of 'archive' in their attempts to document aspects of choreographic cognition through new technologies. For example, bodily-space relations are being replicated through new techniques such as digital scores/annotations, bringing new meaning to sources of evidence and processes of determining archival value where dance is concerned.

The creation of online digital-scores was the focus of the *Motion Bank* project (2010–13). A key collaborator on this project was William Forsythe whose work *One Flat Thing, reproduced* (2006) was documented into 'screen-based visualization' (video, digital artwork, animation, and interactive graphics) that reveal interlocking systems of organization in the choreography (Forsythe 2014). This process informed the process of translating Forsythe's dance 'One Flat Thing' into new 'objects' and ways of visualizing dance in the online platform *Synchronous Objects*.[2] This system affords new ways of 'visualizing dance' through combining digital tools with scientific approaches for exploring choreographic cognition. Forsythe argues that choreography and dancing are two distinct and very different practices and as a result he expresses a particular interest in how the choreographic objective of dance work can be presented as a 'synchronic artefact for detailed inspection' in the same way that other less ephemeral art practices allow. Forsythe's investigations respond to the notion that choreographic ideas are traditionally materialized in 'a chain of bodily action with the moments of its performance being the first, last and only instances of a particular interpretation' (Forsythe, 2014). The emphasis upon ephemerality here serves as a reminder that the archive begins at the end. *Synchronous Objects* emphasizes choreographic structures and spatial relationships between bodies, along with the impetus for an individual dancer's movement. This approach is manifest in digital items such as 'cue scores', 'difference marks' and '3D alignment forms', to name a few. These tools make use of digital inscriptions, abstracted spatial maps and moving images of the cue networks and spatial relationships between dancers to dissect the choreography with a view to providing a visual language for 'physical thinking'.

These tools stem from the original work but emerge and exist in the digital in a new medium, i.e. that which is disembodied. Steve Dixon comments that the body in the virtual environment is no 'less authentic than the live' claiming that it is not 'disembodied from the performer' (2007: 125). Whilst the body is seen to remain as authentic regardless of the media through which it is positioned, the viscerality inherent in the actual experiences of bodies in live spatio-temporal exchanges that are imbued with 'dancerly' knowledge, still evades such mediums of representation. Moreover, fragmented and abstracted approaches to the choreographic 'totality' of a work simultaneously dematerialize the lived, kinaesthetic, experiential qualities of the movement content in its removal of the lived body as the vehicle through which such phenomena are originally enabled. Instead of demystifying the body as a central icon in digital modes of performance, digital documentations in dance, such as those discussed, arguably reinforce the centrality of the body as the medium through which choreographic objects can be deciphered and represented in more abstract, objective forms.

The question of how to effectively preserve embodied practice is continually subject to scrutiny and such technologies have yet to solve this problem. It has been implied that new digital practices aiming to capture the movements of the dancing body overlook the '... aspects of dance that it itself makes invisible, specifically the audience' and moreover, 'it invests in a cultural discourse that imagines dance as archaic and pre-discursive, thus claiming for itself a more direct and unmediated form of documentation' (Pearson 2012:109). This argument expands the possibilities of what is 'documentable' in dance and further destabilizes the tensions between traditional understandings of the archive as logo centric and the potential of the digital environment for embracing ephemeral practice. This implies that the digital further reinstates dance's invisibility from the archive because its structuring of dance through an archival methodology undermines the performing body that precedes the archive (ibid: 112). Moreover, the archival initiatives referred to earlier are imbued with 'a fear of ephemerality' as they exemplify the practice of documenting performance as being 'conducted at the centre of creation itself' whereby 'as you perform you must record, and as you create you must document' (Reason 2006: 84). This is evident in increasing insights into process that are accommodated via the digital. Varied formats of dance documents have also impacted upon the way within which the archive is interacted. The use of the web has afforded new modes of interactivity when accessing the archive, which has ultimately placed 'authority' upon the 'dance viewer'. Julia Hudson claims that as the digital space allows for public commentary and shared interpretations, the spectator 'can be part of the same discussions and meaning creation as the dance professional' (2012: 291). The idea of authority also translates to the Digital Dance Archives' repository,[3] which enables a 'visual search' in addition to conventional text-based searching. The software system developed using computer science enables users to search 'for shape, colour, gesture and patterns of movement in still and moving image materials' (Digital Dance Archives).

The collective experience as preservation

The examples referred to in the discussion presented so far expose how practices of digital dance archiving are looking to the dance-making process as a mechanism for offering a more complete record of dance works for posterity. In terms of the archival methodology, these modes of documenting dance practice still function as an act of transference and subsequently re-impose traditional archival functions of ascribing value to and appraising archival documents. Dance reconstruction practices are processes within which the archive is implicated as a source of historical evidence of dance's past. Notions of the body as an archive are enabling an extension of what can be constituted as 'archival knowledge' in a similar vein to that in digital repositories. Through my direct observations of the reconstructive practices of contemporary dance repertory company, Phoenix Dance Theatre, the archival value of experiential, embodied traces of the past can be explored. Processes of revising historic repertoire as undertaken by the company expose the necessary use of lived, embodied, spatio-temporal relationships that facilitate the re-staging of historic dance repertoire and therefore highlight their archival value. In particular, where dance vocabulary is recalled from the original experience of learning/devising, the company's methodology raises questions about the 'primary' evidence available across the archive and the body archive for such purposes. Foster explains that dances rely on 'knowledge [that is] bone-deep in the dancers' physicality – the product of years of dedicated practice to specific aesthetic and social values' that 'integrate the knowledge seamlessly into the fabric of the dance' and that 'the formation of physicality they have undertaken in learning to dance cannot be separated from other aspects of the performance' (2011: 215–16). McFee suggests this sense of integrated knowledge is typical of how 'learning and understanding occur within the context of a *company* whose members were trained in that manner of delivering the choreography' (2012: 8). Such understandings are cultivated through shared experiences which enable the 'production and reproduction of knowledge by the virtue of "being there" as a part of the transmission' (Taylor 2003: 20).

These ideas relate to how the dynamics and practices of a company can be said to inform the ability for dancers to work together to recall choreography. In discussion with various company members, it was frequently claimed that choreography was remembered through 'a *sense* of working together'. This relates to how Foster positions the body and dance as inclusive of the training and cultivation of a practice. The 'sense' of working together is capable of facilitating the recollection of embodied knowledge and is multi-layered as is evident where dancers from the first generation of the company's existence (1981–9) have sought to revive historic dance repertoire. The collective action of the dancers relates to what Alberto Melucci calls the 'process of collective identity' (1995). This sociological model upholds that 'a network of active relationships' affirms a group identity through 'participation in collective action . . . endowed with meaning . . .' which 'mobilize emotions' (ibid.: 45). This particular generation of dancers, working in 2012 were returning to their choreographic practice two decades later than the original time of creation. During the process, social and hierarchical relationships formed triggers to movement recollection and were fostered through spatial arrangements and ritualistic processes such as warming up the body and participating in regular dance technique classes. Within such processes, the group arranged themselves in familiar patterns, with the original choreographer standing in front of the other dancers and directing the collective action, for example.

Studies in dance and neurocognition indicate that immediate, internal experiences of spatial encounter are the enablers of action and reinstate that that 'thinking, understanding and learning' for the dancer begins with the body (Bläsing 2010: 76). Moreover, such bodily-space relations are layered with haptic and sensorial moments capable of functioning as mnemonic tools, just as archival materials have been considered as triggers or 'touchstones that lead to the recollection of past events' (Millar 2006: 114). A primary aid to remembering within Phoenix's revival process was through the sensation of touch. Memory aids were solicited through shared presence and sensory feedback received through touch inherent in the movement actions. In phenomenological terms, the body is understood as a 'temporal structure of experience' (Merleau-Ponty 1962: 97) and can be understood as deeply connected to the spatial environment within which it dwells. Within the milieu of bodily experience, concepts of lived experience such as these are suggestive of layers of knowledge that might be stored in the body archive. The spatial encounters between dancers facilitated retrieval of 'dancerly' knowledge. For example, when a group of dancers are rehearsing a movement phrase they will rely upon a relationship that exists ephemerally in the form of spontaneous moments of eye contact, sensory feedback, shadowing and negotiating the space collectively. Dancers also depend upon the sound of breath, sensing weight, touch and movement impetus to successfully work together physically in space. These ephemeral markers are exclusive to the lived moment of practice and are difficult to transcribe or interpret into conventional mediums of 'evidence' as per the archive's requirements. Such an observation reinforces the difference between the digital environment where elements of embodied practice are fragmented and represented in abstract visual imagery. Moreover, whilst these components are becoming more intertwined with the time of making and seek to unveil some of the tacit, embodied cognition inherent in dance practice, they still exist outside of the original context of the work and in a non-ephemeral mode. Therefore, in terms of archival provenance, the preservation of the original context through embodied practice is arguably more aligned with this principle than these digital manifestations of process.

The interplay of nostalgic memory within this milieu also adds another dynamic to the notion of the body archive. According to Leo Spitzer, reminders of past environments couched in sounds and sights can function as mnemonic devices (1999: 94). The revival work undertaken by Phoenix constructed familiar elements of sight, sounds and touch that enabled the reappearance of former roles and social ordering of the past choreographic experiences. The process enabled layers of knowledge triggered through emotion, empathy and a perceived spiritual connection across the group. In interview discussion, dancer Edward Lynch stated how 'a company can unify and come together ... not just in body and not just in movement but also in spirit ...' (2013). Lynch commented that such connections were made concrete during studio practice and fellow group member Villmore James likened the process to 'reliving ... memories in the studio' (2011). As Spitzer claims, nostalgic memory functions when 'recall and reaction act as a "connector" ... stimulating a variety of responses to the past' (1999: 96–7). Therefore, the simultaneity of shared spatio-temporal studio practice emerges as central to processes of recall and remembrance.

The future of the dance archive

Digitally-based archival documents as referred to in this chapter expose new layers of knowledge through synonymously intervening with process and illustrate how the gap between knowledge and the 'knower' might be reduced. However, translating knowledge inherent in process-based work into digital documents arguably perpetuates the archival tradition of 'fixing' and locking down mediated knowledge. These digitally enhanced documents often emphasize embodied cognition or 'physical thinking' through presenting the function of such knowledge as it is manifest in the final 'product'.

The dancing body, as lived phenomena is the point of acquisition for movement and choreographic process. As the examples of work undertaken by Phoenix illustrate, the body as a storehouse intertwines embodied, spatial, collective and memorial knowledge unlocking potential evidence that has not yet succumbed to the archive as a result of its ephemerality.

The lived practices facilitate the re-emergence of contextual information through a transformative process that secures evidence of historic dance practice. This tacitly invisible, non-verbal and ineffable information potentially contributes new archival provenances for dance.

Documenting Dance: Tools, Frameworks and Digital Transformation

Sarah Whatley

Dance is a complex, three-dimensional expression of the human body and for this reason, artists and scholars have been challenged to find modes of 'capture' that preserve and provide access to dance long after the live event. The recurrent theme that the 'materiality of dance is inextricably bound up with its own immaterial dimension'[1] has produced an ongoing tension between dance and the documents that the dance might produce. But this tension has produced some imaginative responses, often from dance scholars and choreographers working together. Their experiments with notation, scores and more recently with digital technologies have provided new ways to document and archive dance, and to access the many processes involved in the production of dance. This chapter will survey methods that have been developed over time attempt to document dance, noting the extent to which they have become standardized and modified, or adapted to suit different dance practices. Further, it will examine how the introduction of new tools and frameworks has transformed the approach to documenting dance. Within this context, discussion will also focus on the contribution that digital technologies have had on how dancers document their work and share their making process, and the impact this has had on their creative strategies and in turn, the new ways in which audiences experience dance and engage with the documents that are generated through the dance. With reference to digital dance tools that have offered new ways to conceptualize dance, the chapter will explore how these resources have brought dance artists and researchers together to explore new modes of documenting dance in physical and virtual spaces.

Historic practices: iconography, notation and scoring dance

The rich ways in which dance has been documented through symbols, marks, on staves and in idiosyncratic diagrams, demonstrate how mapping the dance to record, preserve or reconstruct dance has been a continual concern over the centuries. Many documents are already multimodal, combining words, pictures and different materials. Each document also tells us something about the context of the dance, the dancers or dancing, and may communicate something about those who document. Attempts to devise a dance iconography have also seen a variety of notation systems emerge and then often disappear over time, beginning as early as the fourth century with a form of notation that documented the Tamil *bharatnatyam*. In general, dance notation systems have been designed in response to need and as required by a particular field or function, so operate within a specific context. In these processes of bodily inscription we can see what dance theorist Elizabeth Dempster observes, that some stories are told and some bodies are silenced.[2] Natalie Lehoux, a scholar of dance notation, assesses this as a 'demand-driven response',[3] which can be seen exemplified by the characteristics of the Beauchamps-Feuillet notation system, designed specifically to record the ornate style of baroque dancing commissioned by French king, Louis XIV. This was a time of supreme monarchic control. Susan Leigh Foster provides a vivid description of this time and its impact on the relationship between dance and writing, observing that '[a]ll social classes, but especially aristocrats, rely on systems of corporeal signification to convey status and identity'[4] and that '[b]oth forms of inscription circulate within a rigidly fixed social and political hierarchy'.[5] With a definite purpose for its creation, the exclusive nature of this highly stylized form of notation renders itself useful only to this precise context. Fast-forward to the beginning of the twentieth century and choreographers during the Diaghilev period (1909–29) began experimenting with notation methods. Michel Fokine made adaptations to the Stepanov notation method whilst Vaslav Nijinski created his own notation system to record his first ballet for Diaghilev in 1912, *L'après Midi D'un Faune*. (The score was subsequently deciphered and translated into Labanotation in the late 1980s by notation experts Ann Hutchinson-Guest and Claudia Jeschke.[6]) A short time later, the dance artist and theorist Rudolph Laban (1879–1958) established a more sequential, linear symbolic language for analyzing and documenting dance, creating 'Labanotation' – a notation system that was devised as a way to track, record and analyze movement patterns and has been valuable for many movement analysts not only in dance but also in many other practices and subject domains, including theatre, sports and physical therapies.

Whereas the use of stick figure systems might provide a more pictorial impression of motion in how they resemble the human form, Laban's system is built on abstract symbols that are organized to represent body action, direction, time and spatial properties so whilst rigorous in their description they are conceptually more difficult to comprehend. Consequently, even this system is not widely used and rarely used by the choreographer herself, so presents different kinds of questions about its validity, and claim for universality, rooted as it is within the Western theatre tradition, and more specifically European modern dance. Nonetheless, dance notation systems, whilst largely dependent on professional notators, are valuable for providing 'the capacity to archive and preserve historical dance works, to foster the development of contemporary works and to contribute to a richer dance heritage'.[7]

All are an attempt to provide a dance literacy and a legacy for our dance culture, showing how dance notation systems are striving for some kind of objectivity even if, as notation expert Victoria Watts notes, dance notation does much more than document a particular choreographic work. She points out that 'each score contains a record of the movement under observation and also a trace of how the notator thought about and understood what she observed'.[8] So whilst dance notations may reveal the limitations of writing, these marks on the page mediate the process of transformation and as interdisciplinary design expert Alan Blackwell observes: 'We are familiar to the point of unconsciousness with the nature and function of such notations as a communicative score, acting as surrogate when the designer is no longer present, and allowing performers or manufacturers to interpret a (more or less) authorized work'.[9]

Methods for documenting dance, or scripting dance as a form of writing in, through and of the body have thus taken many forms and have tried in various ways to capture and leave a legible trace of dance's kinetic and aesthetic properties. The purpose of these traces is similarly varied. Dance notation systems, whether those that are in more common usage, such as Labanotation, Benesh (used predominantly to record and document the ballet repertoire), Eshkol-Wachman (used now more in scientific research), or a handful of others that are less widely practiced, remain a valuable method for documenting dance. The purpose of these more codified methods is primarily to preserve the dance for analysis or revival or reconstruction, using symbols that abstract the moving body into marks on a page (or screen),[10] enhancing dance's value as it enters our records of cultural heritage. But where methods are more idiosyncratic then the intention and purpose of the document might be more personal. They may follow highly individualized methods, incorporating sketches, words, drawings as well as personalized symbols, which often attempt to capture and transmit something of the felt experience of the dance as much as the spatial, temporal and dynamic properties.

Such a varied corpus of documents reflects the richness of dance but also emphasizes the challenge in capturing this multidimensional, embodied and expressive practice in a way that adequately safeguards its future. The motivation for documenting is as varied as its purpose. Dancers and choreographers work on and through the body, rarely creating any 'hard copy' document of the dance as it is formed and performed. Unlike composers, playwrights and painters, who make their creation tangible in physical form as it is made (through musical score, written text, artefact etc.), the dancer often relies on someone else to document and produce a record of the dance at the time of making. The dancer/choreographer is often less concerned (or has less resource) for documenting the work once made although it is common practice to collect photographs, videos, sketches, personal texts and other residues of the live event as 'proof' of its existence even if it cannot substitute for the lived experience – and is not principally to preserve the work for the purposes of reconstruction at another time. But for archivists and dance historians, what is left behind in the form of a document is highly valuable. Not only is the document evidence that the dance existed, the process of documentation may become a new area of scholarly and artistic practice, a 'new cultural technique'[11] that relies on careful methods of collection and curation.

Documents and documentation

As different strategies for documenting dance continue to be explored it seems that finding a standardized approach that is adequate for all dance forms and practices is unlikely. Whilst notation, where it exists for some dance works might be recognized as a reasonably accurate document of the dance and for identifying and preserving dance,[12] there are relatively few notated scores for any dances beyond the mainstream large-scale repertory dance companies. Smaller touring companies and independent dancers are more likely to rely on more personalized approaches to documenting their dances. Dances that are part of an oral traditional and exist as intangible practices, or dances that are designed to be 'open works',[13] intentionally variable from one performance to the next, may produce a score as document but this on its own may not be regarded as sufficient for reconstruction or preservation even if the most 'appropriate' record of a dance work. Additional documents may be produced and collected (images, text, etc.) so together provide a more extensive set of documents pertaining to a work or works but the dance itself may remain elusive, slipping through and between these disparate objects to resist a complete capture of the work. Moreover, for dance works that are immersive, interactive, site-specific or in some other way highly dependent on a particular spatial/geographical/temporal context then any document that emerges through its creation and performance is likely to be partial at best.

Whilst there is not space to discuss the myriad forms of dance production and the numerous records they have produced, all of these contributions and innovations also raise questions about what *is* the dance document, and what documentation strategies, if any, emerge that are particular to dance or which draw on other methods.[14] The distinction between the document and documentation is particularly interesting in the context of dance because of the challenge of claiming that the ephemeral event is in itself a document rather than (or in addition to) the translation or transformation from an embodied, live event to a static representation/object.

The debate about the ontological status and nature of the document is raised by those working in Information Management and Library Studies who are concerned with collecting, curating, organizing and making documents accessible. The word 'document' summons up a physical object if not a printed text, even though Paul Otlet (1868–1944) challenged this narrow view by citing a range of other forms of the document (such as sculptures) as 'anything that is the product of human thought' and 'bearing traces of human activity'.[15] Clearly dance and its products fit into this definition. Another information management theorist, Michael Buckland looks back to Briet's much praised essay[16] and seems to stand by her definition of a document as intentionally an object and indexed in relation to others, but notes that if the document refers to 'organised physical evidence'[17] then this must perhaps include events, processes, objects, images as well as texts.[18] However, a common view is that the document is as a minimum also associated with fixity. Fixing the dance in material form (film, image, score, notation etc.) means that the document is what lasts and accrues value as a fact or true representation of something otherwise immaterial. As dance documents have proliferated in a variety of forms, one feature or characteristic of many of these new documents is that they attempt to retain this quality of ephemerality and deliberately create multiple versions and resist fixing in a single authoritative form.

Buckland draws attention to the problematic of defining a digital document 'unless we remember the path of reasoning underlying the largely forgotten discussions of Otlet's objects and Briet's antelope'.[19] But Otlet and Briet could not have imagined the impact of digital forms on documentation nor of dance and ephemeral practices entering the debate and asking what new kinds of documents the metaphysical properties of dance might generate. Moreover, in the digital sphere, some versions of the dance document might only emerge through the user's interaction with it, otherwise existing only in digital code rather than in the image/text/video that it generates. This debate is important as methods continue to be developed, not least because of the opportunities afforded by digital technologies, which encourage new and innovative approaches to documenting dance.

Documenting dance: from analogue to digital methods

For the reasons outlined, dance has struggled to find a robust presence within our records of cultural heritage. There is a paucity of filmed records that predate the digital age and criticism continues that dance lacks a robust and 'universally' understood method of notation so dance continues to rely heavily on embodied memory and the passing of the material of dance through the dancing bodies of subsequent generations. However, the analogue records that have been collected speak to and resonate with our present day efforts and it is a number of recent dance projects that have harnessed digital code to document dance in the form of digital scores (scores which are sometimes created after, sometimes before, or alongside the dance), digital archives and other digital objects. The dancer or choreographer, working in collaboration with researchers and other discipline experts, creating another form of artistic output but which also creates some tangible record of an ephemeral form even if not intended for preservation or reconstruction, often initiates these digital objects. Such documents have created valuable dance resources 'for understanding human perception, complex systems of interaction, and moving ideas'.[20]

Choreographer William Forsythe, who has initiated a number of projects that have used digital technologies for inscribing, recording and transmitting his dance practice, sets out in his essay on 'Choreographic Objects' that 'it becomes conceivable that the ideas now seen as bound to a sentient expression are able to exist in another durable, intelligible state'.[21] These digital dance objects find ways to illuminate and access dance in new ways and frequently act as a catalyst for artistic creation.[22] In other words, as deLahunta, claims, 'the page becomes an interactive object inextricably linked with the processes of dance making.'[23] Paradoxically, the proliferation of affordable digital recording devices and the ease of sharing digital content means that we are now actually generating more documents of dance than ever before. The growth of this activity and the concurrent increasing interest in what it means to document dance, and the questions around documentation in the process of preservation and transmission of dance, has been the subject of several publications and special issues of academic journals in recent times.

The relationship between methods of dance preservation, reconstruction and documentation first gained momentum around the turn of the millennium with the publication of a significant collection of writings on this theme that emerged out of a conference at the University of Roehampton, UK, in 1997: *Preservation Politics: Dance Revived, Reconstructed, Remade.*[24] The chapters cover topics that had hitherto not been discussed or shared in this way – spanning traditional notation methods, and papers that questioned the ontological nature of dance. This volume was followed by several dance revival and reconstruction projects as an act of dance preservation (for example, Martin Nachbar's 2008 production 'Urheben Aufheben' and Richard Move's return to several Martha Graham works in the 1990s[25]) and led to dance sociologist Helen Thomas to describe what we witnessed at the end of the twentieth century as a 'minor industry in dance preservation.'[26] What was emerging was a parallel process of reaching back to recover and remake dances from the past with a desire to use a variety of documenting processes to generate new dances for the present day.

Jordan's collection appeared before digital technologies had begun to have much impact on the question of how to document dance. But that was soon to change. Merce Cunningham had begun to experiment with the computer as a tool for creating choreography[27] so it was less about recording or documenting dance, but in 1999 Forsythe released *Improvisation Technologies: A Tool for the Analytical Dance Eye* as a training instrument for his dancers and the first use of computer-augmented representation of choreographic structuring. Made originally for CD-ROM it provided an interactive tool for accessing his own approach to creating movement. The tool was 'intended to facilitate exploration of movement organization principles of individual bodies'.[28] Its influence on subsequent methods for documenting dance was significant. Forsythe's tool simultaneously demonstrated that dance could be documented in ways that retained the particular choreographic aesthetic and sensibility of the artist in an immediate and highly visual way, and showed the immense potential for interactive and multi-media platforms to participate in developing highly creative ways to document dance.

As technology has evolved more projects have developed in the wake of Forsythe's that are often collaborations between artists, researchers and technology experts, and which have experimented with new and playful methods for documenting dance. For example, the TKB web-based archive project led by Carla Fernandes and her team at the New University of Lisbon attempted to 'create a new paradigm for the documentation of performing arts'.[29] Following an extended period of working collaboratively with Portuguese-based choreographers Rui Horta and Stephan Jurgens, Fernandes described how for Jurgens, '[c]ollaborating on developing and testing the design of the TKB Creation-Tool was particularly interesting for him, as multimodal video annotation is presently the most efficient way to support and document the workflow of the artists' processes in this field'.[30] The project combined the experience and 'insights of contemporary creators with scientific theories from cognitive linguistics and new media studies in order to come to an original model of visualization and dissemination of performing arts productions'.[31]

The documents that are now emerging through the creation and production of dance thus reveal more about the thinking and methods of all those involved in dance. Moreover, many documents in both analogue and digital form aim to reveal 'hidden aspects' of dance creation through scores and graphic visualizations that aim to transmit and communicate the dynamic aspects of dance creation and performance. Consequently, as the mode of the dance document has become more experimental and sophisticated (sometimes drawing on established notation methods) precisely *what* was documented also evolved. A desire and enthusiasm for documenting dance, often directly at the time of the dance being created rather than only when the dance was performed, has led to a range of process documents, recording the work of the whole creative team involved in producing dance (composers/designers etc.). For example, British choreographer Siobhan Davies created an online dance documentation project, *Side-by-Side* (2012) in which she invited two artists; dance artist Laila Diallo and craft artist, Helen Carnac to work alongside each other to investigate the process of working together over a six-week residency. Described as 'an investigation into making'[32] that had no finished product, the two artists documented their creative process through image, text, film and object, which was curated for a web-based archive of process documents. What is more usually a private and unseen stage in the process of dance making was what became the 'work' so blurring the distinction between the dance 'work' and the documents that record the 'work'. Moreover, by making public the documents in a form that is carefully curated and designed, the site reveals its approach to collecting and organizing the documents, in effect revealing a documentation strategy that foregrounds 'process', not least because the site continued to change as the process unfolded, replacing rather than archiving historical process documents.

Side-by-Side followed a project I led in collaboration with Davies, *Siobhan Davies RePlay* (*RePlay*); a digital archive of Davies's choreography.[33] It was the first of its kind in terms of providing a digital archive of a single choreographer's output up until that point, and as it turns out, on into the future. As an online dance resource, fully searchable and including some relatively simple tools, such as a digital scrapbook, users can see all the media related to any one production, see material that would otherwise be inaccessible, such as rehearsal tapes, and have access to some of the creative processes towards making some of the works including videos, image, text and a significant range of documents that record the artists' making process. One purpose of the archive was to create an important contribution to dance documentation, by 'find[ing] ways to allow those who have not had a direct experience with the performance to get as close as possible to the essential aspects of the experience.'[34]

We also experimented with accumulating a range of materials to create prototype visualizations of two different choreographies, *Bird Song* (2004) and *In Plain Clothes* (2006). We named them 'Kitchens', as a reference to gathering the 'ingredients' of a work, the traces of the making process, and through a designed interface, providing access to the layers of the choreographic process, to show how the work is 'cooked'. Each experimented with how graphic scores, combining material from the dancers, designers and many others involved in creating the dance, could offer a visual representation of each dance, as an alternative method for documenting dance.

RePlay is one of several dance projects that have responded to the digital turn by experimenting with new ways to represent dance content through using computational processes, interactive technologies and digital media to offer a systematic approach to dance documentation. Some are focused particularly on the artist's own making and thinking process. Emerging around the same time as *RePlay*, William Forsythe's *Synchronous Objects*, Emio Greco Pieter Sholten's *Capturing Intention* project, and Wayne McGregor's *Choreographic Language Agent* all experimented with documenting dance in various forms and formats. Each takes a different approach so the 'object' or resource that is created is particular to the artist, project and the production team. So whilst Forsythe's *Synchronous Objects* is a highly sophisticated website that provides a range of documents that respond in visual form to a single dance (*One Flat Thing, reproduced*) to illuminate its complex organizational structures, in particular that of 'counterpoint', *Capturing Intention* has produced a multimedia tool, which incorporates Labanotation and now a system of 'pre-choreographics' to enhance engagement with Greco's movement language.

New projects combining analogue and digital methods for documenting dance have since been realized, including, Steve Paxton's *Material for the Spine*, offering a glimpse into Paxton's pedagogy and approach to improvisation, *A Choreographer's Score* (Anne Teresa de Keersmaeker) and Forsythe's *Motion Bank* project. Led by Scott deLahunta, *Motion Bank* builds on *Synchronous Objects* by producing an on-line publication of a bank of digital dance scores developed with the dance artists Deborah Hay, Jonathan Burrows and Matteo Fargion, Bebe Miller, and Thomas Hauert working in conjunction with interaction designers, programmers and computer scientists. The artists were 'invited on the basis of their distinctive, articulate and diverse approaches to creating dance works'.[35]

The aim of the project was to 'explore how digital technology can be uniquely applied to the challenge of documenting, analysing, notating and presenting dance'[36] by archiving the choreographers' conceptual approaches along with video recordings and three-dimensional data documenting the performances and the depictions created by the designers. Each digital score reflects the particular aesthetic and choreographic characteristics of the artist so each provides a unique approach to recording and visualizing the dance. The technology experts described their work as involving 'videoing the dancer's positions, movements and shapes from different angles simultaneously.

As a result, our visual computing methods will help to document and preserve dance and choreography three-dimensionally and offer new impulses to the development of and access to digital content'.[37]

Writing the dance: documenting the digital

What links these aforementioned projects is a desire to experiment with methods to promote the knowledge that resides within dance and which through an accretion of materials in various documented forms could support increased access to dance, particularly when using digital technologies and platforms. Their outcomes and reflections on them have themselves been documented in a number of edited collections, including those that focus on archiving performance,[38] dance preservation[39] and several themed journal issues that have all drawn on a wide theoretical and conceptual framework for deepening thought about documenting, preserving and archiving dance. Many writings recall and interrogate theories that have had wide impact within the performance and dance studies communities[40] and test the extent to which their highly influential claims on the interdependency between performance and documentation and 'what it means to see performance through its documentation'[41] hold true in the field of dance.

The issue of RTRSRCH entitled <*Notation*> included contributions that 'address topics that share features with notation-related practices often at the friction point between artistic intention and embodied knowledge: presence and cultural memory'.[42] Two issues of the *International Journal of Performance Arts and Digital Media* (9: 1 and 10: 1) continue this theme by specifically focusing on modes of documenting performance and documentation strategies more widely. In the first of these, writing ranges across an in-depth survey and analysis of notation systems (Lehoux), to reflections on projects that have explored how performance transforms through the transition from analogue to digital modes (Bermudez Pascual; Whatley), to contributions, some from working artists, that document more experimental approaches to scoring dance (Gourfink; Brown, Niemetz, Medlin, Scoones; Durning and Waterhouse). These 'artist pages' are introduced through a reflective piece from Johannes Birringer who remarks upon the 'concerted efforts that are under way to document, analyze, display and propel choreographic processes and languages to a much wider audience, thus also making available a diverse range of unique methods of scoring, recording, teaching and conceptualizing movement within an expanding international culture of performance and mediated arts (with the role of online dance platforms and archives gaining an ever greater significance)'.[43] By including several highly visual and score-like contributions the aims was to promote a variety of approaches that combined text and image in playful ways to reflect how 'the potential of artist-initiated projects comes from the drive to invent, or attempt invention, of ways to appropriately express thinking and concepts discoverable in a particular artwork or in the principles of a certain creative process'.[44] These experiments also responded to Susan Leigh Foster's question posed in the mid-1990s though still pertinent today, 'What if the body of the text is a dancing body, a choreographed body?'[45]

Van Saaze and Dekker's article reflects on their experience of building a documentation model designed for recording the performance *Extra Dry* by Dutch-based dance company Emio Greco PC.[46] Explaining that the documentation model has multiple functions and meanings for different parties, they draw on social theory to describe the model as resembling a 'boundary object'; 'an object or construct that is flexible enough to enable collaboration between heterogeneous disciplines or groups'.[47] They further argue that the strength of the model is in its flexibility and how it is able to draw together 'different sets of knowledge emerging from various disciplines'.[48] This is particularly valuable for practitioners and scholars when considering that many projects concerned with documenting dance involve multidisciplinary teams, and focus as much on working processes as the performance itself. Taken as a whole, the contributions to this journal move 'between questions about what happens before live performance (pre-performance), to what happens after (mediating its preservation), [which] means that a certain temporal fluidity is intrinsic to all of the projects discussed'.[49]

The second issue, *Interdisciplinary Approaches to Documenting Performance* is broader in scope than focusing only on dance but the themes covered are apposite. In particular, Sant makes the point in his editorial that '[w]e need to question the relegation of the cultural significance of performance documentation or the activity of documenting performance as secondary to the artists' works'.[50] He further points out that 'documentation is not about the contents or qualities of a document but the making, preservation and potential reuse of the document – from a noun associated with documentary evidence to a verb describing the act of creating and collection documents'.[51] This is a welcome reminder that dance documentation is not simply the collective noun for 'document' but should be a thoughtful, creative process. Several contributions also draw attention to web archives and the increasing role of technology in not only documenting performance but in providing a new platform that creates the performance.

A more recent publication, *On An/Notations*, a special issue of *Performance Research* (2015), picks up some of these same themes with a focus on the role of annotation and its relationship with notating and archiving performance. Many papers at least mention if not chart the evolution of dance notation systems (Gallier; Blades) to offer a consideration of the importance of scores and archives in how artists and researchers create, recreate and/or document dance (Hansen with House; Crocker, Gansterer and Greil). For example, Gallier's paper 'Notating for an Audience' advocates for choreographic scores to be available for spectators to decipher for themselves to awaken choreographic thinking.[52] Three choreographic scores[53] provide a focus for Hetty Blades' paper that examines the connections between 'notation' and 'annotation'. Blades argues that whilst notation systems 'such as Labanotation are composed from the position of the dancer ... the annotator inscribes on top of, as opposed to in the place of, the dancing body'.[54] She concludes that some annotations 'concentrate on relations and space, opening up possibilities for highlighting that is not perceptible in performance or recording, such as traces and internal experiences'[55] suggesting that annotation is a valuable mode of documenting what other approaches might overlook.

Clarissa Bardiott discusses an open-source digital environment for performing arts that she has developed, *ReKall*, that is designed to fulfill two aims; 'helping artists to document their works so that they can restage them, at the same time compensating for the obsolescence of digital technology; and helping researchers study the genesis and creation of stage productions in the context of natively digital documents and Large Data'.[56] The environment leads to Bardiott arguing for denotation ('distant reading') to follow notation and annotation remarking that '[d]istant reading steps away from the document itself, and this makes it possible to identify models and motifs and relationships between them when considering a very large corpus of documents'.[57]

Contemporary strategies and methods for documenting dance

Given the range and diversity of dance and the documents that the dance produces, it is not straightforward to categorize these varying approaches. Neither do they point towards a single or even several identifiable documentation strategies. As technology advances and dance draws on the expertise from other disciplinary practices, the methods continue to expand. However, what links all these approaches is a commitment to evolve processes that reflect if not capture the particular properties and characteristics of an artist's work, or that of a community of dance practitioners. With this range in mind, and broadly speaking, documentation as a management process might take the form of notations, experimental texts, digital scores and visualizations, or archives. Clearly, these categories often overlap; notations and scores may form the basis of experimental texts, and archives may comprise notations, digital scores and visualizations (etc.) but grouping may provide the basis for thinking about how they give rise to particular documentation strategies and may contribute to thinking more broadly about the value of documentation as a systematic or standard process in relation to dance.

In addition to established notations, which attempt to document features at a micro and macro level, there are more idiosyncratic modes of dance notation. For example, dance practitioner Nancy Stark-Smith's 'Underscore' is a framework, containing more than twenty phases, each with a name and graphic symbol, for practising and researching dance improvisation, and particularly contact improvisation. The symbols take the form of glyphs, unique to the 'Underscore', providing a visual guide to that stage (for example, 'arriving energetically', 'preambulation' and 'pow-wow'). It is a distinctive notation, particular to her approach to improvisation and practised by the contact improvisation community worldwide.[58]

The texts that have been included in the journals mentioned earlier are part of a growing number of experimental texts that are written and designed by the dancer her/himself, often multimodal in form that decentralizes the text itself by foregrounding the artist's own methods of documenting performance. The intention is to explore ways to document (artistic) practice. The emphasis is thus not on the text *per se* but the extent to which the text provides access to evidence of the performance, and the relationship between writing and moving.[59]

Digital scores and visualizations record all or part of the dance in visual form and include those discussed earlier, such as *Synchronous Objects, Motion Bank,* and the 'kitchens' in *RePlay*. But it can be extended to the outputs of motion tracking technology, such as motion capture, which can be a powerful tool for analyzing human movement but in dance has been used more productively as a tool for creating visualizations as artistic output than as a tool for documenting dance. Visualizations provide an abstraction and transformation of the dance, often designed to reveal particular aspects of the dance so more interpretive than representative of the dance. Scores may have open features and focus more on the macro level, or might attempt to score at a more micro level, concentrating on particular selected features of the dance (the duration, structure, etc.) for example, the focus on cueing in the digital scores of *Synchronous Objects*).

In simple terms, archives are an organized collection of documents. Dance archives might include image, audiovisual content, text and much more. Recent experiments with archiving dance within digital environments have produced imaginative ways to collect, curate, organize and visualize the documents within the archive. New forms of digital dance inscriptions can also reconfigure the traditional concept of the archive. Whilst dance artists often find the notion of creating an archive seductive, many also resist the idea of fixing their history in a form other than in the principal medium of dance; the body. More single artist archives are emerging (e.g. The Digital Pina Bausch Archive)[60] whilst other digital repositories collect together several archives (e.g. Digital Dance Archives, Numeridanse.tv).[61]

Conclusion

This chapter has attempted to provide an overview of some of the ways in which choreographers, dancers, researchers, designers and technology experts, frequently working together, have developed methods to document dance. Many of the examples that have been referred to offer new ways to document and share the *process* of making dance, not only of the dance in performance. As new initiatives in the documentation of dance, they intentionally traverse analogue, digital and embodied methods of transmission and offer new ways to think about how dance is visualized, remembered, interpreted and transformed.

Notation systems remain an important method and indeed some more recent projects have integrated established notation systems to enrich digital dance resources, potentially increasing the value of notation as a tool for documenting dance. Digital technologies continue to have a significant impact on documentation strategies and means that dance is beginning to generate more records for the benefit of future generations. But these records are not necessarily collected systematically due to what Laura Molloy has identified as a lack of digital curation (including digital preservation) awareness amongst (a small sample of) performance and live arts practitioners working outside institutional contexts.[62] Added to this is the fragility of digital technology, coupled with the unpredictability of technological change and the inevitable obsolescence of digital formats, which means that these records may be more vulnerable than their analogue counterparts.

As in other performance and live art disciplines, there are ongoing debates about the relationship between performance and its documentation. On the one hand, the ontological nature of dance as an ephemeral, disappearing art form leads some to resist any form of documentation and criticize notation and other documents that emerge out of the dance as fixing what is a fluid form that cannot, or should not be 'pinned down'. However, as Van Saaze and Dekker point out, an opposite view is also held by some, whereby 'documentation is heralded as a potential redeemer of performance's disappearance. Here documentation is considered as a way out of performance's ephemeral character and embraced as a means to counter transience and safeguard repertoire for the future'.[63] But questions remain about *what* should be documented and preserved, who is responsible for its preservation and what is the purpose and impact of preservation on artists, institutions and cultural organizations.

But there is progress. More documents are being created in more imaginative ways that attempt to get closer to the specificity of the individual dance or dancer, whilst offering models that might be more widely applied. But we need to find ways to take care of these documents, to collect, organize and store in robust and well-managed ways whilst making them available, long into the future for the benefit of successive generations of practitioners and scholars.

Notes

Chapter 1

1 See more at: http://www.dcc.ac.uk/digital-curation/what-digital-curation
2 Detailed explanation of the Digital Curation Centre's Curation Lifecycle Model is available at http://www.dcc.ac.uk/resources/curation-lifecycle-model
3 See http://www.jisc.ac.uk/whatwedo/programmes/mrd/rdmtrain/cairo.aspx
4 Described at http://www.vads.ac.uk/kaptur/about.html
[All entries accessed 21 July 2015].

Part One: Contexts for Documenting Performance

1 For the sake of transparency, I should disclose the fact that I am an active Wikimedian: I have been a registered/volunteer Wikipedia editor since 2010. Between 2013 and 2015 I was also employed as the education programme organizer by Wikimedia UK, a registered charity that supports and promotes Wikipedia and the other Wikimedia projects, and the volunteers who write, edit and curate the content of the projects.
2 Wikidata is a free linked database with millions of data items that anyone can edit. In 2016, Wikidata held over 18 million data items and was already becoming one of the world's largest repositories of basic data that can be read by both humans and machines. All stuctured data held in this database is available under a Creative Commons CC0 licence at http://www.wikidata.org.
3 Wikimedia Commons is a database of over 31 million freely useable media files to which anyone can contribute. All the files are kept under a Creative Commons-Attribution-Share Alike license at http://commons.wikimedia.org. Images, videos and sound files on Wikipedia are housed in this database.

4   A basic understanding of the various similarities and differences between copyright (dealt with by Jeanine Rizzo in chapter 4) and public copyright licences such as the Creative Commons licenses is very useful. See also https://creativecommons.org/licenses/ for detailed explanation on Creative Commons licenses. Such licences are not intended to provide free content but rather content that can be used freely. The distinction here may seem subtle but it pertains mainly to the idea that knowledge is more useful if it is more readily accessible to more people who may find some use or other for it.

5   This is one of Briet's central examples in *What is Documentation?*

Chapter 2

1   Susan Crane (ed.), *Museums and Memory*, Redwood City: Stanford University Press, 2000, p. 2.

2   Crane, Susan, *Ibid.*, p. 1.

3   Mary Carruthers, *The Book of Memory: a study of memory in medieval culture,* Cambridge: Cambridge University Press, 1990, p. 16.

4   Richard Schechner, *Performance Studies: an introduction*, London and New York: Routledge, 2006, p. 225.

5   Samuel Beckett cited by Alvarez, José Carlos, '25 anos de Museu Nacional do Teatro: do sonho, da memória e do efémero', in Claudia Figueiredo (ed.), *Museologia.pt*, n°4, Lisboa: IMC, 2010, p. 46.

6   George Banu, cited in José Carlos Alvarez (ed.), *Documentation des Arts du Spectacle dans une société en mutation – Documentation/ Actes*, Lisboa: SIBMAS, 1994, p. 22.

7   José Oliveira Barata cited in Alvarez, *Op. Cit.,* p. 50.

8   Osório Mateus cited in Alvarez, *Op. Cit.,* p. 56.

9   Joan Gibbons, *Contemporary Art and Memory: images of recollection and remembrance*, London and New York: I.B. Tauris, 2007, p. 118.

10 Stephen Bann, *The Clothing of Clio*, Cambridge: Cambridge University Press, 1984, p. 35.

11 Diana Taylor, *The Archive and the Repertoire: performing cultural memory in the Americas,* Durham and London: Duke University Press, 2003, pp. 19–20.

12 Umberto Eco, *A Definição da Arte*, [s.l.], U. Mursia & C., 1968, p. 226.

13 Diana Taylor, *Op. Cit.*, p. 20.

14 From the author's own notes taken during the ICOM project.

15 Emile Zola in Paulo Filipe Monteiro, *Drama & Comunicação*, Coimbra: Imprensa Universitária de Coimbra, 2010, p. 271.

16 Alfred Jarry in Paulo Filipe Monteiro, *Op. Cit.*, p. 271.

17 Maria Augusta Babo, 'Do corpo protésico ao corpo híbrido', in Maria Lucília Marcos, Cascais, António Fernando (org), *Revista de Comunicação e Linguagens – Corpo, Técnica, Sujectividades*, Lisboa: FCSH-UNL, 2004, p. 26.

18 Marita Sturken, *Tangled Memories: the Vietnam war, the AIDS epidemic and the politics of remembering*, Los Angeles: University of California Press, 1997, p. 12.

Chapter 3

1 http://enicpa.info/

2 http://www.sibmas.org/

3 http://www.teatro.es

4 http://www.digitaltheatre.com

5 http://www.dance-archives.ac.uk

6 http://www.europeana.eu/portal/

7 http://icom.museum

8 http://www.glopac.org

9 http://dublincore.org/

10 http://www.amico.org/AMICOlibrary/dataDictionary.html

11 http://www.getty.edu/research/publications/electronic_publications/cdwa/

12 https://www.loc.gov/standards/vracore/

13 http://www.eclap.eu

[All entries accessed 21 July 2015].

Chapter 4

1 'Copyleft is a strategy of utilising copyright law to pursue the policy goal of fostering and encouraging the equal and inalienable right to copy,

share, modify and improve creative works of authorship. Copyleft (as a general term) describes any method that utilizes the copyright system to achieve the aforementioned goal. Copyleft as a concept is usually implemented in the details of a specific copyright license, such as the "GNU General Public License" (GPL) and the "Creative Commons Attribution Share Alike License". Copyright holders of creative work can unilaterally implement these licenses for their own works to build communities that collaboratively share and improve those copylefted creative works'. See also http://copyleft.org

2 By the process of dance notation, such as the Beauchamp-Feuillet notation, and Labanotation.

3 Choreography can be fixed by an audio-visual recording, but if discussing how choreography could classify as a literary work, the answer would be dance notation.

4 Legally, the term is 'fixation', however, here the preferred term is 'fixity' in order not to cause confusion for readers who may be unfamilar with legally specific terminology.

5 Creation Records vs. News Group Newspapers [1997] EMLR 444.

6 As decided by Peterson J in University of London Press vs. Oxford University Press, [1916] 2 Ch 601.

7 See http://www.npr.org/sections/thetwo-way/2016/01/07/462245189/federal-judge-says-monkey-cant-own-copyright-to-his-selfie [accessed 30 March 2016].

8 Whis was rejected by US courts in the case Feist Publications vs. Rural Telephone Service 499 US 340 (1991) in favour of the creative spark test.

9 Ladbroke (Football) Ltd vs. William Hill (Football) Ltd [1964] 1 All ER 465.

10 In author's rights systems historically.

11 Infopaq (Case C-5/08) and Football Dataco (Case C-604/10) cases.

12 Directive 96/9/EC.

13 WIPO Performances and Phonograms Treaty, 1996 (http://www.wipo.int/wipolex/en/treaties/text.jsp?file_id=295477).

14 Phonographic Performance Limited.

15 Article 7 of the EU Database Directive.

Chapter 5

1 This title paraphrases Lynn Hershman Leeson's comment that the truth 'is always apparent in the flaws [. . .] it's in the crack in the wall, not the replication of it' (Giannachi et al. 2012b: 228).

2 *Roberta Breitmore*'s dates appear as 1973–9 on Hershman Leeson's website, as well as in the ZKM retrospective, but in a recent interview in San Francisco the artist indicated that the artwork started in 1972 (Hershman Leeson 2015).

3 The Dante Hotel on Hotwire Island in Second Life is currently offline (http//slurl.com/secondlife/Hotwire/111/110/28), but the exhibition about Roberta Breitmore can be visited in Second Life: http://maps. secondlife.com/secondlife/Hotgates/162/115/54 [accessed 09/04/2016].

4 E-mail to Gabriella Giannachi dated 30/11/2015, private archive. Apart from the re-mediations mentioned above, and 'reincarnations', like *Lamp Test* (2005), *Roberta in Black Face* (2005), among others, there are a number of less known documents, including birthday cards, which form the 'Anonymous Social Constructions' series, e.g., cards from Hillary and Bill Clinton (1992), Nancy and Ronald Regan (1992) and Richard Nixon (1992); a set of comics about Roberta by Spain Rodriguez (1975); and essays such as Roger Penrose's extract on black holes and a list of artworks by Arturo Schwartz, including 'The Alchemical' (1978).

5 Lynn Hershman Leeson's artworks at MoMA, http//www.moma.org/ collection/artists/39696 [accessed 08/12/2015].

6 The complete Roberta 'inventory' consists of approximately 200 documents/works (e-mail to Gabriella Giannachi dated 01/12/2015, private archive).

7 Kelli Dipple, 'Reasons for acquiring', Lynn Hershman Leeson, PC 10.4, A31490, Tate Archive.

8 Kelli Dipple, 'Lynn Hershman Leeson Notes', e-mail to Frances Morris, 09/07/2009, PC 10.4, A31490, Tate Archive.

9 The group consisted of Lucas Battich, Molly Bower and Nina van Doren, Michaela Lakova, Hélia Marçal, Thomas Walskaar and Julie Boschat Thorez. For more information see http//li-ma.nl/site/article/capturing-moment-where-net-art-and-performance-meet [accessed 13/11/2015].

10 For more information see: http//pzwiki.wdka.nl/mediadesign/
Archiving_grad_projects_2013 [accessed 13/11/2015].

11 Quote from Julie Boschat Thorez's research webpage, http//pzwiki.wdka.
nl/mediadesign/User:Jules/jodiatstedelijk [accessed 13/11/2015].

Part Two: Ways of Documenting Performance

1 Storify is available online at storify.com

Chapter 7

1 See Jones (1997) and Auslander (2006).

2 Such as in Erickson (1999) who suggests using black-and-white images
so the photograph acts merely as a supplement (p. 98).

3 The use of the word 'languages' in this context is not intended to imply a
simple linguistic – or even structuralist – understanding of either
photographic or performance practice, but instead to indicate the
multitude of communicative devices through which each medium
constructs meanings or relationships in either its production or reception.

4 A concept explored in Pelosi (2011: xx): 'During the course of a creative
work, an artist will have multiple intentions, including a meta-intention of
the overall work and many micro-intentions as the art progresses. This
journey has become known as the creative trail and is included in many
intentist works . . . This layering is on occasion referred to as Palimpsestism.'

5 Those seeking a more in depth history of performance photography are
referred to Joel Anderson's *Theatre and Photography* (2015).

6 *The Experience of Time in Modern Culture* is a research project run by
the University of Warwick, with the Universität Constant, University of
Nottingham and University of Durham. The project 'deals with cultural
and intellectual responses to time, or more specifically to changes in the
human experience and consciousness of time within modernity, from ca.
1800 to the globalized and digitalized present' (www2.warwick.ac.uk/
fac/arts/modernlanguages/research/german/time/).
[All entries accessed 21 July 2015].

7   If likened to Derrida's *énonciation* and *énonce*, or the difference between the indicative active present to the utterance and then a later statement of that utterance. For more, see Derrida (1988: 19).

8   Although the emphasis here is on linguistic translation, it should be noted that the study of translation engages with wider acts of cultural translation and transmission, where these linguistic principles are applied to cultural ideas, identities and memories, and also to performative events (see Aaltonen 2000).

9   For further discussion on the relationship between fine art moments, photography, and theatre documentation, see Skinner (2015).

Chapter 9

1   Available at: https://archive.org/index.php

2   Available at: http://www.dance-archives.ac.uk/

3   Available at: http://www.realtimearts.net/realtimedance

4   For example, see essays by Rachel Fensham and Sarah Whatley in G. Borggreen and R. Gade eds (2013), *Performing Archives/Archives of Performance*, Copenhagen: Museum Tusculanum Press.

5   Available at: http://web.archive.org/web/*/http://www.ps122.org/

6   Available at: http://web.archive.org/web/*/performancespace.com.au

7   For example this detail of Franklin Furnace's Friday Webcasts from 1999 http://web.archive.org/web/19990302034654/http://www.franklinfurnace.org/

8   For example Chris Goode's blog that is archived from 2007 onwards http://web.archive.org/web/20160212085818/http://beescope.blogspot.com/

9   Available at: http://www.history.ac.uk/projects/digital/AADDA

10 Available at www.webarchive.org.uk/

11 Available at http://pandora.nla.gov.au/

12 Available at https://www.loc.gov/webarchiving/

13 Available at http://www.emulator-zone.com/

14 Available at https://web.archive.org/web/*/http://www.youtube.com

15 Available at: http://www.alexa.com/
      [All entries accessed 21 July 2015].

16 This is an education project set up specifically to encourage schools to engage with web archiving available at: https://www.archive-it.org/k12/
17 See thematic special collections on topics such as 9/11 and the 2000 American presidential elections, which are curated by the IA's in-house archivists.

Chapter 10

1 See http://gallery.adm.ntu.edu.sg/Exhibitions/About/27 for details
2 Artist Adam Nash and curator Laurene Vaughan are the co-authors of this chapter.

Chapter 11

1 www.artscouncil.org.uk/media/uploads/pdf/NT_Live_NESTA_case_study.pdf [accessed 30 December 2015].
2 www.theguardian.com/stage/theatreblog/2015/oct/16/benedict-cumberbatch-hamlet-nt-live-barbican [accessed 30 December 2015].
3 www.barbican.org.uk/theatre/event-detail.asp?ID=17809 [accessed 2 January 2016].
4 It should be noted that as the live cinema screenings have no edited output, should an actor corpse, for example, this would appear in both the stage and screened versions, with their sharing of the same experience. In this sense, the theoretical sharing of the live elements between live stage and live screen is justified.
5 The concept of double bodies is considered by Matthew Causey in his 2006 *Theatre and Performance in Digital Culture: From simulation to embeddedness*, Routledge.
6 www.express.co.uk/entertainment/theatre/595375/Benedict-Cumberbatch-star-Hamlet-Barbican [accessed 3 January 2016].
7 www.telegraph.co.uk/news/newstopics/howaboutthat/3519640/Pianists-dying-wish-fulfilled-as-David-Tennant-uses-his-skull-in-Hamlet-performance.html [accessed 3 January 2016].

8   Naturally the identity of the skull was eventually revealed and latterly used in the television dramatisation of *Hamlet* from the RSC (www.telegraph. co.uk/culture/theatre/6644720/David-Tennant-to-revive-partnership-with-real-skull-for-BBCs-Hamlet.html [accessed 21 July 2016].

9   www.telegraph.co.uk/culture/theatre/6644720/David-Tennant-to-revive-partnership-with-real-skull-for-BBCs-Hamlet.html [accessed 21 July 2016].

10 www.whatsonstage.com/london-theatre/news/benedict-cumberbatch-hamlet-nt-live_37195.html; ntlive.nationaltheatre.org.uk/productions/ntlout10-hamlet [accessed 3 January 2016].

11 www.whatsonstage.com/london-theatre/reviews/hamlet-benedict-cumberbatch-review_38587.html [accessed 3 January 2016].

12 ntlive.nationaltheatre.org.uk/productions/ntlout10-hamlet [accessed 4 January 2016].

13 thewoostergroup.org/hamlet [accessed 20 July 2016].

14 Questionnaires contained questions concerning engagement with paradocumentation before, during and after the broadcast, as well as requesting information about the primary reasons for attending the broadcast. A total of 183 questionnaires were returned. Data was collated and free-text responses were categorised.

15 twitter.com/search?q=%23CumberHamlet [accessed 4 January 2016].

Chapter 12

1   All quotations from Shakespeare's *Hamlet* come from The Arden Shakespeare edition (Third Series): Ann Thompson and Neil Taylor eds (2006), *Hamlet*, The Arden Edition of the Works of William Shakespeare, London: Bloomsbury.

2   The Asian Shakespeare Intercultural Archive is a collaborative archive created by two major Shakespeare projects together with individual scholars, practitioners, and translators: 'Relocating Intercultural Theatre' followed by 'Digital Archiving and Intercultural Performance' (Singapore Ministry of Education Academic Research Fund Tier 2 and National University of Singapore) and 'A Web Archive of Asian Shakespeare Productions' (until 2015, Gunma-Nagoya City Universities; until

2010, Gunma-Doho Universities). The website for the project is at
http://a-s-i-a-web.org.

Chapter 13

1 The CWA is available at http://www.cwa-web.org
2 Claire Holt, *Art in Indonesia: Continuities and change* (Ithaca: Cornell
University Press, 1967).
3 Matthew Kirschenbaum, *Mechanisms: New media and the forensic
imagination* (Cambridge: MIT Press, 2008).
4 Kirschenbaum, *Mechanisms*, 20.
5 Stamford Raffles, *The History of Java* (London: Black, Parbury, and Allen,
Booksellers to the East-India Company and John Murray, 1817).
6 Ibid.
7 Ibid.
8 Nancy Florida, *Writing the Past, Inscribing the Future: History as prophecy
in colonial Java* (Durham: Duke University Press, 1995).
9 Carel Poensen, 'De Wajang', *Mededeelingen vanwege het Nederlandsche
Zendelinggenootschap* [Publications of behalf of the Netherlands
Missionary Society] XVI (1872).
10 Quoted in Willem Huibert Rassers, *Panji, The Culture Hero: A structured
study of religion in Java* (The Hague: M. Nijhoff, 1959).
11 Rassers, *The Culture Hero*.
12 Akitoshi Shimizu and Jan van Bremen, *Wartime Japanese Anthropology
in Asia and the Pacific* (Osaka: National Museum of Ethnology, 2003).
13 See Laurie Jo Sears, *Shadows of Empire: Colonial discourse and Javanese
tales* (Durham: Duke University Press, 1996) and Hendrik Kleinsmiede,
'Watching Wayang with Spinoza: Mentalism and (Written) Language in
Nonnative Scholarship on Wayang as Evidence of Paradigmatic
Constraint', in *Puppet Theater in Contemporary Indonesia: New
approaches to performance events,* ed. Jan Mrázek (Ann Arbor: University
of Michigan, Centers for South and Southeast Asian Studies, 2002).
14 Gerrit Knaap, *Cephas, Yogakarta: Photography in the service of the sultan*
(Leiden: KITLV Press, 1999).

15 Knaap, *Cephas.*

16 Karel Vanhaesebrouck, 'Theatre, Performance Studies and Photography: A history of permanent contamination', *Visual Studies* 24, no. 2 (2009): 99.

17 Victoria Maria Clara van Groenendael, *The Dalang Behind the Wayang: The role of the Surakarta and the Yogyakarta dalang in Indonesian-Javanese society* (Dordrecht: Floris Publications, 1985).

18 Ibid.

19 Ibid.

20 Kathryn Emerson, *Rama's Crown: Text of Wayang Kulit Tale, performed in three dramatic styles* (Jakarta: Indonesia Lontar, 2013).

21 Diana Taylor, 'Save as . . . Knowledge and Transmission in the Age of Digital Technologies' keynote address at the 2010 Imagining America conference, Seattle.

Chapter 14

1 The Western Australian New Music Archive is dedicated to collecting and celebrating the history of 'new music' as a distinct and specific iteration of Western art music practice, which emerged in the early to mid-twentieth century. Whilst linked to classical and chamber music tradition, it uses the modernist notion of progress with regard to composition and performance practice, and it has come to encompass a diverse range of styles and approaches. As such it belongs to a musical discourse that is distinct from other forms such as popular or folk musics.

2 This project has been facilitated by an Australian Research Council grant and the support of Western Australian new music organization Tura. The collection is curated by the Artistic Director of Tura, Tos Mahoney in association with the lead investigator on the project, Cat Hope.

3 The portal is located at www.wanma.org.au

4 The initial curation of content for the archive was undertaken by Tura and was based on a collection of material that had been reformatted from physical to digital form. There is a large number of other images that can and hopefully will be added to the archive as it progresses.

Chapter 15

1   Available at http://archive.circusoz.com
2   See http://www.circusarchive.net
    [Both accessed 21 July 2015].

Chapter 16

1   Peter Hulton has long been a leading creator of such works, through the
    Arts Archives (2015) at Exeter and more recently as the digital producer
    of several of the projects mentioned here. For additional examples of
    academic publications involving DVDs, see Camilleri (2015: 28) and
    Spatz (2015a: 242-47).
2   Video here refers to integrated audiovisual recording, as in common
    usage, not to silent video.
3   As I write this in early 2016, I am in the early stages of putting together a
    new *Journal of Embodied Research*. This will be the first peer reviewed,
    open access journal dedicated to the scholarly video essay as a medium
    for sharing knowledge in performance and related fields.
4   Those engaged in Practice as Research in the UK will understand the
    importance of producing assessable research documents for external
    assessment. But anyone who is interested in establishing a rigorous
    epistemological basis for embodied and artistic practice within academia
    will recognize the importance of such documents with regard to peer
    review and other mechanisms of synchronic and diachronic rigour
    (Spatz 2015a: 234–42).

Chapter 17

1   In 'Disciplines of the Text/Sites of Performance' (1995) and 'Antigone's
    Bones' (2008) W.B. Worthen further reasons and problematizes the
    opposition assumed between the embodied repertoire and the text/

archive as connected with the opposition perceived between performance and theatre studies.

2   Through a week of workshops, Tufnell 'Le[d] participants', including Evans' students, 'through a sequence of somatic exercises and improvisations in response to specific initial stimuli (object, material, idea or body-based), which would then lead to creative writing responses. The written work would later be reintegrated into creative improvisation, typically, for instance, as another form of stimulus' (Evans 2007: 72).

3   Barba points out that 'to speak of the performer's "energy" means using a term which lends itself to a thousand misunderstandings' (1995: 17). Similarly, Zarrilli will frequently highlight, in the training space, the problematic lack of precision and vagueness bound up with the term, 'energy', and will sometimes refer to the more specifically positioned, Chinese *qi* and Japanese and Korean *ki*, instead. However, whilst acknowledging these problems, here, as in the training space, it becomes pragmatic to use the widely deployed term, energy.

Chapter 18

1   Available at http://www.siobhandaviesreplay.co.uk
2   See http://synchronousobjects.osu.edu
3   The Digital Dance Archives can be found at http://www.dance-archives.ac.uk
    [All entries accessed 21 July 2015].

Chapter 19

1   Scott deLahunta and Norah Zuniga Shaw, 'Constructing Memories: Creation of the choreographic resource', *Performance Research*, vol. 11: 4 (2006), 53.

2   Elizabeth Dempster, 'Women Writing the Body: Let's Watch a Little How She Dances' in E. Goellner and J. Murphy (eds) *Bodies of the Text: Dance*

as theory, literature as dance (New Brunswick: Rutgers University Press, 1995), 22.

3 Natalie Lehoux, 'Dance Literacy and Digital Media: Negotiating past, present and future representations of movement'; *International Journal of Performance Arts and Digital Media*, vol. 9:1 (2013), 156.

4 Susan Leigh Foster, 'Textual Evidences' in E. Goellner and J. Murphy (eds), *Bodies of the Text: Dance as theory, literature as dance* (New Brunswick: Rutgers University Press, 1995), 233.

5 Foster, 'Textual Evidences', 234.

6 Helen Thomas, 'Reconstruction and Dance as Embodied Textual Practice' in A. Carter, A. (ed.) *Rethinking Dance History: A reader* (London: Routledge, 2004), 37.

7 Lehoux, 'Dance Literacy and Digital Media', 2–3.

8 Victoria Watts, 'Archives of Embodiment: Visual culture and the practice of score reading' in M. Bales and K. Eliot (eds), *Dance on Its Own Terms: Histories and methodologies* (Oxford: Oxford University Press, 2013), 372.

9 Alan Blackwell, Scott deLahunta, Wayne McGregor and John Warwicker, 'Transactables'; *Performance Research* 9 (2) (2004), 69.

10 Software such as *LabanWriter* and *LabanAssist* exists to edit, manage and simplify the use of Labanotation (Lehoux, 2013).

11 Corina MacDonald, 'Scoring the Work: Documenting Practice and Performance in Variable Media Art', *Leonardo*, 42 (1) (2009), 59.

12 Graham McFee, *The Philosophical Aesthetics of Dance: Identity, performance and understanding* (Hampshire: Dance Books, 2011).

13 Sarah Rubidge, 'Identity and Open Works' in S. Jordan (ed.) *Preservation Politics. Dance Revived, Reconstructed, Remade* (London: Dance Books, 2001).

14 Dance Heritage Coalition, Inc. *Dance Documentation; A Practical Guide* http://www.danceheritage.org/DocumentingDance.pdf

15 Paul Otlet (1934), cited in Michael Buckland 'What is a "Document"?', *Journal of the American Society for Information Science (1986–1998)* vol. 48:9 (1997), p. 805.

16 Suzanne Briet, *Qu'est-ce que la documentation?* (Paris: EDIT, 1951).

17 Suzanne Briet (1951), cited in Buckland, 'What is a "Document"?' p. 804.

18 Ibid., p. 804.

19 Ibid., p. 808.

20 deLahunta and Zuniga Shaw, 'Constructing Memories', p. 62.

21 William Forsythe (2009) http://www.williamforsythe.de/essay.html.

22 Blackwell, deLahunta, McGregor, Warwicker, 'Transactables', p. 67.

23 Ibid., p. 67.

24 Stephanie Jordan (ed.) *Preservation Politics. Dance Revived, Reconstructed, Remade* (London, Dance Books 2001).

25 I discuss these projects and their impact on dance archiving and dance reconstruction in Whatley (2015).

26 Thomas, 'Reconstruction and Dance as Embodied Textual Practice', p. 32.

27 Cunningham's *Lifeforms* was choreographic software developed in the late 1980s as a way to generate movement possibilities beyond the imagination of human mind and body.

28 William Forsythe and Scott deLahunta, *Motion Bank Brochure and Logo Generator* http://motionbank.org/sites/motionbank.org/files/mb_brochure.pdf (2011) p. 10

29 Carla Fernandes and Stephan Jurgens, 'Video annotation in the TKB project: Linguistic meets choreography meets technology' *International Journal of Performance Arts and Digital Media* vol 9: 1 (2013) p. 122.

30 Ibid., p. 124.

31 ibid., p. 122.

32 See http://www.siobhandavies.com/sidebyside/. I discuss this project in more detail in Whatley, S. (2014).

33 *RePlay* launched in 2009 after 30 months development with funding from the Arts and Humanities Research Council. See http://www.ahrc.ac.uk

34 Dance Heritage Coalition, *Dance Documentation,* p. 59.

35 Forsythe and deLahunta, *Motion Bank Brochure and Logo Generator*, p. 12.

36 Ibid., p. 12.

37 Michael Zollner and Jens Keil, *Motion Bank Brochure and Logo Generator* http://motionbank.org/sites/motionbank.org/files/mb_brochure.pdf (2011) p. 23.

38 Rune Gade and Gunhild Borggreen (eds), *Performing Archives/Archives of Performance* (Copenhagen: Museum Tusculanum Press, 2013).

39 Lynn Brooks and Joellen Meglin (eds) *Preserving Dance Across Time and Space* (Abingdon: Routledge, 2013)

40 notably Phelan (1993); Schneider (2001); Auslander (2006, 2009).

41 Vivian van Saaze and Annet Dekker, 'Surprising usages of a documentation model: On the notions of boundary objects and beyond', *International Journal of Performance Arts and Digital Media* vol. 9:1 (2013), p. 100.

42 Bertha Bermudez and Scott deLahunta 'Introduction', *RTRSRCH;* <*Notation*> vol. 2:2 (2010), p. 00.

43 Johannes Birringer 'What score? Pre-choreography and post-choreography', *International Journal of Performance Arts and Digital Media* vol. 9:1 (2013), p. 7.

44 Scott deLahunta and Sarah Whatley, 'Choreographic documentation', *International Journal of Performance Arts and Digital Media* vol. 9:1 (2013), p. 4.

45 Foster, 'Textual Evidences', p. 234.

46 Natalie Lehoux, 'Dance literacy and digital media', p. 156.

47 van Saaze and Dekker, 'Surprising usages of a documentation model: On the nations of boundary objects and beyond', p. 102.

48 Ibid., p. 110.

49 deLahunta and Whatley, 'Choreographic documentation', p. 4.

50 Toni Sant 'Interdisciplinary approaches to documenting performance', *International Journal of Performance Arts and Digital Media* vol. 10:1 (2014), p. 4.

51 Ibid., p. 6.

52 Emilie Gallier 'Notation for the Audience: The reading movement as way to implicate spectators', *Performance Research* vol. 20:6 (2015), p. 15.

53 *Synchronous Objects for One Flat Thing, reproduced* (Forsythe et al. 2009), *Using the Sky* (Motion Bank and Hay 2013) and *A Choreographer's Score: Fase, Rosas danst Rosas, Elena's Aria, Bartók* (De Keersmaeker and Cvejić 2012).

54 Hetty Blades 'Affective Traces in Virtual Spaces: Annotation and emerging dance scores', *Performance Research* vol. 20:6 (2015), p. 33.

55 Ibid., p. 33.

56 Clarisse Bardiott 'Rekall: An environment for notation/annotation/denotation', *Performance Research* vol. 20:6 (2015), p. 83.

57 Ibid., p. 83.

58 See http://nancystarksmith.com/underscore

59 For example deLahunta, S. and Bastien, M. (eds) (2007), deLahunta, S. (ed.) (2007), Burrows, J. (2010), Lee, R and Pollard, N. (2006).

60 See http://www.pinabausch.org/en/archive/the-digital-archive

61 See http://www.dance-archives.ac.uk; http://numeridanse.tv/en/

62 Laura Molloy 'Digital curation skills in the performing arts – an investigation of practitioner awareness and knowledge of digital object management and preservation', *International Journal of Performance Arts and Digital Media* vol. 10:1 (2014), p. 19.

63 van Saaze and Dekker, 'Dance Literacy and Digital Media', p. 100.

Bibliography

Aaltonen, S. (2000), *Time-Sharing on Stage: Drama translation in theatre and society*, Clevedon, Buffalo, Toronto, Sydney: Multilingual Matters Ltd.

Abbott, D. (2015), '"Cut me to pieces" Shakespeare, fandom, and the fractured narrative', *Proceedings of the Digital Research in the Humanities and Arts*, 2014.

Abbott, D. and E. Beer (2006), *AHDS Performing Arts Scoping Study*, www.ahds.ac.uk/performingarts/pubs/scoping-study-2006.pdf [accessed 13 December 2015].

Alexander, B.K. (2012), 'Archiving Performance/Performance as Archive: A hybrid book review and performance commentary on E. Patrick Johnson's Sweet Tea', *Text and Performance Quarterly* 32 (3): 269–84.

Allegue, L., S. Jones, B. Kershaw and A. Piccini eds (2009), *Practice as Research in Performance and Screen*, book with DVD-ROM, Basingstoke: Palgrave.

Allen, J. (2010), 'Depth-charge in the Archive: The documentation of performance revisited in the digital age', *Research in Dance Education* 11 (1): 61–70.

Alvarez, José Carlos ed. (1994), *Documentation des Arts du Spectacle dans une société en mutation – Documentation/ Actes*, Lisboa: SIBMAS.

Alvarez, José Carlos (2010), '25 anos de Museu Nacional do Teatro: do sonho, da memória e do efémero', in Claudia Figueiredo (ed.), *Museologia.pt*, no. 4, Lisboa: IMC.

Anderson, J. (2015), *Theatre & Photography*, London: Palgrave Macmillan.

Artaud, A. (1958), *The Theater and its Double*, trans. M.C. Richards, New York: Grove Press.

Arts Archives (2015), online: www.arts-archives.org

Arts Council (2011), *Digital Broadcast of Theatre: Learning from the pilot season, NT Live,* www.artscouncil.org.uk/media/uploads/pdf/NT_Live_NESTA_case_study.pdf [accessed 30 December 2015].

ArtsLaw, 'Information Sheets: Copyright, online: www.artslaw.com.au/info-sheets/info-sheet/copyright/ [accessed 3 December 2015].

Auslander, P. (1999, 2008), *Liveness: Performance in a mediatized culture*, New York and London: Routledge.

Auslander, P. (2006), 'The Performativity of Performance Documentation', *PAJ: A Journal of Performance and Art* 84 (3), September: 1–10.

Auslander, P. (2008), 'Live and Technologically Mediated Performance', in Tracy C. Davis (ed.), *The Cambridge Companion to Performance Studies*, Cambridge: Cambridge University Press.

Auslander, P. (2009), 'Reactivation: Performance, mediatization and the present moment' in M. Chatzichristodoulou, J. Jefferies and R. Zerihan (eds), *Interfaces of Performance*, Farnham: Ashgate.

Auslander, P. (2012), 'Digital Liveness: An historico-philosophical perspective', *PAJ: A Journal of Performance and Art*, 34: 3: 3–11.

Austin, J. (1962), *How to do Things with Words*, Oxford: Oxford University Press.

Australian Bureau of Statistics (31/3/15) 3218.0 Regional Population Growth, Australia, 2013–14, online: www.abs.gov.au/ausstats/abs@.nsf/mf/3218.0/ [accessed 2 December 2015].

Babo, M.A. (2004), 'Do corpo protésico ao corpo híbrido', in Maria Lucília Marcos, Cascais, António Fernando (org), *Revista de Comunicação e Linguagens – Corpo, Técnica, Sujectividades*, Lisboa: FCSH-UNL.

Baetans, J. (2009), 'Is a Photograph Worth a Thousand Films?' *Visual Studies* 24 (2): 143–8.

Balduzzi, M. (2013), 'Massimiliano Balduzzi: Physical Training for Performers', six videos, online: vimeo.com/album/2328479 and www.routledgeperformancearchive.com

Bann, S. (1984), *The Clothing of Clio*, Cambridge: Cambridge University Press.

Barba, E. (2005 [1995]), *The Paper Canoe: A guide to theatre anthropology*, London: Routledge.

Barbican (2015), *National Theatre Live: Hamlet*, www.barbican.org.uk/theatre/event-detail.asp?ID=17809 [accessed 2 January 2016].

Bardiott, C. (2015), 'Rekall: An environment for notation/annotation/denotation', *Performance Research* 20 (6): 82–6.

Barker, M. (2004), 'News, Reviews, Clues, Interviews and Other Ancillary Materials: A critique and research proposal', *Scope: An Online Journal of Film and Television Studies*, online: www.nottingham.ac.uk/scope/documents/2004/february-2004/barker.pdf [accessed 17 January 2016].

Barker, M. (2013), *Live to Your Local Cinema: The remarkable rise of livecasting*, Basingstoke, Palgrave Macmillan.

Barry, P. (2002 [1995]), *Beginning Theory* (2nd ed.), Manchester, New York: Manchester University Press.

Barthes, R. (1975), *The Pleasure of the Text*, trans. R. Miller, New York: Hill and Wang.

Barthes, R. (1977), *Image-Music-Text*, Glasgow: Fontana.

Barthes, R. ([1981] 2000), *Camera Lucida*, R. Howard (trans), London: Vintage Classics.

Barthes, R. and S. Heath (1977), *Image, Music, Text*, New York: Hill and Wang.

Bartlett, V. (2014) 'New medium, old archives? Exploring archival potential in The Live Art Collection of the UK Web Archive', *International Journal of Performance Arts and Digital Media* 10 (2): 91–103.

Batchen, G. (1999), *Burning With Desire: The conception of photography*, Cambridge MS: MIT Press.

Bay-Cheng, S. (2012) 'Theatre is Media: Some principles for a digital historiography of Performance', *Theater* 42 (2): 27–41.

Belfiore, E. and O. Bennett (2008), *The Social Impact of the Arts: An intellectual history*, Basingstoke: Palgrave Macmillan.

Bellini, P. and P. Nessi (2014), 'Modeling Performing Arts Metadata and Relationships in Content Service for Institutions', *Multimedia Systems*, 21 (5):427–49, doi:10.1007/s00530-014-0366-0.

Bellos, D. (2011), *Is that a Fish in Your Ear? Translation and the meaning of everything*, London: Penguin.

Benjamin, W. (1968), 'The Work of Art in the Age of Mechanical Reproduction', in Walter Benjamin, *Illuminations*, London: Fontana.

Bennett, L. (2013), 'Texting and Tweeting at Live Music Concerts: Flow, fandom and connecting with other audiences through mobile phone technology', in K. Burland and S. Pitts (eds), *Coughing and Clapping: Investigating audience experience*, Farnham: Ashgate.

Bentkowska-Kafel, A., H. Denard and D. Baker eds (2012), *Paradata and Transparency in Virtual Heritage*, Abingdon: Ashgate.

Bermudez P.B. (2013), '(Capturing) Intention: The life of an interdisciplinary research project', *International Journal of Performance Arts and Digital Media*; 9 (1): 61–81.

Bermudez, P.B. and S. deLahunta (2010), 'Introduction', *RTRSRCH* <*Notation*>, 2 (2): 00–01.

Berne Convention, 1886.

Birringer, J. (2013), 'What Score? Pre-choreography and post-choreography', *International Journal of Performance Arts and Digital Media* 9 (1): 7–13.

Blackwell, A., S. deLahunta, W. McGregor and J. Warwicker (2004), 'Transactables', *Performance Research* 9 (2): 67–72.

Blades, H. (2015), 'Affective Traces in Virtual Spaces: Annotation and emerging dance scores', *Performance Research* 20 (6): 26–34.

Blau, H. (1990), *The Audience*, London: Johns Hopkins University Press.

Blank, T.J. (2012), *Folk Culture in the Digital Age: The emergent dynamics of human interaction*, Boulder: University Press of Colorado.

Bläsing, B. (2010), 'The Dancer's Memory: Expertise and cognitive structures in dance', in B. Bläsing, M. Puttke and T. Schack (eds), *The Neurocognition of Dance: Mind, movement and motor skills*, Hove: Psychology Press.

Bluedorn, A.C. (2002), *The Human Organization of Time: Temporal realities and experience*, Redwood City, CA: Stanford University Press.

Boal, A. (2006), *The Aesthetics of the Oppressed*, Abingdon: Routledge.

Le Boeuf, P., M. Doerr, C.E. Ore, S. Stead eds (2015), Definition of the CIDOC Conceptual Reference Model, www.cidoc-crm.org/docs/cidoc_crm_version_6.2.pdf

Boyd, D. and K. Crawford (2012), 'Critical Questions for Big Data', *Information, Communication and Society* 15 (5): 662–79.

Briet, S. (1951), *Qu'est-ce que la documentation?* Paris: EDIT.

Briet, S. (2006 [1951]), *What is Documentation?: English translation of the classic French text*, trans. Ronald E. Day, Laurent Martinet and Hermina GB Anghelescu, Lanham, MD: Scarecrow.

British Library, *The British Library Collection Development Policy for Websites*, online: www.bl.uk/reshelp/pdfs/modbritcdpwebsites.pdf [accessed 31 October 2013].

Brooks, L. and J. Meglin (2013), *Preserving Dance Across Time and Space*, Abingdon: Routledge.

Brown, Adam D., Yifat Gutman, Lindsey Freeman, Amy Sodaro and Alin Coman (2009), 'Introduction: Is an interdisciplinary field of memory studies possible?' *International Journal of Politics, Culture, and Society* 22 (2): 117–24.

Brown, C., A. Miemetz, M. Medine and R. Scoones (2013), 'Score for Collaborative Production Process of REVOLVE', *International Journal of Performance Arts and Digital Media* 9 (1): 40–3.

Buckland, M. (1997), 'What is a "Document"?' *Journal of the American Society for Information Science (1986–1998)* 48 (9): 804–9.

Burdick, A., J. Drucker, P. Lunenfeld, T. Presner and J. Schnap (2012), *Digital_Humanities*, Cambridge MA: MIT Press.

Burrows, J. (2010), *A Choreographer's Handbook*, Abingdon: Routledge.

Camilleri, F. (2015), 'Towards the Study of Actor Training in an Age of Globalised Digital Technology', *Theatre, Dance and Performance Training* 6 (1): 16–29.

Campbell, L. (2014), 'Beyond Pollock: On visual art objects as non-traditional forms of performance document', *International Journal of Performance Arts and Digital Media* 10 (1): 35–47.

Carlson, M. (2003), *The Haunted Stage: The theatre as memory machine*, Ann Arbor: University of Michigan Press.

Carruthers, Mary (1990), *The Book of Memory: A study of memory in medieval culture*, Cambridge: Cambridge University Press.

Causey, M. (2006), *Theatre and Performance in Digital Culture: From simulation to embeddedness*, London: Routledge.

Charlton, T.L., L.E. Myers and R. Sharpless eds (2006), *The Handbook of Oral History*, Oxford: AltaMira Press.

Chrysochou, P. (2014), 'Semiotics, Theatre, and the Body: The performative disjunctures between theory and praxis', *Semiotica* 202: 641–55.

Cixous, H. (1981a), 'Castration or Decapitation?' trans. A. Kuhn, *Signs: Journal of Women in Culture and Society* 7 (1): 41–55.

Cixous, H. (1981b), 'The Laugh of the Medusa', in E. Marks and I. de Courtivron (eds), *New French Feminisms* (trans. K. Cohen and P. Cohen), Brighton: The Harvester Press.

Cixous, H. (1987), 'Reaching the Point of Wheat, or a Portrait of the Artist as a Maturing Woman', *New Literary History* 19 (1): 1–21

Cixous, H. (1991a), '*Coming to Writing' and Other Essays*, D. Jenson (ed.), S. Cornell; D. Jenson, A. Liddle, S. Sellers (trans), Cambridge MA: Harvard University Press.

Cixous, H. (1991b), *Readings: The poetics of Blanchot, Joyce, Kafka, Kleist, Lispector and Tsvetayava*, V. Conley Andermatt(trans. and ed.), Minneapolis: University of Minnesota Press.

Cixous, H. (1993), 'Without End no State of Drawingness no, rather: The executioner's taking off', C.A.F. MacGillivray (trans.), *New Literary History* 24 (1).

Cixous, H. (1998a), 'In October 1991 ...', in Hélène Cixous, *Stigmata: Escaping Texts* (trans. Keith Cohen), London: Routledge.

Cixous, H. (1998b), 'Writing Blind: Conversation with the donkey' in H. Cixous, *Stigmata: Escaping Texts* (trans. E. Prenowitz), London: Routledge.

Cixous, H. (2002a), 'The Book as One of its Own Characters' (trans. C. Porter), *New Literary History* 33 (3), 403–34.

Cixous, H. (2002b), '"You Race Towards that Secret, which Escapes": An interview with Martin McQuillan', *The Oxford Literary Review* 24: 185–201.

Cixous, H. (2004), '"Magnetizing the World": An interview with Hélène Cixous', in S. Sellers (ed.), *The Writing Notebooks of Hélène Cixous*, London: Continuum.

Cixous, H. and M. Calle-Gruber (1997), 'We are Already in the Jaws of the Book: Inter Views', in H. Cixous and M. Calle-Gruber, *Hélène Cixous, Rootprints: Memory and life writing*, Eric Prenowitz (trans.), London: Routledge.

Clarke, P. and J. Warren (2009), 'Ephemera: Between archival objects and events', *Journal of the Society of Archivists* 30 (1), Oxford: Routledge.

Clausen, B. (2005), 'After the Act. The (Re)Presentation of Performance Art', *Coll. Theory Series*, 3, Vienna: Museum Moderner Kunst Stiftung Ludwig; Nürnberg and Vienna: Verlag für moderne Kunst.

Clemens, J. and A. Nash (2015), 'Being and Media: Digital ontology after the event of the end of media', *Fibreculture Journal* 24.

Collingwood, R.G. (1946), *The Idea of History*, Oxford: Oxford University Press.

Conner, Lynne (2013), *Audience Engagement and the Role of Arts Talk in the Digital Era*, Basingstoke: Palgrave Macmillan.

Connerton, Paul (1989), *How Societies Remember,* Cambridge: Cambridge University Press.

Conquergood, D. (1998), *Beyond the Text: Toward a performative cultural politics*, in Dailey, S.J. (ed.), *The Future of Performance Studies: Visions and revisions*, Indiana: National Communication Association.

Copyright Act [2000], Malta.

Copyright, Designs and Patents Act, UK, accessed at www.legislation.gov.uk/ukpga/1988/48/section/3

Crane, Susan ed. (2000), *Museums and Memory*, Redwood City: Stanford University Press.

CRASSH (2015), Cambridge Centre for Digital Knowledge, online: www.crassh.cam.ac.uk/programmes/cambridge-centre-for-digital-knowledge

Creation Records vs. News Group Newspapers [1997] EMLR 444.

Crocker, E., N. Gansterer and M. Greil (2015), 'Notion of Notation><Notation of Notion (artists' pages)', *Performance Research* 20 (6): 53–7.

Crouch, Tim (2011), '*The Author*: Response and Responsibility', *Contemporary Theatre Review* 21: (4): 416–22.

Cvejic, B. (2015), 'From Odd Encounters to a Prospective Confluence: Dance-philosophy, *Performance Philosophy*, 1.

Daily Express (2015), *There's nothing like a Dane: Benedict Cumberbatch starring as Hamlet at the Barbican*, www.express.co.uk/entertainment/theatre/595375/Benedict-Cumberbatch-star-Hamlet-Barbican [accessed 3 January 2016].

The Daily Telegraph (2008), *Pianists dying wish fulfilled as David Tennant uses his skull in Hamlet performance*, www.telegraph.co.uk/news/newstopics/howaboutthat/3519640/Pianists-dying-wish-fulfilled-as-David-Tennant-uses-his-skull-in-Hamlet-performance.html [accessed 3 January 2016].

The Daily Telegraph (2009), *David Tennant to revive partnership with real skull for BBC's Hamlet*, www.telegraph.co.uk/culture/theatre/6644720/David-Tennant-to-revive-partnership-with-real-skull-for-BBCs-Hamlet.html [accessed 21 July 2016].

Dance Heritage Coalition, Inc. (2006), *Dance Documentation: A practical guide*, online: www.danceheritage.org/DocumentingDance.pdf [accessed 10 December 2015].

Database Directive 96/9/EC.

Davis, J., K. Normington, G. Bush-Bailey, J. Bratton (2011), *Researching Theatre and Historiography*, in B. Kershaw, H. Nicholson (eds), *Research Methods in Theatre and Performance*, Edinburgh: Edinburgh University Press.

Day, R.E. (2014), *Indexing it All. The [Subject] in the Age of Documentation, Information, and Data*, Cambridge MA: MIT Press.

de Keersmaeker, A.T. and B. Cvejic (2012), *A Choreographer's Score: Fase, Rosas Danst Rosas, Elena's Aria, Bartok*, Brussels: Mercatorfonds.

Dekker, A. (2013), 'Enjoying the Gap. Comparing Contemporary Documentation Strategies', in C. Saba, J. Noordegraaf, B. Le Maître and V. Hediger (eds), *Preserving and Exhibiting Media Art: Challenges and perspectives*, Amsterdam: University of Amsterdam Press.

deLahunta, S. ed. (2007), *SwanQuake the User Manual*, Plymouth: Liquid Press.

deLahunta, S.N. and Zuniga Shaw (2006), 'Constructing Memories: Creation of the choreographic resource', *Performance Research* 11 (4): 53–62.

deLahunta, S. and M. Bastien eds (2007), *Capturing Intention: Documentation, analysis and notation research based on the work of Emio Greco, PC*, Amsterdam: Emio Greco PC and AHK/Lectoraat.

deLahunta, S. and S. Whatley (2013), 'Choreographic Documentation', *International Journal of Performance Arts and Digital Media* 9 (1): 3–5.

deLahunta, S., K. Vincs and S. Whatley (2015), *On An/Notations*, *Performance Research* 20 (6).

Dempster, E. (1995), 'Women Writing the Body: Let's watch a little how she dances', in E. Goellner and J. Murphy (eds), *Bodies of the Text: Dance as theory, literature as dance*, New Brunswick: Rutgers University Press.

Derrida, J. (1988), 'Signature, Event, Context', *Limited Inc*, Evanston: Northwestern University Press.

Derrida, J. (1994), *Specters of Marx: The state of the debt, the work of mourning, and the new international*, Peggy Kamuf (trans.), London and New York: Routledge.

Derrida, J. (1996), *Archive Fever: A Freudian impression*, Eric Prenowitz (trans.), Chicago: University of Chicago Press.

Doerr, M. (2003), 'The CIDOC Conceptual Reference Module: An ontological approach to semantic interoperability of metadata', *AI Magazine* 24 (3): 75–92, www.aaai.org/ojs/index.php/aimagazine/article/view/1720

Doerr, M. and N. Crofts (1999), 'Electronic Esperanto: The role of the oo CIDOC Reference Model', *Archives and Museums Informatics*, ICHIM 1999, doi:10.1.1.61.2748.

Dolan, J. (2005), *Utopia in Performance: Finding hope at the theater*, Ann Arbor: University of Michigan Press.

Dourish, P. (2001), *Where the Action Is*, Cambridge MA: MIT Press.

Dourish, P. and G. Bell (2011), *Divining a Digital Future: Mess and mythology in ubiquitous computing*, Cambridge MA: MIT Press.

Durning, J. and E. Waterhouse (2013), '77 Choreographic Proposals: Documentation of the evolving mobilization of the term choreography', *International Journal of Performance Arts and Digital Media* 9 (1): 44–51.

Eames, S.M. (1964), 'Primary Experience in the Philosophy of John Dewey', *The Monist* 48 (3): 407–18.

Eco, U. (1968), *A Definição da Arte* [s.l.], U. Mursia & C.

Edwards, E. (2004), 'Ephemeral to Enduring: The Internet Archive and its role in preserving digital media', *Information Technology & Libraries* 23 (1): 3–8.

Ehn, P. (2008), 'Participation in Design Things', conference proceedings Participatory Design Conference, CPSR/ACM Indiana University, USA: 92–101.

E&I (2015), Experiments & Intensities digital book series, online: www.experimentsandintensities.com, Winchester: University of Winchester Press.

Emerson, K. (2013), *Rama's Crown: Text of Wayang Kulit Tale, performed in three dramatic styles* Jakarta: Indonesia Lontar.

Erickson, J. (1999), 'Goldberg Variations: Performing distinctions', *PAJ: A Journal of Performance and Art* 21 (3): 98.

Etchells, T. (1999), *Certain Fragments: Contemporary performance and forced entertainment*, London: Routledge.

Evans, M. (2007), 'Another Kind of Writing: Reflective practice and creative journals in the performing arts', *Journal of Writing in Creative Practice* 1 (1): 69–76.

Evening Standard (2015), *Benedict Cumberbatch pleads with fans to stop filming his Hamlet performances*, www.standard.co.uk/showbiz/celebrity-news/benedict-cumberbatch-pleads-with-fans-to-stop-filming-his-hamlet-performances-a2352276.html [accessed 13 December 2015].

Falk, John H. (2009), *Identity and the Museum Visitor Experience*, California: Left Coast Press.

Feist Publications vs. Rural Telephone Service 499 US 340 (1991).

Fernandes, C. and S. Jurgens (2013), 'Video Annotation in the TKB Project: Linguistic meets choreography meets technology', *International Journal of Performance Arts and Digital Media* 9 (2): 115–34.

Florida, N. (1995), *Writing the Past, Inscribing the Future: History as prophecy in colonial Java*, Durham: Duke University Press.

Flusser, V. (2000 [1983]), *Towards a Philosophy of Photography*, London: Reaktion Books.

Football Dataco (Case C-604/10).

Forsythe, W. (1999), *Improvisation Technologies: A tool for the analytical dance eye*, Berlin: Hatje Cantz.

Forsythe, W. (2009), *Choreographic Objects – an essay*, online: www.williamforsythe.de/essay.html [accessed 10 December 2015].

Forsythe, W. and S. deLahunta (2011), *Motion Bank Brochure and Logo Generator*: 10–19, online: motionbank.org/sites/motionbank.org/files/mb_brochure.pdf [accessed 10 December 2015].

Fortier, M. (2002), *Theory/Theatre: An introduction*, London: Routledge.

Foster, S.L. (1995a), 'Choreographing History', in S.L. Foster (ed.), *Choreographing History*, Bloomington and Indianapolis: Indiana University Press.

Foster, S.L. (1995b), 'Textual Evidences' in E. Goellner and J. Murphy (eds), *Bodies of the Text: Dance as theory, literature as dance*, New Brunswick: Rutgers University Press.

Foucault, M. (1978), 'The Incitement to Discourse', in *The Will to Knowledge: The history of sexuality* 1, New York: Pantheon Books.

Freshwater, H. (2003), 'The Allure of the Archive', *Poetics Today* 24 (4): 729–58.

Freshwater, H. (2009), *Theatre and Audience*, Basingstoke: Palgrave Macmillan.

Friedman, J. (2006), *Fractious Action: Oral history-based performance*, in T.L. Charlton, L.E. Myers and R. Sharpless, *Handbook of Oral History*, Oxford: AltaMira Press.

Gade, R. and G. Borggreen eds (2013), *Performing Archives/Archives of Performance*, Copenhagen: Museum Tusculanum Press.

Gaines, S.M., G. Eglinton, and J. Rullkötter (2009), *Echoes of Life: What fossil molecules reveal about earth history*, Oxford: Oxford University Press.

Gallier, E. (2015), 'Notation for the Audience: The reading movement as way to implicate spectators', *Performance Research* 20 (6): 12–16.

Garde-Hanson, J. (2009), 'My Memories?: Personal digital archive fever and Facebook', in J. Garde-Hansen and A. Hoskins (eds), *Save As . . . Digital Memories*, New York: Palgrave Macmillan.

Gardner, L. (2010), 'Theatre: Wake up to the digital age!', *The Guardian*, 20 April, online: www.theguardian.com/stage/theatreblog/2010/apr/18/theatre-digital-twitter-facebook-social-media [accessed 22 March 2016].

Giannachi, G. (2017), *Archive Everything: Mapping the everyday*, Cambridge: The MIT Press.

Giannachi, G., H. Lowood, G. Worther, D. Price, D. Rowland and S. Benford (2012), 'Documenting mixed reality performance: The case of CloudPad', *Digital Creativity* 23–3–4: 159–75.

Giannachi, G., N. Kaye and M. Shanks (2012), *Archaeologies of Presence*, London and New York: Routledge.

Giannachi, G. and N. Kaye (2011), *Performing Presence: From the live to the simulated*, Manchester: Manchester University Press.

Gibbons, Joan (2007), *Contemporary Art and Memory: Images of recollection and remembrance*, London and New York: I.B. Tauris.

Gindler, E. (1995), 'Gymnastik for People Whose Lives Are Full of Activity', in D. Hanlon Johnson (ed.), *Bone, Breath and Gesture: Practices of embodiment*, The Charlotte Selver Foundation (trans.), North Atlantic: Berkeley.

GloPAC (2006), Application Profile for GloPAD Performing Arts Metadata Schema, www.glopac.org/about/ApplicationProfile5-1.pdf

Goffman, E. (1959), *The Presentation of Self in Everyday Life*, New York: Doubleday.

Gorsky, M (2015), 'Sources and Resources into the Dark Domain: The UK Web Archive as a source for the contemporary history of public health', *Social History of Medicine* 28 (3): 596–619.

Gourfink, M. (2013), 'Dance, Borrow, Create? From the breath to ideas, from ideas to gestures', *International Journal of Performance Arts and Digital Media* 9 (1): 14–30.

Graham, J. and J. Sterrett (1997), 'An institutional approach to collections care of electronic art', *WAAC Newsletter* 19 (3), online: cool. conservation-us.org/waac/wn/wn19/wn19-3/wn19-310.html [accessed 12/13/2015].

Grant, Catherine (2002), 'Private Performances: Editing performance photography', *Performance Research* 7 (1): 34–44.

Green, L., T. Mahoney, C. Hope and L. MacKinney (2014), 'Publishing an Archive: A meta-narrative of (be)longing', *Proceedings of Australian and New Zealand Communication Association Conference*, Melbourne, VIC. ANZCA: 1–15.

Grotke, A. (2011), 'Web Archiving at the Library of Congress', *Computers in Libraries*, 31 (10) available at: www.infotoday.com/cilmag/dec11/Grotke. shtml

Groys, B. (2008), *Art Power*, Boston: MIT Press.

The Guardian (2015), *Benedict Cumberbatch's Hamlet comes into its own on the screen*, www.theguardian.com/stage/theatreblog/2015/oct/16/ benedict-cumberbatch-hamlet-nt-live-barbican [accessed 30 December 2015].

Halbwachs, M. (1992), *On Collective Memory*, Chicago: Chicago University Press.

Hallnas, L. and J. Redstrom (2002), 'From Use to Presence: On the expressions and aesthetics of everyday computational things', *ACM Transactions on Computer-Human Interaction* 9 (2), June: 106–124.

Hamilton, P. and L. Shopes (2008), *Oral History and Public Memories*, Philadelphia: Temple University Press.

Hansen, P. with C. House (2015), 'Scoring the Generating Principles of Performance Systems, *Performance Research* 20 (6): 65–73.

Hantelmann, von D. (2010), *How to Do Things with Art*, Zürich/Dijon: JRP/ Ringier & Les presses du reél.

Heddon, D. (2014), *Performing the Archive Following in the Footsteps*, in R. Gough, H. Roms (eds), *On Archives and Archiving, Performance Research* 7 (4): 64–77.

Henning, M. (1995), 'Digital Encounters: Mythical pasts and electronic presence' in Martin Lister (ed.), *The Photographic Image in Digital Culture*, London: Routledge.

Hensen, S. (1993), 'The First Shall Be First: APPM and its impacts on American archival description, *Archivaria* 35 Spring: 64–70.

Heritage Sandbox (2012), 'Like Theatre, The Memory of Theatre will be Experienced as an Event, a Social Event [online article], retrieved from: http://old.react-hub.org.uk/heritagesandbox/projects/2012/memory-of-theatre/journal/like-theatre-the-memory-of-theatre-will-be-experienced-as-an [accessed September 2015].

Hershman L.L. (1996), *Clicking In: Hot links to a digital culture*, Seattle: Bay Press.

Hershman L.L. (2015), interview with Gabriella Giannachi, 29 August 2015, private archive.

Hodge, A. (2013), *Core Training for the Relational Actor*, DVD-ROM, London and New York: Routledge.

Holden, C. (2015), 'The Definition of the Work Entity for Pieces of Recorded Sound', *Cataloging and Classification Quarterly* 53 (8): 873–94

Holland, P. (2006), 'On the Gravy Train: Shakespeare, memory and forgetting', in P. Holland (ed.), *Shakespeare, Memory and Performance*, Cambridge: Cambridge University Press.

Holt, C. (1967), *Art in Indonesia: Continuities and change*, Ithaca: Cornell University Press.

Hope, C., L. MacKinney, L. Green, M. Travers, T. Mahoney (2015), 'The Western Australian New Music Archive: Performing as remembering', in A. Harris, N. Thieberger and L. Barwick (eds), *Research, Records and Responsibility: Ten Years of PARADISEC,* Sydney: UNSW Press.

Hoyle, B. (2010a), 'Lloyd Webber sequel incurs scorn of online "phans"', *The Times*: 5 March, online: www.thetimes.co.uk/tto/arts/stage/article2462880.ece [accessed 17 January 2016].

Hoyle, B. (2010b), 'Andrew Lloyd Webber Insists It'll Be All Right on the Night', *The Times*, 6 March, online: www.thetimes.co.uk/tto/arts/stage/article2463152.ece [accessed 17 January 2016].

Hudson, J. (2012), Access and Collective Memory in Online Dance Archives, *Journal of Media Practice* 13 (3): 285–301.

Hulton, D. and M. Kapsali (2016), *Yoga and Actor Training*, DVD-ROM, London and New York: Routledge.

Infopaq (Case C-5/08).

International Federation of Library Associations, and Institutions (1998), section on cataloguing, Standing Committee. 'Functional requirements for bibliographic records: final report', Ed. IFLA Study Group on the Functional Requirements for Bibliographic Records. Vol. 19, KG Saur Verlag Gmbh & Company, 1998.

Jackson, A. (2015), 'Towards a Macroscope for UK Web History', *UK Web Archive Blog*, web log post, online: http://britishlibrary.typepad.co.uk/webarchive/2015/06/towards-a-macroscope-for-uk-web-history.html [accessed 13 September 2015].

James, V. (2011), Interview with Laura Griffiths, Phoenix Dance Theatre, Leeds, UK, 11 November.

JAR (2015), *Journal for Artistic Research*, online: www.jar-online.net

Jay, M. (1994), *The Denigration of Vision in Twentieth Century French Thought*, Berkeley: University of California Press.

Jenkins, H. (2006), *Convergence Culture*, New York: New York University Press.

Jensen, D. and L. Westbrook (2013), 'I Was a Tino Sehgal Interpreter', https://www.cca.edu/news/2013/04/15/i-was-tino-sehgal-interpreter [accessed 13 September 2016].

Jones, A. (1997), '"Presence" in Absentia: Experiencing performance as documentation', *Art Journal* 56 (4): 11–18.

Jordan, S. ed. (2001), *Preservation Politics. Dance Revived, Reconstructed, Remade,* London: Dance Books.

JoVE (2015), *Journal of Visualized Experiments*, online: www.jove.com

Kelsey, D, and L. Bennett (2014), 'Discipline and Resistance on Social Media: Discourse, power and context in the Paul Chambers "Twitter Joke Trial"', *Discourse, Context and Media* 3: 37–45.

Kennedy, D. (2009), *The Spectator and the Spectacle: Audiences in modernity and postmodernity,* Cambridge: Cambridge University Press.

Kidd, J. (2011), 'Performing the Knowing Archive: Heritage performance and authenticity', *International Journal of Heritage Studies* 17 (1): 22–35.

Kietzmann, J.H., K. Hermkens, I.P. McCarthy and B.S. Silvestre (2011), 'Social Media? Get Serious! Understanding the Functional Building Blocks of Social Media', *Business Horizons* 54 (3): 241–51.

Kimpton, M. and J. Ubois (2006), 'Year-by year: From an archive of the internet to an archive on the internet', in J. Masanès (ed.), *Web Archiving,* New York: Springer.

Kirschenbaum, M. (2008), *Mechanisms: New media and the forensic imagination*, Cambridge MA: MIT Press.

Kleinsmiede, H. (2002), 'Watching Wayang with Spinoza: Mentalism and (written) language in nonnative scholarship on wayang as evidence of paradigmatic constraint', in Jan Mrázek (ed.), *Puppet Theater in Contemporary Indonesia: New approaches to performance events*, Ann Arbor: University of Michigan, Centers for South and Southeast Asian Studies.

Knaap, G. (1999), *Cephas, Yogakarta: Photography in the service of the sultan*, Leiden: KITLV Press.

Kopytoff, I. (1986), 'The Cultural Biography of Things: Commoditization as a process', in A. Appadurai (ed.), *The Social Life of Things: Commodities in a Cultural Perspectiv*, Cambridge: Cambridge University Press.

Kriebel, S.T. (2007), 'Theories of Photography: A short history', in James Elkins (ed.), *Photography Theory*, London: Routledge.

Kristeva, J. (1984), *Revolution in Poetic Language*, M. Waller (trans.), New York: Columbia University Press.

Kuhn, A. (2002 [1995]), *Family Secrets: Acts of memory and imagination*, London: Verso.

Kuhn, B. (2011), 'Operatic Hyperreality in the Twenty-First Century Performance Documentation in High-Definition Quality', *Word and Music Studies* 12, (2011): 191–210.

Ladbroke (Football) Ltd. vs. William Hill (Football) Ltd, [1964] 1 All ER 465.

Laurenson, P. and V. Van Saaze (2014), 'Collecting Performance-based Art: New challenges and shifting perspectives', in O. Remes, L. MacCulloch, and M. Leino (eds), *Performativity in the Gallery. Staging Interactive Encounters*, Bern: Peter Lang.

Lave, J. and E. Wenger (1991), *Situated Learning: Legitimate peripheral participation*, Cambridge: Cambridge University Press.

Lee, R. and N. Pollard (2006), *Beached: A Common Place Book,* London: ResCen.

Lehoux, N. (2013), 'Dance Literacy and Digital Media: Negotiating past, present and future representations of movement', *International Journal of Performance Arts and Digital Media* 9 (1): 153–74.

Levin, L. (2009), 'Review Essay: The performative force of photography', *Photography and Culture* 2 (3): 327–36.

Lister, M. (1995), *The Photographic Image in Digital Culture*, Abingdon: Routledge.

Loukes, R. (2006), '"Concentration" and Awareness in Psychophysical Training: The practice of Elsa Gindler', *New Theatre Quarterly* 22 (4): 387–400.

Löwgren, J. and E. Stolterman (2004), *Thoughtful Interaction Design: A design perspective on information technology*, Cambridge, MA: MIT Press.

Luboh, A. (2010), 'Making Art Out of an Encounter', *New York Times*, 15 January, online: www.nytimes.com/2010/01/17/magazine/17seghal-t.html?_r=0 [accessed 12/01/2015].

Lynch, E. (2013), Interview with Laura Griffiths, Phoenix Dance Theatre Meeting Room, Leeds, UK, 24 January.

MacDonald, C. (2009), 'Scoring the Work: Documenting practice and performance in variable media art', *Leonardo* 42 (1): 59–63.

Masanès, J. (2006), 'Web Archiving Issues and Methods', in J. Masanès (ed.), *Web Archiving*, New York: Springer.

McAuley, Gay (2008), 'Photography and Live Performance Introduction', *About Performance* 8: 7–13.

McFee, G. (2011), *The Philosophical Aesthetics of Dance: Identity, performance and understanding*, London: Dance Books.

McFee, G. (2012), 'In Remembrance of Dance Lost', *Choros International Dance Journal* 1, Spring: 1–13.

McKechnie, S., and J. Stevens (2009), 'Visible Thought: Choreographic cognition in creating, performing, and watching contemporary dance', in J. Butterworth and L. Wildschut (eds), *Contemporary Choreography: A critical reader*, London and New York: Routledge.

McKernan, L. 'The Disappearing Archive', *Luke McKernan Weblog*, online: http://lukemckernan.com/2016/01/03/the-disappearing-archive/ [accessed 1 May 2016].

McGeeney, E. (2015), 'Live Tweeting and Building the Digital Archive: #NFQLR – Who and What is it For?' *International Journal of Social Research Methodology* 18: (3): 307–19.

Media Commons (2015), *[in]Transition: Journal of Videographic Film and Moving Image Studies*, online: http://mediacommons.futureofthebook.org/intransition

Mee, E.B. (2013), 'Hearing the *Music of the Hemispheres*', *TDR: The Drama Review* 57 (3) 148–50.

Melrose, S. (2006), '"Not Yet, and Already no longer": Loitering with intent between the expert practitioner at work, and the archive', *ResCen, Performance as Knowledge*. 3 May, The Portico Rooms, Somerset House, London, online: www.rescen.net/archive/PaK_may06/PaK06_transcripts4_1.html [accessed 9 February 2011].

Melucci, A. (1995), 'The Process of Collective Identity', in H. Johnston and B. Klandermans (eds), *Social Movements and Culture*, London: UCL Press.

Merleau-Ponty, M. (2002 [1969]), *The Phenomenology of Perception*, London: Routledge.

Millar, L. (2006), 'Touchstones: Considering the relationship between memory and archives', *Archivaria* 61: 105–26.

Miller, D. and P. Le Boeuf (2005), '"Such Stuff as Dreams Are Made On": How does FRBR fit the performing arts?' *Cataloging and Classification Quarterly* 39 (3–4): 151–78.

Mitchell, J. (1999), 'Capturing Emotion in Motion', *Dance Magazine*, December 1999: 66–75.

Mitchell, W.J.T. (1994a), *Picture Theory*, Chicago: Chicago University Press.

Mitchell, W.J.T. (1994b), *The Reconfigured Eye: Visual truth in the post-photographic era*, Cambridge, MA: MIT Press.

Mitchell, W.J.T. (2005), *What Do Pictures Want?: The lives and loves of images*, Chicago: Chicago University Press.

Moisdon, S. (2003), '« moi je dis, moi je dis. . . . » [en]' online: http://janmot.com/text.php?id=21 [accessed 12/08/2015].

Moggridge, B. (2007), *Designing Interactions*, Cambridge, MA: MIT Press.

Molderings, H. (1984), 'Life is no Performance: Performance by Jochen Gerz', in Gregory Battcock and Robert Nickas (eds), *The Art of Performance: A critical anthology*, New York: E.P. Dutton.

Molloy, L. (2014), 'Digital Curation Skills in the Performing Arts: An investigation of practitioner awareness and knowledge of digital object management and preservation', *International Journal of Performance Arts and Digital Media* 10 (1): 7–20.

Monks, A. (2010), *The Actor in Costume*, UK: Palgrave Macmillan.

Monteiro, P.F. (2010), *Drama & Comunicação*, Coimbra: Imprensa Universitária de Coimbra.

Moretti, F. (2000), 'Conjectures in World Literature', *New Left Review* 1: 54–68.

Moretti, F. (2007), *Graphs, Maps, Trees; Abstract Models for Literary History*, London: Verso.

Moretti, F. (2013), *Distant Reading*, London: Verso.

Morgan, R.C. (2010), 'Thoughts on Re-Performance, Experience and Archivism', *PAJ: A Journal of Performance and Art* 96, 32, (3): 1–15.

Morris, Jacqui and Mark Morris (directors & producers) (2013), *McCullin*. [documentary film] BBC Imagine (series editor: Alan Yentob).

Motion Bank (2013), A Project of the Forsythe Company, online: motionbank.org [accessed 9 December 2015].

Muñoz, J.E. (1996), 'Ephemera as Evidence: Introductory notes to queer acts, women and performance', *A Journal of Feminist Theory*, 8 (2): 5–16.

National Library of Australia, *National Library of Australia Policy and Practice Statement*, online: http://pandora.nla.gov.au/policy_practice. html [accessed 19 October 2015].

National Theatre (2015), National Theatre Apps, www.nationaltheatre.org. uk/form/national-theatre-apps [accessed 14 December 2015].

National Theatre Live (2012), *OFFICIAL Statement re: Frankenstein DVD/ Bootleg Recordings*, http://ntlive.tumblr.com/post/27833520736/official-statement-re-frankenstein-dvdbootleg [accessed 14 December 2015].

National Theatre Live (2015), *Hamlet*, http://ntlive.nationaltheatre.org.uk/ productions/ntlout10-hamlet [accessed 14 December 2015].

NEJM (2015), 'Videos in Clinical Medicine', *New England Journal of Medicine*, online: www.nejm.org/multimedia/medical-videos

Nemiroff, D. (2005), 'Performances for Camera: Montreal and Toronto in the 1970s and 1980s', in France Choinère and Michèle Thériault (eds), *Point & Shoot: Performance and photography*, Montreal: Dazibo.

Odin Teatret South West Residency (2004), Exeter Phoenix Arts Centre, 1–4 May.

Palmer, Sean B (undated), The Fenton Photographs [website], online: http:// sbp.so/fenton [accessed: 9 April 2015].

Participant F (2005), Audio-visual interview with the Author, Exeter, 6 July.

Pavis, P. (2006), *Analyzing Performance: Theater, dance and film*, Ann Arbor: University of Michigan Press.

Paxton, S. (2008), *Material for the Spine: A movement study*, DVD-ROM, Brussels: Contredanse.

Pearson, J. (2002), 'Stilling Bodies/Animating Texts', *Performance Research* 7(4): 59–63.

Pearson, M., and M. Shanks (2001), *Theatre/Archaeology: Disciplinary dialogues*, London: Routledge.

Pelosi, V. (2009), *Intentism: Resurrection of the Artist*, London: Intentism Publishing House.

Pelosi, V. (2011), 'A Word On Intentist Art Practice', in Adrian Haak Jr (ed.), *The Search For Intentist Art: A Collection of Interviews with Contemporary Intentist Artists*, London: Intentism Publishing House.

Pérez, E. (2014), 'Experiential Documentation in Pervasive Performance: The democratization of the archive', *International Journal of Performance Arts and Digital Media* 10 (1): 77–90.

Phelan, P. (1993a), *Unmarked: The politics of performance*, London and New York: Routledge.

Phelan, P. (1993b), 'The Ontology of Performance: Representation without reproduction', in P. Phelan, *Unmarked: The politics of performance*, London: Routledge.

Phelan, P. (2010), 'Haunted Stages: Performance and the photographic effect', in Jennifer Blessing and Nat Trotman (eds), *Haunted: Contemporary photography/video/performance*, New York: Guggenheim Museum.

Poensen, C. 'De Wajang' [The Wayang] (1872), *Mededeelingen vanwege het Nederlandsche Zendelinggenootschap* [Publications of behalf of the Netherlands Missionary Society] XVI.

Pogue, D. (2009), 'Should You Worry About Data Rot?', *New York Times*, 26 March.

Pollock, D. (1990), 'Telling the Told: Performing like a family', *Oral History Review* 18 (2): 1–36.

Pollock, D., S.S. Nethercott, N.O. Leighton, C.H. Bailey eds (1990), *Oral History Review*, 18 (2).

Portelli, A. (1991), *The Death of Luigi Trastulli and Other Stories: Form and meaning in oral history*, Albany: State University New York Press.

Postlewait, T. (2009), *The Cambridge Introduction to Theatre Historiography*, Cambridge: Cambridge University Press.

Raffles, S. (1817), *The History of Java*, London: Black, Parbury and Allen, Booksellers to the East-India Company and John Murray.

Rassers, W.H. (1959), *Panji, The Culture Hero: A structured study of religion in Java*, The Hague: M. Nijhoff.

Read, C. (2015), email correspondence, Barbican Centre, London.

Reason, M. (2006), *Documentation, Disappearance and the Representation of Live Performance*, Basingstoke: Palgrave Macmillan.

Reason, M. (2008), 'Dance, Photography and Kinaesthetic Empathy' online paper: www.watchingdance.org/research/documents/ MRphotographypaperedit.pdf [accessed 10 July 2014].

Reason, M. (2010), 'Asking the Audience: Audience research and the experience of theatre', *About Performance* 10: 15–34.

Reason, M. and K. Sedgman (2015), 'Editorial Introduction: Themed section on theatre audiences', *Participations* 12 (1): 117–22.

Redström, J. (2008), 'RE:Definitions of Use', *Design Studies* 29(4): 410–23.

Reeve, S. (2005), 'Guiding through Movement: Workshop and seminar presentation', *The Changing Body Seminar Series: The bodymind in contemporary training and performance*, University of Exeter, 19 January.

Reeve, S. (2006a), 'The Next Step: Eco-somatics and performance', unpublished paper presented at *The Changing Body Symposium: The Bodymind in contemporary training and performance*, University of Exeter, 6–8 January: 1–20.

Reeve, S. (2006b), 'Journey: Valley to Rock to Sea: Environmental Movement Workshop', Langton Matravers, Dorset, 13–15 May.

Reeve, S. (2006c) 'Strata: Autobiographical Movement' Workshop, Wootton Fitzpaine Village Hall, Dorset, 24 June.

Reeve, S. (2008), 'The Ecological Body', PhD Thesis, University of Exeter.

Reeve, S. (2012a), 'Sea Moves Workshop', Charmouth, West Dorset, 23–4 June.

Reeve, S. (2012b), 'Space-Site-Environment-Place Workshop', Greta Berlin's Sculpture Garden, Charmouth Forest, Near Wootton Fitzpaine, Dorset, 8–9 September.

Richards, M. (2012), 'This Progressive Production: Agency, durability and keeping it contemporary', *Performance Research: A Journal of the Performing Arts* 15 (5): 71–7.

Ricoeur, P. (1984, 1990), *Time and Narrative*, Chicago: Chicago University Press.

Rinehart, R. and J. Ippolito (2014), *Re-collection: Art, new media, and social memory*, Cambridge: MIT Press.

Ritchin, F. (2009), *After Photography*, New York: W.W. Norton.

Roms, H. (2008), *What's Welsh for Performance?* Cardiff: Trace Samizdat Press.

Roms, H. (2010), *Remembering Performance – Performing Memory: An oral history of performance art in Wales*, in N. Leclercq, L. Roisson, A.R. Jones (eds), *Capter L'essence Du Spectacle [Capturing the Essence of Performance]*, Brussels: P.I.E.-Peter Lang S.A.

Rubidge, S. (2001), 'Identity and Open Works' in S. Jordan (ed.), *Preservation Politics. Dance Revived, Reconstructed, Remade*, London: Dance Books.

Rubin Suleiman, S. (1991), 'Writing Past the Wall: Introduction to *Coming to Writing*', in D. Jenson (ed), S. Cornell et al. (trans.), '*Coming to Writing' and Other Essays*, Cambridge: Harvard University Press.

Salter, C. (2010), *Entangled: Technology and the transformation of performance*, Cambridge, MA: MIT Press.

Sant, T. (2014), 'Interdisciplinary Approaches to Documenting Performance', *International Journal of Performance Arts and Digital Media* 10 (1): 3–6.

Saorín, T. (2010), 'Catalogación de objetos culturales y difusión digital del patrimonio', Anuario ThinkEPI 5 (October), EPI SCP, Barcelona, Spain: 168–72, online: http://hdl.handle.net/10760/15949

Sapir, M. (1994), 'The Impossible Photograph: Hippolyte Bayard's Self-portrait as a Drowned Man', *Modern Fiction Studies* 40 (3): 619–29.

Schechner, R. (2003), *Performance Theory*, New York: Routledge Classics.

Schechner, R. (2006), *Performance Studies – An introduction*, London and New York, Routledge.

Schmale, E. (2005), 'Gindler Work: Sensory Awareness Workshop', University of Exeter, 4–9 January.

Schneider, R. (2010), 'Performance remains', *Performance Research* 6 (2): 100–108.

Schneider, R. (2011), *Performing Remains: Art and war in times of theatrical reenactment: on performing remains*, London and New York: Routledge.

Schöch, C. (2013), 'Big? Smart? Clean? Messy? Data in the Humanities', *Journal of the Digital Humanities* 2 (3): 2–13.

Sears, L.J. (1996), *Shadows of Empire: Colonial discourse and Javanese tales*, Durham: Duke University Press.

Sedgman, K. (2016), *Locating the Audience: How people found value in National Theatre Wales*, Bristol: Intellect Ltd.

Seely Brown, J. and P. Duguid (2000), *The Social Life of Information*, Boston: Harvard Business School Publishing.

Sellers, S. (2004), 'Introduction', in S. Sellers (ed.), *The Writing Notebooks of Hélène Cixous*, London: Continuum.

Senelick, L. (1997), 'Early Photographic Attempts to Record Performance Sequence', *Theatre Research International* 22 (3): 255–64.

Shaughnessy, N. (2012), *Applying Performance: Live art, socially engaged theatre and affective practice*, New York: Palgrave Macmillan.

Shields, D.S. (undated), Broadway Photographs [website], online: http://broadway.cas.sc.edu/ [accessed: 15 April 2015].

Shimizu, A. and J. van Bremen (2003), *Wartime Japanese Anthropology in Asia and the Pacific*, Osaka: National Museum of Ethnology.

Siobhan Davies RePlay (2009), online: www.siobhandaviesreplay.com [accessed 9 December 2015].

Skinner, A. (2015), *Meyerhold and the Cubists: Perspectives on painting and performance* (Bristol: Intellect/Chicago: Chicago University Press).

Sontag, S. (1979), *On Photography*, Harmondsworth: Penguin.

Sorensen, V. (2015), 'The Mood of the Planet', *Everything is Data Catalogue*, Singapore: NTU Gallery.

Spatz, B. (2015a), *What a Body Can Do: Technique as knowledge, practice as research*, London and New York: Routledge.

Spatz, B. (2015b), 'Sequence of Four Exercise-Actions', *Theatre, Dance and Performance Training* website, posted 6 November 2015, online: http://theatredanceperformancetraining.org/2015/11/sequence-of-four-exercise-actions-physical-training-led-by-ben-spatz

Spatz, B. (2014), 'Massimiliano Balduzzi: Research in physical training for performers', *Theatre, Dance and Performance Training* 5 (3): 270–90.

Spitzer, L. (1999), 'Back Through the Future: Nostalgic Memory and Critical Memory in a Refuge from Nazism', in M. Bal, J. Crewe, L. Spitzer, *Acts of Memory: Cultural recall in the present.*

Spooner, P. (2015), 'Beginner's Guide to Web Archives Part 3', *UK Web Archive Blog*, web log post, online: http://britishlibrary.typepad.co.uk/ webarchive/2015/06/beginners-guide-to-web-archives-part-2.htm [accessed 13 September 2015].

Sterne, J. (2009), 'The Preservation Paradox in Digital Audio', in K. Bijsterveld and J. van Dijck, *Sound Souvenirs: Audio technologies, memory and cultural practices*, (2009): 55–65.

Stuckey, H., M. Swalwell, A. Ndalianis and D. de Vries (2015), 'Remembering and Exhibiting Games Past: The popular memory archive', in *Transactions of the Digital Games Research Conference, Special Issue: The inaugural DiGRA Australia conference.* Australia: ETC Press.

Sturken, M. (1997), *Tangled Memories: The Vietnam war, the AIDS epidemic and the politics of remembering*, Los Angeles: University of California Press.

Sturken. M. and L. Cartwright (2003), *Practices of Looking: An introduction to visual culture*, Oxford: Oxford University Press.

Suchman, L.A. (2007), *Human-Machine Reconfigurations: Plans and situated actions* (2nd ed.), Cambridge: Cambridge University Press.

Synchronous Objects (2009), online: http://synchronousobjects.osu.edu/ [accessed 9 December 2015].

Tagg, John (1988), *The Burden of Representation: Essays on photographies and histories*, Minneapolis: University of Minnesota Press.

Taylor, D. (2003), *The Archive and the Repertoire: Performing cultural memory in the Americas.* Durham: Duke University Press.

Taylor, D. (2007), 'Performed Practice, Embodied Knowledge', paper presented and documented at *The Articulate Practitioner – Articulating Practice*, International Forum, University of Wales, Aberystwyth, July 2005, DVD-ROM, produced and compiled by J. Greenhalgh and M. Brookes, Performance Research Books: An E-Publication.

Taylor, D. (2010), 'Save as . . . Knowledge and Transmission in the Age of Digital Technologies' keynote address at the *Imagining America Conference*, Seattle.

Taylor, H. (2013), 'AADDA Report: Sentiment Analysis and the Reception of the Liverpool Poets', *Domain Dark Archive weblog*, 16 October 2013,

online: http://domaindarkarchive.blogspot.co.uk/2013/10/researchers-
final-reports-1.html [accessed 15 December 2015].

Taylor, H. (2015), 'Do online networks exist for the poetry community?',
School of Advanced Study Online Repository, online: http://sas-space.sas.
ac.uk/6105/#undefined [accessed 1 May 2016].

TDPT (2015), *Theatre, Dance and Performance Training*, blog, online:
http://theatredanceperformancetraining.org

Thomas, H. (2004), 'Reconstruction and Dance as Embodied Textual
Practice', in A. Carter (ed.), *Rethinking Dance History: A reader*, London:
Routledge.

Tillett, Barbara B. (2010), 'RDA. Antecedentes y aspectos de su
implementación', Presentación en la Conferencia Regional de Catalogación,
Universidad Autónoma San Luis Potosí: México, marzo 2009.

Tromble, M. and L. Hershman Leeson (ed.) (2005), *The Art and Films of
Lynn Hershman Leeson: Secret agents, Private I*, Berkeley: The University
of California Press.

Trower, S. ed. (2011), *Place, Writing, and Voice in Oral History*, New York:
Palgrave Macmillan.

Turner, V. (1985), *The Anthropology of Performance*, New York: PAJ
Publications.

Twitter (2016), twitter.com/search?q=%23CumberHamlet [accessed 4 January
2016].

University of London Press vs. Oxford University Press [1916], 2 Ch 601.

University of Warwick (2014), *The Experience of Time in Modern Culture*
(research project), online: www2.warwick.ac.uk/fac/arts/
modernlanguages/research/german/time/ [accessed 13 December
2015].

van Groenendael, V.M.Cl. (1985), *The Dalang Behind the Wayang: The role of
the Surakarta and the Yogyakarta dalang in Indonesian-Javanese society*,
Dordrecht: Floris Publications.

Vanhaesebrouck, K. (2009), 'Theatre, Performance Studies and Photography:
A History of Permanent Contamination', *Visual Studies* 24 (2).

van Saaze, V. (2015), 'In the Absence of Documentation. Remembering Tino
Sehgal's Constructed Situations', *Revista de História da Arte*, 04: 55–64,

online: http://revistaharte.fcsh.unl.pt/rhaw4/RHAw4.pdf [accessed 09/12/2015].

van Saaze, V. and A. Dekker (2013), 'Surprising Usages of a Documentation Model: On the notion of boundary objects and beyond', *International Journal of Performance Arts and Digital Media* 9 (1): 99–113.

Vaughan, L. (2015), 'Performance, Practice, Presence: Design Parameters for the Living Archive, in David Carlin and Laurene Vaughan (eds), *Performing Digital, Multiple Perspectives on a Living Archive,* Farnham: Ashgate.

Watts, V. (2013), 'Archives of Embodiment: Visual culture and the practice of score reading', in M. Bales, and K. Eliot (eds), *Dance on Its Own Terms: Histories and methodologies*, Oxford: Oxford University Press.

Weber, T. (2010), 'Why Companies Watch Your Every Facebook, YouTube, Twitter Move', BBC, 10 October, online: www.bbc.co.uk/news/business-11450923 [accessed 17 January 2016].

Wegner, D.M. (1986), 'Transactive Memory: A contemporary analysis of the group mind', in B. Mullen and G.R. Goethals (eds), *Theories of Group Behavior*, New York: Springer-Verlag, 185–205.

Wegner, D.M. (1995), 'A Computer Network Model of Human Transactive Memory', *Social Cognition* 13 (3): 319–39.

West End Whingers (2010), 'Review – Love Never Dies, Adelphi Theatre': 2 March, online: http://westendwhingers.wordpress.com/2010/03/02/review-love-never-dies-adelphi-theatre [accessed 17 January 2016].

Whatley, S. (2013), 'Siobhan Davies RePlay: (Re)visiting the digital archive', *International Journal of Performance Arts and Digital Media* 9 (1): 83–98.

Whatley, S. (2014), 'Digital Inscriptions and the Dancing Body: Expanding territories through and with the archive', *Choreographic Practices* 5 (1): 121–38.

Whatley, S. (2015), 'Materiality, Immateriality and the Dancing Body: The challenge of the *inter* in the preservation of intangible cultural heritage', in M. Causey, J. Frieze and E. Meehan (eds), *Through the Virtual Toward the Real: The performing subject in the spaces of technology,* Basingstoke: Palgrave Macmillan.

Whatley, S. and R. Varney (2009), 'Born Digital: Dance in the digital age', *International Journal of Performance Arts and Digital Media* 5 (1): 51–63.

WhatsOnStage (2015a), *Hamlet (Barbican) – 'Benedict Cumberbatch rings the changes'*, www.whatsonstage.com/london-theatre/reviews/hamlet-benedict-cumberbatch-review_38587.html [accessed 3 January 2016].

WhatsOnStage (2015b), *Benedict Cumberbatch Hamlet to be screened globally through* NT *Live*, www.whatsonstage.com/london-theatre/news/benedict-cumberbatch-hamlet-nt-live_37195.html [accessed 3 January 2016].

Whitelaw, M. (2009), 'Visualising Archival Collections: The visible archive project', *Archives and Manuscripts* 37 (2): 22–40.

Wing, B. (1996), 'Glossary', in H. Cixous and C. Clément, *The Newly Born Woman*, London: I.B.Tauris.

Woolley, M.J. (2014), 'Documenting Performance Art: Documentation in practice', *International Journal of Performance Arts and Digital Media* 10 (1): 48–66.

The Wooster Group (2016), *Hamlet*, http://thewoostergroup.org/hamlet [accessed 20 July 2016].

Worthen, W.B. (1995), 'Disciplines of the Text/Sites of Performance', *The Drama Review* 39: (1): 13–28.

Worthen, W.B. (2008), 'Antigone's Bones', *The Drama Review* 52 (3): 10–33.

WIPO Performances and Phonograms Treaty (1996).

Yong, Li Lan, Eng Hui Alvin Lim, Ken Takiguchi, Chee Keng Lee, Hyon-u Lee, Ha-young Hwang, Michiko Suematsu and Kaori Kobayashi (2015), *Asian Shakespeare Intercultural Archive (A|S|I|A)*, 2nd edition, National University of Singapore. In English, Chinese, Japanese, online: www.-a-s-i-a-web.org

Zarrilli, P. (1988), 'For Whom is the "Invisible" not Visible?: Reflections on Representation in the Work of Eugenio Barba', *The Drama Review* 32 (1): 95–106.

Zarrilli, P. (1990), 'What Does it Mean to "Become the Character": Power, Presence, and Transcendence in Asian in body Disciplines of Practice', in R. Schechner and W. Appel (eds), *By Means of Performance: Intercultural studies of theatre and ritual*, Cambridge: Cambridge University Press.

Zarrilli, P. (2002 [1995]), 'On the Edge of a Breath, Looking', in P. Zarrilli (ed.), *Acting (Re)Considered,* 2nd ed., London: Routledge.

Zarrilli, P. (2009), *Psychophysical Acting: An intercultural approach after Stanslavski,* book with DVD-ROM by Peter Hulton, London and New York: Routledge.

Zollner, M. and J. Keil (2011), *Motion Bank Brochure and Logo Generator:* 23, online: motionbank.org/sites/motionbank.org/files/mb_brochure.pdf [accessed 10 December 2015].

Index

Tables are denoted by the use of *italic* page numbers. Illustrations are denoted by the use of **bold** page numbers.

Kean, Edmund 171
Keersmaeker, Anne Teresa de 295
Kidd, J. 225
Kietzmann, Jan H. 122
Kirschenbaum, Matthew 204
Kitchens (choreographies) 294
Klein, Yves 98
Knowing through pleasure 267–70
knowledge, embodied 278–9, 280, 281
knowledge, exchange of 30, 39
Kristeva, Julia 261

Labanotation 285, 286, 299
Laban, Rudolph 285
Lakova, Michaela 75
Leclaire, Serge 257
legal deposit libraries 136
legal protection, of performance 47–60
legislation, web archiving 140
Lehoux, Natalie 284
Le Noyé (Bayard) 95–7
libraries 30, 219, 222, 223 67
libraries, archives and museums (LAM) domain 29–30
library and information science (LIS) 13, 15, 35, 288–9
Library of Congress 141
Lightweight Information Describing Objects (LIDO) 31
Lim, Alvin Eng Hui 162, 189–201
Lister, Martin 94
literary production, understanding 145–6
Live Art Collection of The UK Web Archive (Bartlett) 132
liveness 114–15, 168, 174, 192, 228–30
See also audience, live
live performances 150, 190, 242
live-streaming, of events 126–9, 165–87
Lloyd Webber, Andrew 119–20, 121
Loukes, Rebecca 265

Love Never Dies (musical) 119–21
low culture 140
Lubow, Arthur 70
Lynch, Edward 280–1

McFee, Graham 278
McGeeney, E. 125
McGregor, Wayne 294–5
McKernan, Luke 139
McLuhan, Marshall 150, 151
Mahoney, Tos 223
Man A (Gibson/Martelli) 149, 156–7
MARC (Machine-Readable Cataloguing) 35
Marçal, Hélia 75
marketing materials 32, 114, 175, 178, 216–18
Martelli, Bruno 149
martial arts 260
Martínez, Alberto Pendón 15, 29–45
Masanès, Julien 132, 136
material forms 23, 289
Material for the Spine (Paxton) 295
Mateus, Osório 21
MAYK (theatre production company) 84
Meene, Hellen van 99
Melrose, S. 272
Melucci, Alberto 279
memories, embodied 26–8, 192–3, 280, 290
Memory of Theatre (project, 2012) 84–92
memory studies 13–14, 19–28, 26–8, 84–92, 199
metadata 31, 33, 34, 222, 247
metamemory 81
metaphorical archives 171
metonym, and the synecdoche 22
M.H. de Young Memorial Museum (San Francisco) 66–7, 68
microblogging, live 80, 124–9
mind, as a theatre 199
mirror/window analogies 110–11
Mishkin, Herman 102